Cast Member Confidential

CHRIS MITCHELL

CITADEL PRESS
Kensington Publishing Corp.
www.kensingtonbooks.com

CITADEL PRESS BOOKS are published by

Kensington Publishing Corp.
119 West 40th Street
New York, NY 10018

All Kensington titles, imprints, and distributed lines are available at special quantity discounts for bulk purchases for sales promotions, premiums, fund-raising,
educational, or institutional use. Special book excerpts or customized printings
can also be created to fit specific needs. For details, write or phone the office of
the Kensington special sales manager: Kensington Publishing Corp., 119 West
40th Street, New York, NY 10018, attn: Special Sales Department; phone 1-800-
221-2647.

CITADEL PRESS and the Citadel logo are Reg. U.S. Pat. & TM Off.

First printing: January 2010

10 9 8 7 6 5 4 3 2

Printed in the United States of America

Library of Congress Control Number: 2009930447

ISBN-13: 978-0-8065-3128-1
ISBN-10: 0-8065-3128-2

PREFACE

All my life, Disney has been a kind of sanctuary for me, a place that felt safe when everything else was going fuzzy. The music, the movies, the characters—every element so well thought out, it was hard to believe I couldn't simply jump through a chalk drawing to get to a world where animals sang and danced. So when I hit a rocky road in my life, and desperately needed some magic to solve or at least escape my problems, I turned to the Magic Kingdom for sanctuary and solace.

In many ways, Disney World is just like one of those animated movies in which everything seems more colorful, more extravagant. It's a place where everyone is welcome. Whether you're a pirate or a princess or an anarchic runaway, Disney provides a dress code, teaches you how to behave, and gives you all the tools you need to live happily ever after.

But there's danger in losing yourself to a fantasyland of fairies and flying carpets because at some indecipherable moment that fantasy becomes your reality, and the moral code that used to define you blurs. When the only limit is imagination, life can get very strange, very quickly.

The people I met while I worked at the park were good people. Every one of them signed legal agreements with Disney promising not to talk about their behind-the-scenes experiences. Because I worked for a third-party subcontractor, I signed no such agreement. While I intend to hold nothing back in telling you my story, I have a responsibility to protect the identities of my otherwise innocent fellow Cast Members.

The people in this book are real, but I have changed their characteristics to mask their true identity from the Corporation. In some instances, I have combined characteristics of people I met and created composite characters. The events in this memoir really occurred. The incidents that happened to me, I describe as accurately as possible. Stories I heard, I present as folklore. At Disney, as in every society, the legend and lore passed down through oral storytelling are a vital part of the cultural experience, so I didn't leave that out. In certain instances, I have ascribed folkloric episodes to actual (or composite) persons for ease of storytelling. I didn't include the many rumors that I couldn't confirm to my satisfaction.

From my first day as a Disney World Cast Member, people wanted to know what it was like to be a part of Walt's great machine. I would try to describe the onstage atmosphere or the backstage culture or the after-hours social events, but I could never quite capture the essence. How could I describe a cartoon dream world? What could I say to make them understand the challenging circumstances that drove me there in the first place? The only way to explain it is to start at the beginning.

You are about to discover what really happens behind the scenes at Disney World. Please keep your hands and arms inside at all times. Things are about to get a little bumpy. . . .

ACKNOWLEDGMENTS

My gratitude goes out to the people who helped shape this book: to my mother whose strength and courage I will admire forever, to my family, who has always been incredibly supportive, even when my actions made no sense at all, to my agent, Nancy Love, and my editor, Richard Ember. To the beautiful and talented Ann Christianson, who patiently read a thousand versions of this manuscript, and to Shane Coburn, who helped shape my most convoluted thoughts into words. Most of all, I want to thank the people I can't name on these pages, the Disney Cast Members who would get fired or worse if the Corporation found out about their involvement: to the Madame of the Safe House and Spiderguy and the Girl of Paradise Cove, thank you for taking the risk and letting me in on your secrets. My biggest thanks of all to Walt Disney, whose vision has meant so much to so many.

Cast Member
Confidential

Zip-a-Dee-Doo-Dah

Nobody has ever died at Disney World.

I discovered this curious truism on a trip to Orlando the year Tony Hawk landed the 900. I was there for work at the time, interviewing a professional rollerblader who worked as a stunt monkey in the Tarzan show.

It was a perfect September evening in Frontierland. The sky was North Shore blue and cloud free from Saint Pete's Beach in the west to Cocoa in the east. Butterflies were dancing to the banjo music, chasing beehives of hot pink cotton candy and buckets of popcorn that shone like doubloons in the last rays of the setting sun. It was a waxed planter day, a point break day, a powdery double-diamond day where anything at all was possible.

I was leaning up against a railing, the murky water of Tom Sawyer's Island at my back, when a baritone recording announced the beginning of the Magic Kingdom parade. Music rose up out of the landscaping and parade floats began to appear. My interview subject, Nick, had assured me that I would recognize him when the Tarzan float rolled up, and sure enough, he was hard to miss, dressed in a unitard of brown fur, doing cartwheels and flips in his Rollerblades. The audience was entertained by the stunt monkey, but they were enthralled with the dreadlocked bodybuilder in the loincloth, earnestly flexing his muscles on top of the float. Tarzan was the star of this show.

I could hardly hear myself think over the din of the Tarzan soundtrack, but I had no problem hearing the woman next to me when she belted out a glass-shattering scream. She was pointing at the dark expanse of lagoon that separated the flowerbeds of Frontierland from Tom Sawyer's Island, screeching like she had just found a crocodile in her cereal bowl. As I watched, the surface of the lagoon broke, and two tiny arms clawed the air, only for a second, before disappearing once again beneath the water.

I'm not a heroic person. While I'd like to say I was motivated by altruism that day in Frontierland, I was driven by what, in my case, is a more primal instinct: I sensed the opportunity to break the rules and get away with it. So I took it.

I kicked off my shoes and jumped the railing. The spot where the child had appeared was less than ten feet away, bubbles spritzing the surface where he had gone under. I aimed in that general direction and dove.

Immediately, I regretted my decision. The water tasted like diesel and expired spinach and smelled like El Porto after a sewage spill. I shot to the surface and tried not to retch. When my eyes focused, I discovered that I wasn't alone. A crowd of people was standing at the edge of the lagoon, and there were at least three in the water with me. The woman was at the railing, bawling into her hands.

I was looking for the shortest distance to the shore when I heard a triumphant shout behind me, and the crowd of tourists cheered. A man in the water held up a terrified boy who was, miraculously, still wearing a pair of mouse ears. Several people helped me over the railing onto the grass bank of Frontierland where the frantic woman was already clutching her boy and his savior.

The lifesaver, I realized then, was none other than Tarzan, who moments earlier had been riding his float, grinning as if he'd just been acquitted. He was six feet tall with broad shoulders and a Neanderthal forehead. Up close, I could see that his head of twisted dreadlocks was actually a wig. He was covered from head to toe in bronze makeup, and shadows had been artfully applied to exaggerate his musculature. He hugged the woman and put his hand on the boy's head.

"Keep boy safe," Tarzan said in broken English. "Children most important thing in world." He turned around and, for a moment, we stood face to face. "Tarzan very brave. But everybody can be hero." Then he winked at me and bounded through the crowd. The people parted, cheering as he vaulted back up onto his float, where he was joined by a woman in a yellow pinafore who batted her eyelashes at him and kissed him on the cheek.

The parade resumed and the crowd around me went back to eating waffle cones and buying souvenirs as if a cartoon character saving a drowning child were just another amusement park spectacle like a barbershop quartet or a sunburned German.

Afterward, I met Nick in the Disney parking lot and asked him about the experience. He responded to my amazement with an uninspired shrug. Just another day at the office. We drove to the skate park, where we spent the next couple of hours shooting sequences of switch-up grind tricks, then tagged the alleys off Orange Blossom Trail. When we ran out of Krylon, we picked up a couple of Red Bulls from a convenience store and sat down on a curb to do the interview.

As a general rule, I don't pass judgment on anyone. In my interviews, I ask challenging, often uncomfortable questions, but I don't moralize, demonize, or indemnify. People are complicated; that's why crayons come in boxes of sixty-four. When researching a subject, I start with her or his digital persona. People usually lie in their "About Me" section, but their choice of avatar is, if not immediately revealing, at least an honest foreshadowing of their true character. Nick's avatar was a slick version of himself—shirtless, with spiked hair and a studded belt. His ringtone was Snoop Dogg's "Mind On My Money." His screen name was SaintNicksRevenge. It wasn't a lot to go on, but considering we both grew up in a skate park, we were family. We spoke the same language.

"People say Nick Elliot sold out," I said into the Dictaphone.

"Three years ago, he was the X Games Champion. Now, he's run off and joined the circus. What do you say to them?"

Nick kept his cool. "I get paid to skate," he said. "And that's all I really care about. Fuck them."

"But you're skating for *the* Corporation," I goaded. "You're a wage slave to Disney Inc. How is that satisfying?"

He finished his Red Bull and crumpled the can. "I know what you're thinking. You look around Disney World, and you see crowds of sweaty-ass tourists, singing animals, sweatshop-manufactured merchandise, and you think this must be the lamest place in the world. But you're just seeing the surface, bro. You wouldn't believe the shit that goes on here behind the scenes."

"Disney has a dark side?"

"Dark as dysentery. What do you want? Opium? Koala bears? How about an Uzbeki mail-order bride? I'm telling you, this is the real Neverland Ranch. Michael ain't got nothing on the Mouse."

"You know," I said. "Radical accusations against Disney have been made before, but nothing has ever been proven. A lot of people consider it conspiracy theory propaganda."

Nick checked his watch. "In less than twenty minutes, I can introduce you to a guy who sells acid out of his Pooh costume. He's at Epcot right now."

"So, is that the real reason then? You've found a place where you can lead a double life?"

For the first time, Nick's cool exterior cracked. "This is going to sound totally fucking lame—in fact, turn off the tape recorder. I don't want this to go in the interview." I pretend to do it. "This place has real Magic—I'm serious. There's almost no crime. Nobody ever dies here. Have you noticed you don't see those bright green exit signs anywhere? Or telephone lines? It's not because they forgot; it's because they make their own rules here. This is what utopia would look like if it were run by eight-year-old architects."

"I still don't see what's in it for you."

"Being a pro skater ain't easy, dude. My sponsors are constantly

on my ass. The kids expect me to rip *all the effing time.* I eat ibupro-
fen like Skittles. But here . . . here, not even the Grim Reaper can
touch me. All I ever wanted to do was skate, and now I've found
something better. I've found a place where I can be a kid forever.
Besides, the bud that comes through this place is the kindest you've
ever had."

My whole flight home, I thought about what Nick had said and
what I had witnessed. Nick Eliot was the guy every kid in Rollerblades wanted to be. He had a pro skate and a video game character,
and yet here he was, working for Disney, proselytizing about magic
like an apostle. As an action sports journalist, I was well aware of
my responsibility to temper all claims of purity with a dose of ironic
realism. I skated through Hollywood during the 1992 riots, video-
taping skate tricks while looters robbed stores in the background. I
did tequila shots before DARE half pipe shows. I protested my own
values as a counterpoint to Absolutism.

And yet, I couldn't find a cynical twist for my encounter with
Tarzan. I had watched a storybook hero save a child from drowning
in a place that claimed nobody had died there since it first opened
its doors in October 1971—no crime; no natural disasters; no unhappy endings. Was it possible that Disney was the next step in our
evolution as a civilization? Nick believed. Either I was involved in
one of the most convincing scams of the century or Disney was truly
blessed with a legacy of immortality.

There are times when even the most jaded journalist needs to
believe in Magic. For me, this was one of those times.

Heigh-Ho

Disney heroes don't have mothers—Snow White, Pinocchio, Aladdin, Ariel—they all come from broken homes. Mowgli was raised by wolves, Princess Aurora by fairies. Cinderella had a wicked *step*mother, Alice had a nanny, and Lilo only had an older sister to watch over her. Bambi's mother was shot by hunters. Dumbo's mom was locked up in a cage. The Lost Boys, a gang of parentless runaways, led by the ultimate motherless hero, were always trying to convince Wendy to be their mother. I suppose, Disney is sending the message that you don't have to have a perfect nuclear family to be a hero, but I preferred to see it the other way around: in order to be a hero, you had to be an orphan . . . or a bastard.

From the moment I arrived in Orlando, I was aware that I was entering a manufactured community. The highways were dazzlingly clean, decorated with palm trees and hibiscus flowers, which, even in late January, were bursting with color. Gleaming rental cars jumped lane dividers like frisky salmon churning beneath tall billboards that advertised entertainment at every off-ramp. The sky was as blue as a Costa Rican wave, the air robust with the smells of fragrant orange blossoms and reclaimed water. And everywhere I looked, people were smiling, like convicts who had just staged a daring escape and couldn't quite believe they had gotten away with it. Rolling down the windows of my Jeep, I inhaled Florida and counted a million ways my Florida life would be better than its California prequel. It took less than forty-eight hours to get an interview at Walt Disney World.

It was exactly 3:00 P.M. when I stepped out of the Magic Kingdom monorail. All around me, unseen speakers played that song from *Snow White*, where the dwarfs are going to work in the mines. I had known the lyrics by heart as a kid, but in college, I relearned them as an ode to an easy sorority (Chi-O, Chi-O, it's off to bed we go.), and that was the version running through my head. Families thundered past me, people of all sizes and colors and abilities, eager to cross the turnstile into the land beyond. The Pearly Gates, I thought to myself. Nirvana. The images made me laugh, but I swallowed the false sentiment. This was my world now, and I didn't want to pollute it with disenchantment. Gray clouds were just beginning to darken the sky above the Will Call kiosk as I stepped up to the window. I carried a saddlebag with my portfolio and a copy of the *Orlando Sentinel*, folded open to the Classifieds section.

Experienced photographers wanted for Disney theme park. Must be outgoing. Please provide résumé and portfolio on request.

Under the listing, I had scribbled the words "Orville. 3:00. Magic Kingdom. <u>DO NOT</u> be late!"

To signify my dedication to the photographic profession, I wore a neatly trimmed goatee and just a hint of disdain in my scowl. My hair was pulled back into a ponytail, held in place with a black band, which made me look, I felt, *artistic*. The Disney security guard looked me over for a full minute before directing me to a row of office trailers on the edge of the theme park property. He shadowed me the whole way, his anxious hand hovering above his hip as I walked up the stairs to the photography trailer and opened the door. As the door closed behind me, I heard the first fat raindrops hit the rooftop.

"I'm looking for Orville," I announced.

"And you would be?" The man behind the desk was so large he seemed to be overflowing out of his chair.

"I'm a photographer," I said. "We have a three o'clock."

He ducked his head so that he could peer at me over his spectacles. I counted one two three chins. "Meeting," he said.

"I beg your pardon."

"You said 'we have a three o'clock.' " He smiled proudly. "I finished your sentence."

I checked my watch—3:05. Either my pupils were contracting or the clouds were rolling in thicker, but the trailer walls were definitely sliding closer. "Is Orville here?"

"Sure thing." The man stood up and crossed the trailer. "Follow me."

He invited me to sit at a Formica workbench, then disappeared. The trailer was actually a compact lab about twenty feet square. It was quiet inside, only the purring of the air conditioner as a soothing soundtrack. It smelled of photo chemicals, a rank, pungent odor that was guaranteed to turn the stomach of nonphotographers but one that set me at ease. The center of the lab was occupied by a massive film-processing machine, which hummed and clicked and spat out photos more or less constantly. The rest of the lab consisted of a three-foot-wide walkway that separated the machine from dozens of filing cabinets and bookshelves around the perimeter.

I opened my portfolio on the table and laid out tear sheets from some of my more successful shoots. When I looked up, I was surprised to see the same enormous man was easing himself into a chair next to me, surveying my work.

"So you must be Orville," I surmised.

"Good lighting here." He pointed to a headshot of a guy whose entire face was painted silver. "Did you use a gel to get that blue tint?"

"I used a blue-based film," I said. "And I had it cross processed."

He was already on to the next one. "How did you get this ghost-like image?"

It was an action shot, a skater on a handrail, taken at dusk. "I used a slow shutter speed," I explained, "and mounted the camera on a tripod."

"There's a flash right about"—he pointed to a spot out of frame—"here. At quarter, maybe half power."

"Right on the money," I said.

He nodded and flipped through my shots, pausing every so often to ask about one detail or another. His brow was scored with thoughtful lines, his eyes quick to take in the details of each photo in my book. He turned the pages carefully, his sausage fingers tapping at the page just outside the images so as not to smudge the prints. Finally, he shut the book.

"Very nice," he said. He stood up to adjust the processing machine, then transferred a stack of photos to a folder by the door. Outside, the rain was falling harder, but inside the lab, it was cozy. As Orville moved around the room, he turned his body sideways to shuffle between obstacles, a maneuver that did little good since he was about the same width in every direction. Taking his seat again, his expression was inscrutable. "They're called extreme sports, right?"

"It's just a sample," I said. "I can have more photos sent from LA if you want to see them."

"That won't be necessary." He leaned back with his arms behind his head. His white-collared shirt was yellow in the armpits. "Why do you want to work here?"

I was ready for this question. "Because I like photography," I said. "And I like Disney."

His fleshy lower lip gave him the bearing of a spoiled child, pouting for another piece of pie. He blinked his watery eyes slowly behind his spectacles. "But you're a *sports* photographer."

I was ready for this one too. I made a speech about the similarities between portrait and sport photography. "The way I see it," I concluded, "a photographer *needs* to have sports experience to truly understand photography."

Orville nodded. "You think so?"

I nodded enthusiastically. "And I'm hoping to learn more about portraiture from the other photographers here."

Again, the view over the top of the spectacles. Again the chins. One two three. "Bullshit."

I wasn't ready for that one. "Excuse me?"

"The photographers who work here need an instruction manual just to open a box of film. They don't know exposure settings from sunblock. Half the time, they're not even sure which way the lens faces. Now you come waltzing in here with your 'three o'clocks' and your cross-processed prints, and you tell me you *like photography*?" He wrinkled his nose as if he was looking over the edge of a box of kitty litter. "I don't buy it."

I was at a total loss. I looked down at the photos fanned out on the desk and back up at his round face, glowering behind the spectacles.

"I don't know what you want me to say."

"Why are you here?" He crossed his arms across his chest. "What can I—what can *Disney* possibly do for you?"

Six months before, I had been on top of the world. I was the editor of a wildly successful skate magazine; I had a network of friends that I would've killed or died for; my family was healthy; and I was in a relationship with my soul mate. I was unstoppable.

Which was why it was so devastating when, one crisp December morning, my boss called me into his swank LA office and fired me. It seemed that some of my editorial content was, in the words of the Christian Coalition, "offensive, obscene, and patently disgusting." Other critics pointed out that I was a "godless bastard," a point I took as canny observation rather than malicious critique. As an example, he showed me the interview with Nick Elliot, which featured a photo of the prodigy wall riding a tombstone in a Florida cemetery. "I can appreciate an artistic statement," he said in an unappreciative tone, "but you've crossed the line." I was escorted out of the building and told that they would pack up my stuff and send it to me later.

That weekend, while I was still reeling from my sudden loss of executive privilege, my girlfriend phoned to tell me that she had fallen in love with somebody else and would be moving out. She apologized profusely, but she had made up her mind. That was that. In fact, "that" wasn't actually "that." I stalked her for the next three days, sleeping in my Jeep, only to find out that the somebody she left me for was a guy who, up until that exact moment had been *L* on my speed dial, and for maybe five minutes longer, was number 2 in my Top 8.

But the worst news had begun unfolding a few months prior. Sometime during the summer of that year, my mother had become very ill. It was a strange time for me because my parents never openly mentioned it to me, preferring instead to smile through the symptoms as if nothing serious was happening. The first time my mom went into the hospital, my dad said she was getting her appendix removed. The next time, it was a minor cosmetic procedure. Every time her energy sagged, they explained that she'd had a tough day or was coming down with something or just needed a nap. I was caught up in the rituals of my own twenty-something life, so I didn't question any of the symptoms. I assumed a new diet might've been the reason for her weight loss and thinner hair.

Then, on a day that was already strained to the point of breaking, I got a call from my older brother, Michael. "There's something you need to know. And you're going to want to sit down." He explained that our mother was very sick. She had a deadly form of cancer known as lymphoma, which was already in the late stages by the time they detected it.

I couldn't understand a lot of his medical jargon, but I got the gist. Because lymphoma was based in the lymph nodes, the lymph was carrying the cancerous cells though the bloodstream to every organ in her body. Could they remove the lymph nodes? It was too far along. Could they treat each organ? It was too pervasive. In essence, there was no center of operations; hence, no easy surgery to remove the cancer.

Our parents had known about the diagnosis for months, but they didn't want to bother me with all the messy details. Mom and dad had asked him not to tell me, but he thought I should know.

My guts turned to acid, then to worms, then to acid again. Instinctively, I looked for my shadow, but I was inside, naked. The words fought their way out. "Is she okay?"

"Not really, no."

His scientific formality burned like frostbite. "Is she in pain?"

"Yes." He added, "A lot." At that moment, I hated him as much as I ever had. He was talking about our mother the way he used to describe med school cadaver research over dinner—distant, cold—relishing my obvious discomfort. The asshole. Still, he was being honest with me.

"Why didn't they tell me themselves?" I asked.

"You know how Mom is."

"I'm calling her."

"No!" he snapped. "You can't tell them I told you."

I considered this. "You want me to pretend I don't know?"

"Only until she mentions it."

"Any idea how long that might be?"

His voice became brittle, his paper-thin patience disintegrating completely. "Maybe never. Just do me a favor. Promise me you'll wait for Mom to bring it up first."

I promised.

I was crying even before I hung up the phone, childish tears I thought I'd outgrown were cascading down my cheeks. My mother had always been my champion. When my dad was working late or hidden behind his books, it was my mom who was there arranging McDonald's French fries on a crayon-drenched placemat to explain the wonders of addition and subtraction; acting out character voices from *The Jungle Book* story while music rambled out of the living room record player; and dropping me off, picking me up, then dropping me off again at the beach. They were enchanting memories, but they were just snapshots, dusty sepia recollections, brittle and cracked with age. From the past ten years, I had nothing. I wanted to blame her for disappearing from my life, but I knew it wasn't true. I was the one who had disappeared. I had skated away and never looked back.

That night I lay awake in bed sweating, my head crowded with fears of mortality and questions about betrayal. In just three months, my entire wonderful life had fallen to pieces, and I didn't have a single person to confide in. My brother and I had a fairly tempestuous relationship so our conversation made me feel, if anything, *resentful* that they had trusted him with the diagnosis. True, he was a doctor, but he was a pediatrician, not an oncologist, and he wasn't *that* much older than I was.

I was in a sort of suspended animation, gagged by my vow of silence, bound by my own sense of stubborn pride. I felt helpless to do anything for her, weak. And I was humiliated by what I was certain was my parents' recognition of that weakness. It was a selfish and self-centered reaction, the response of a thoughtless child, but in my disoriented state, it made sense. Unable to run to her, I ran away, desperate only to run, to find a Never Land filled with Lost Boys like me who lived in a world without mothers.

As a child, Disney had always embodied the promise of a better life, a pure world where good guys were noble and villains wore black, and the difference between the two was clear. Of course, I was older now and educated, too skeptical to believe in a land of Magic and pixie dust. But at that moment, I was desperate, and a desperate person can justify anything. What I needed, I rationalized, was a happy, hopeful place, a safe harbor with a group of people I could trust, people who would dive into a dirty lagoon to save an innocent life. Friends, family, a job—if this was going to work, I needed to start from scratch with only the purest influences.

"What can Disney do for you?" Orville asked again.

I felt the seconds tick away, but still, my mind was blank, and so I blurted out the first words that came to me. "I didn't know where else to go. I never planned what I'd do if everything went to hell. And so when everything did, in fact, go to hell, I panicked and ran and here I am." My fingers were clenched in my lap, palms aching from the serrated edges of my unevenly chewed fingernails. "I don't want anything from Disney. I'm just trying to find . . . some Magic."

And just like that, the word was out there, hanging in the air between us, shiny and clean and fragile like a bubble. I had crossed a line, and there was nothing I could do about it. I was a godless bastard requesting a reprieve from St. Peter. Orville nodded and leaned back in his chair, and for a moment, there was just the sound of the rain on the roof of the trailer. Then he said, "How soon can you start?"

I signed the contract right there in the photo lab using a Minnie Mouse pen. During the course of my interview, the rain had abated so that by the time Orville ushered me outside, the sky was clear and the air had a damp, clean scent like when you stick your head in a dryer before the load is finished. I felt lighter than air. If somebody had cut me loose, I would've floated up, away from the trailer, beyond the magical kingdom and into the Caribbean sky.

Orville cheerfully pumped my hand, then turned his attention to a stack of books and papers by the door. "Tomorrow," he said, "we're gonna get you started at Disney's Animal Kingdom."

"So I'll be shooting animals?"

His eyes went wide as wheels. "Oh, my ears and whiskers, no! Animals don't buy pictures." He motioned for me to hold out my hands, then started dispensing papers and booklets, thick manuals of information. "Your job will be to work with the characters. You'll take pictures of Mickey and Minnie and Winnie the Pooh and Tigger and anybody else our beloved guests wish to meet. And you'll try to capture a moment on their faces that doesn't look like desperate misery, and then you'll sell the photos back to them at a very reasonable price."

By this time, my arms were full, and the stack of information was getting heavy. "That doesn't sound very magical," I mumbled.

"Magic," he said, "has nothing to do with it."

When You Wish Upon a Star

Walter Elias Disney died alone. According to the reports, there was a physician on duty and some hospital staff nearby, but neither his wife nor his two daughters were present when he finally succumbed to "acute circulatory collapse" on December 15, 1966. This fact is one of the little proofs I cite in my arguments for atheism.

While he was alive and in charge of the theme parks, Walt was very particular about the appearance of his park staff, whom he re-branded Cast Members to make employment feel more like show biz. Among the many regulations in *The Disney Look* book I was violating were body piercing, facial hair, black nail polish. Men's hair could not cover the ears or shirt collar, and sideburns could be no longer than the earlobes. After twenty-five years of stubborn rejection, Disney was finally allowing mustaches, but only the non-threatening kind à la Tom Selleck, Keith Hernandez, or Ned Flanders. No beards. In my case, becoming a Disney Cast Member meant a transformation of near surgical proportions.

First stop: the barber shop, where a thin wisp of a man hacked my artistic locks into a style that my father would approvingly call *sensible*. With a creepy sense of familiarity, I realized that I was now sporting the same hairstyle as my brother, the stunt monkey, Nick,

Donald Rumsfeld, and pretty much every moral majority nut job who ever complained about indecency in my articles.

Sensing an impending identity crisis, I headed back to the "World Famous" Budget Lodge in Kissimmee where I had secured an inexpensive roof over my head. The carpets reeked of suntan lotion and diaper powder, and I'm pretty sure the mattress was filled with stuffed woodpeckers, but it had hot showers and clean towels. Over a sink of soapy water, I extracted my labret for the last time and shaved my goatee. My reflection in the mirror looked like a twelve-year-old version of myself, before Glen Plake and Anthony Kiedis became fashion icons, before my brother transformed himself into an irreconcilable tool, and at the time when my mom would spend hours in the garden, tending her roses and humming tunes from *Mary Poppins* in an authentic English accent.

On my first day of work at Animal Kingdom, I woke up before dawn, showered, shaved, and gelled my freshly shorn hair into place. In time, this would become subconscious ritual, but on this day, it felt exotic, like I was living the life of a real estate broker in suburban Shreveport. The air outside was thick as bacon grease. It clogged my pores and streaked my windows as I raced down I-4.

Before heading to the park, I had to stop at the costume warehouse to pick up my wardrobe. I was certain Disney would stick me in culottes and a gabardine blouse like some old-timey photographer, but the lady behind the counter surprised me with khaki shorts, a khaki, short-sleeved button-down, and a safari hat. I looked like Banana Republic circa 1986, but I was stoked. I immediately started planning ways to mod my outfit with personal touches—a Buzzcocks patch safety-pinned to the shoulder, a Warhol image stenciled on the shorts, a few well-chosen ska buttons on the crown of the hat.

The ink was still wet on my time card when Orville cornered me. "I appreciate that you're making an attempt to personalize your wardrobe, but there are a few details here that just won't wash. First of all, tuck in your shirt."

I made a plea for fashion. "Don't you think that's just a little too neo-Con? Nothing says 'my mommy dresses me' like a tucked-in shirt."

"Don't *you* think I'd come to work in sweats and Genie slippers if Disney allowed it? Second of all, shoelaces must be tied—don't even try to argue that one. And for Pete's Dragon's sake, tighten your belt. Nametag goes on the left side of your shirt. You have to take off *no less than one* of those thumb rings. Lose the chain wallet and put away the sunglasses. Guests need to be able to see your eyes."

I made the wardrobe modifications, and presented myself to Orville, who eyed me like he was sizing up a potential avalanche chute. He ran an exasperated hand down his face. "It's not even nine yet."

The photo lab was already humming with activity. Photographers in khaki uniforms streaked in, dumped canisters of film into the development machine, and ransacked a pile of camera parts before rushing back through the doors. Orville wasn't kidding about the skill level of these amateur shooters; they handled lenses the way toddlers handle kittens, and Orville watched them in periphery, his dry lips drawn tight against his teeth, his fingers skipping across the debossed letters on his nametag every time a lithium battery cracked against the linoleum floor.

I reached for one of the cameras on the countertop. "Nikon, huh? I'm a Canon man myself, but I suppose I can work with this."

Orville held up a pudgy hand. "Not so fast, White Rabbit. You may look the part of a Disney Cast Member, but you have a lot to learn before I can send you out on your own. Put that camera down and follow me." He opened the door and bowed grandly. "It's showtime!"

I stepped through the door of the drab photo lab and into another world. Everywhere I looked, there were brilliant colors and flashing lights. Huge dinosaur skeletons and roller coasters filled with rapturous, screaming children, grinning like newlyweds on Día de Los Muertos. Vendors were in mouse ears selling mouse-shaped toys and mouse-shaped ice creams. There was music everywhere, indistinct theme songs that quickly faded into the auditory topography, and the stench of sodium and high-fructose corn syrup.

It was like crossing the border from some undeveloped country of impoverished manufacturers into an empire of sensational hedonism. Despair didn't exist here. Neither did gloom or desperation or sad endings. Inside the impenetrable fortress of Disney World, fairies, genies, and mermaids were real; parking tickets, dead batteries, and blurry photographs were make believe.

It was my first time "onstage" as a Disney Cast Member, and it was thrilling. In my mind, I had just snuck into Disney World through an open back door, and now I was free to do whatever I wanted—so many gleaming handrails, so many clean surfaces. The smooth pathways banked through the vegetation, disappearing seductively beyond my reach every time I rounded a fresh corner. My shadow tugged at my heels, yearning to be set free with a pair of skates and a spray can. Orville was quick to remind me that I wasn't there to indulge my fantasies.

"There are thousands of details that set the Disney parks apart from other theme parks." His deep baritone suggested he was presenting a well-rehearsed speech in front of an amphitheater of new Cast Members. "Naturally, Disney properties are well tended, their communities virtually crime free, and their roads unblemished by potholes, but these details would be wasted effort without the cheerful smiles of the Disney staff." To demonstrate what he meant, he twisted his face into a stupendous jack-o'-lantern grin. "Now you."

I jerked the corners of my mouth upward the way I do when somebody points a camera my way. Orville's face dropped.

"Let's try something else," he said. "Pretend you're standing in front of a jury, trying to convince them you're *not* a sociopath. . . ."

Nothing was ever so bad in my life that Disney couldn't make it better: a skinned knee, a Little League losing streak. For small things, a simple Disney movie might have been enough. For bigger problems, it took a trip to Disneyland.

This was LA in the 1970s. The new Mickey Mouse Club dominated the after-school airwaves. *Bedknobs and Broomsticks* picked up an Academy Award for best special effects. *Herbie the Love Bug* was on a roll, and *The Apple Dumpling Gang* and *The Witch Mountain* series were the talk of the blacktop. All across America, every Sunday night, entire families fell silent as "When You Wish Upon a Star" signaled the opening credits of *The Wonderful World of Disney*.

For a six-year-old kid, Disneyland was the greatest place on Earth, a destination that was reserved for the most extraordinary of special occasions. Birthday parties qualified. So did Christmas and graduation ceremonies. Of course, I wanted to go to the park every day. I wanted to *live* at Disneyland. Every moment away from my parents was spent conspiring to escape bedtime and vegetables and all the other shackles of childhood regulation so that I could live out my days in wonderland.

I fantasized about inhabiting the Pirates of the Caribbean ride, that had those raucous bazaar scenes with the bawdy wenches and filthy, leering drunkards and the menacing skeletons draped over piles of glittering treasure. I would have given anything to step off the boat and disappear on one of those white-sand islands. To live among the fire-ravaged villages of the Caribbean of my dreams.

But that wasn't all. I wanted to be a part of the Small World ride too. And Mr. Toad's Wild Ride. Tom Sawyer's Island was a preternatural paradise to me, a place where parents never assigned chores and the pontoon bridge replaced homework as life's most challenging obstacle. And that huge wonderful tree house where the Swiss Family Robinson spent their days—I could haunt those branches for hours, transfixed by the sheer ingenuity of a canopied bed or a table made from a tree stump and a supply of water that was pulled from a crude but brilliant coconut husk conveyor.

Leaving the park was impossible. I was that kid in the tram throwing a tantrum all the way through the parking lot, grabbing light posts and car door handles and anything I could get my candy-coated fingers around. My life was at its best right there in Tommorowland.

My father, a sensible man, was an electrical engineer who owned his own computer business. My mother wrote allegorical children's stories about colorful witches. They met during World War II and built their lives in the postwar boom of mid-century America. They used words like "preposterous" and "swingin'" and laughed out loud at the wholesome comedy of *The Lawrence Welk Show*. Already in their autumn years when I was born, they were looking forward to my father's retirement, less than a decade away.

And so it happened, following a gripping spelling bee victory hinging around the word "flotsam," that I found myself awake at sunrise on a Saturday, turning on lights and banging pots and otherwise helping my parents wake up so that we could get to the park for a hard-won celebration. The trip from my front door to Disney's parking booth took forty-five minutes, but it felt like hours. We arrived before the park even opened.

While my dad paid for the tickets, my mother pulled aside one of the Disney staff stationed near the turnstile and whispered a few words in her ear. She smiled and nodded, then leaned down close to my face and whispered, "We have a special honor for boys who win spelling bees. How would you like to be the first one in the park?" My mom gave me a collaborative wink.

I couldn't believe my luck. I was to be allowed inside the gates of the Magic Kingdom before the park even opened. I had somehow found a loophole in the restrictive legislature of child management, and I was determined not to waste my opportunity. Once and for all, I was going to learn the answer to those age-old questions: Where did Mickey and his friends go when they weren't signing autographs or appearing in parades? What did they do when no one was looking?

I stood behind the velvet rope at the bottom of Main Street and imagined I could see Minnie pulling open the curtains of the chocolate shop and Goofy polishing the railings of the Magic Castle. When they drew back the rope and let me go, I broke free of my dad's grasp and ran as fast as I could through the winding streets of Fantasyland, confident that I would find things that no kid before me had ever discovered. By the time my parents caught up with me, two hours later in the Missing Children Office, I was exhausted and elated.

That little peek behind the Disney curtain was a religious epiphany. For the first time, I saw something more than just rides and candy and cartoon characters. I saw a *lifestyle* of happiness and support, a group of people who cared for parents and lost kids they had never even met just because they were sharing the Disney Dream.

"Freeze!" Orville snapped. "That's your Disney smile right there!"

I studied my face in a Tinker Bell mirror hanging in a souvenir kiosk and tried to memorize the feeling, but Orville was already beginning his tour of Disney's Animal Kingdom. There was a section loosely themed around Asia, and one like Africa. The place where we had started was Dinoland, and we finished in an area called Camp Minnie-Mickey, where, Orville explained, I would be spending most of my time behind the lens.

Each land was a neighborhood with its own distinct music, smells, and entertainment. Africa had dense vegetation and tribal drums, indigenous dancers performing subdued erotic movements, and charred meat on skewers. Dinoland was stripped down to look like an archeological dig inexplicably located in a carnival midway. There was nothing surprising about the layout—a Queen's necklace where each land was a crown jewel surrounding the park icon, which in this case was a large artificial tree called The Tree of Life, carved with hundreds of animal images and decorated with thousands of plastic leaves that shivered in the morning breeze. In each section, Cast Members wore costumes that defined their role: embroidered polyester in Asia, dashikis in Africa. Kiosk vendors wore shirts patterned with Rorschach designs and souvenir salespeople wore solids. Every Cast Member played for a team within the Disney franchise, and you could sort the teams by the color of their jerseys.

As we walked the park, Orville lectured me on the Rules of Disney. "When you're in an area with Disney guests, you must make yourself a part of their Magical Experience." Seeing my confusion, he heaved an aggrieved sigh. "You didn't read any of the literature, did you? Don't answer that; you'll spoil whatever Magic I have left today. Listen closely. Cast Members should always keep in mind the following seven Guest Service Guidelines: (1) Make eye contact and smile at each and every guest who enters the park; (2) greet and welcome each guest as they approach; (3) stop and offer assistance even if nobody is asking for it; (4) if you sense that a guest is having a less than Magical moment—are you listening to me?"

"If I sense that a guest is having a less-than-Magical moment." Parroting back the last five seconds of a boring lecture was a skill I had developed around the second month of kindergarten.

Orville sniffed and continued, "If you sense that a guest is having a less-than-Magical moment, provide immediate recovery any way you can; (5) project the appropriate body language on stage at all times; (6) preserve the Magical Experience; and (7) as she or he is leaving the park, thank each guest and invite her or him to return soon."

"Guest Service Guidelines," I repeated, staring at a beautiful girl dressed in a Pocahontas costume, posing for pictures with a group of children. "Got it."

Orville inserted his own considerable frame between the Native American Princess and me. "Let's try a simple exercise. You see those two Japanese women standing there looking at an upside-down map of Universal Studios?"

"Yes."

"Go ask them if they need help."

Some insipid Phil Collins song was trickling out of the vegetation—"Something, something, my heart." It combined the hopeful evangelism of gospel with all the soulful depth of a high school musical.* I moved cautiously to the side of the two women,

---

*While Phil Collins went on to receive two Academy Awards—Best Score and Most Original Song with "You'll Be in My Heart"—for his work on Disney's

trying to recreate my Disney smile from before. The women were in an advanced state of flustered, talking very fast in Japanese and tugging at the soggy map, like grommets fighting over a bong.

"Excuse me," I enunciated. "Can I help you?"

The women looked relieved to see somebody with a nametag. "Toilet?" said one.

"No problem," I said. Remembering one I had just seen, I jerked my thumb over my shoulder. "One hundred yards. On the right."

"Thank you," they chirped together, and ran off.

"Say-o-na-ra!" I said in my best Japanese, then beamed as Orville joined me. "Ta-da!"

"That," he said, "was terrible. Stage presence is of the utmost importance. When onstage, a Cast Member should always display appropriate body language. This means, stand up straight. Don't lean or sit or cross your arms. Keep your hands off your hips and make eye contact with the guest at all times. A Walt Disney World Cast Member never points with a single finger—and he *never* uses a thumb.* Instead, use two fingers." Orville held out his index and middle fingers together. "Or, to be on the safe side, the whole hand in the style of a karate chop."

Just then, a cheer erupted from the crowd, and Mickey Mouse appeared. He was smiling his big grin and walking with that classic Steamboat Willie swagger. Instead of his traditional primary-colored

---

Tarzan, the musical score was generally lambasted by his fans, especially those diehard Genesis fanatics, who felt particularly betrayed by the fact that on one of the film's main songs, "Trashin' the Camp," he performs an instrumental duet with 'N Sync. By the time he composed the score for Disney's *Brother Bear*, his fans had either forgiven him or stopped caring altogether, penning reviews on fansites like "just about memorable" and "not too intrusive."

*In Iran, a thumbs-up gesture means "go fuck yourself." It is impolite to point with the index finger in the Middle and Far East. If you show a Brazilian the "OK" symbol, you're calling that person an asshole. Generally, Disney advocates a policy of no hand gestures, although in a classic "damned if you do, damned if you don't" twist, it is also against the Disney Rules to put your hands in your pockets.

overalls, he was wearing a khaki safari outfit with an outback hat and scout patches on the sleeves. Everywhere he turned, people were adoring him as if he were the Second Coming.

"Is that one of the Mickeys I'll be shooting?" I asked.

The color drained from Orville's face, and he gave his forehead a vaudeville slap. "Oh my stars and garters!" he gasped. "When referring to a character such as Mickey or Minnie, keep in mind that each one is a unique individual and, as such, *must not* be referred to in the plural."

I watched the *one and only* Mickey Mouse disappear behind a Cast Members Only door, then reappear a few seconds later, looking mightily refreshed and maybe a little taller. "Aha!" I pointed with two fingers. "How do you explain that?"

"Each performer can only last so long in their costume in this heat," Orville said. "So when we make the exchange, you have to come up with a plausible reason why each character disappears for a spell."

"Like he's got a phone call?" I ventured.

"Absolutely not," Orville said. "A Cast Member should never let on that one of the characters is doing something 'out of character.' When Tigger leaves the autograph line every thirty minutes, he isn't taking a Powerade break; he is going to the Hundred Acre Wood for bouncing practice. Brer Fox is checking the briar patch, etcetera."

"So maybe Mickey got a phone call . . . from his Hollywood agent who just cast him in a provocative but tasteful new movie with leading lady Jessica Rabbit."

Orville frowned at me. "I think it's better if you don't say anything at all. Come on, I'll show you the backstage commissary."

I began to imagine Disney World as a kind of friendly monarchy, something along the lines of Monaco or the United Arab Emirates, with its opulent kingdoms built around shimmering resort hotels, or like a religion. The Church of Jesus Christ of Latter-day Saints has strict appearance guidelines, as do Jehovah's Witnesses and pretty much all sects of Islam. A Cast Member who peppers his speech with smiling courtesies doesn't think about that choice any more

than a Muslim thinks to praise Allah throughout his daily conversations. Wearing a conservative hairstyle is no more taxing than the
Orthodox Jewish custom of wearing side curls.

I was half paying attention to Orville's monologue as we entered
the cafeteria and got in line, so I didn't really notice the beautiful
Pocahontas until I bumped into her, nearly knocking over her Diet
Coke.

"Double-u, tee, fuck," she growled.

"Sorry about that," I said. Instead of her yellow Indian princess
dress, she had on an Adidas tracksuit, and her long, dark hair was
tied up in a bun, but it was definitely the same girl I had seen in the
park, smiling and signing autographs. She had the body of a dancer,
athletic and elegant, and a regal jawline. Her face was done in thick
makeup, rouged cheeks with long, dark eyelashes. She had eyes like
my ex, fickle globes that changed color with every mood swing. She
didn't say anything, so I added, "First day. I'm a little clumsy here in
the Church of Disney."

"Excuse me?" Her lip curled when she said this.

"Well, not literally. I mean. You have to admit it's *sort of* a religious
experience, right? These outfits. The characters. All deities in the Disney pantheon, and Walt's Papa Zeus." Pocahontas's face was blank.
"It's Disneyism," I babbled, now committed to my theme, "and Orlando is the Holy Land." I felt off balance. I was suddenly very con-
scious of my short hair and vintage Banana Republic wardrobe.

"You don't know what you're talking about," Pocahontas growled,
her now gray eyes churning like storm clouds. "Disney is about family values. Not religion."

I was flexing my arms, biting my cheeks, letting myself get riled
up the way I swore I wouldn't if I ever found myself face to face with
my ex-best friend. "Kids eat Mouse burgers like they're taking Holy
Communion, learning the Gospel of Walt: 'Tigger is real.' 'There's
only one Mickey.' You deceive children into believing you're a Native
American princess. What kind of values are you teaching these
kids?"

The flush rose from her tan chest, up her neck, and into her cheeks where it glowed like hot coals through the heavy stage makeup. She looked me up and down with unconcealed contempt. "Let me explain something to you, *photographer.*" She spat the word as if it was a bug that had flown into her mouth. "Piaget stated—and I *believe*—that the unconscious, or semiconscious characteristics of imagination must be stimulated early and often in a child's development to ensure proper cognitive development as an adult. What we do as Cast Members aids in the development of a healthy, productive society." She went on like this for a while, spouting social theories that echoed sociology lectures I hadn't paid attention to in college and couldn't understand now. I was acutely aware of other Cast Members in the commissary watching or pretending not to watch, entertained by my abject humiliation. Eventually, the tirade stopped and it was my turn. Orville was smiling as he turned his gaze on me.

"Children are idiots," I countered.

Pocahontas stormed off. I paid for my lunch and found a seat at one of the long tables. Five minutes later, Orville was still smiling at me over the top of his sandwich.

"That didn't go the way I expected," I said.

"It went pretty much exactly the way I expected," Orville said.

"She took it so personally."

"There's something you have to understand about your fellow Cast Members," he said, and I knew he was about to say something serious because I could clearly count his chins. One two three. "Disney World employs forty thousand people from all corners of the globe. They come to Orlando and work for minimum wage, and they don't care about the money. They work here because Disney makes them *feel* something: nostalgia, pride, love . . . Whatever it is, it's real, and it keeps them here for their entire lives." He pushed his plate away from him. "Cynical journalist types, on the other hand, don't last long here."

"You think I'm a troublemaker."

"If I thought you were *real* trouble, I wouldn't have hired you. We have a state-of-the-art security system with cameras, uniformed guards, and undercover 'foxes' who are trained to take you down long before you become a problem." He pushed his spectacles up on his nose and winked. "But I know that won't be necessary with you. I can see your momma taught you well."

His words summoned memories of my mother. I tried to picture her as she was when I was eight: vital, energetic, laughing at my ridiculous Baloo impressions, a spatula in her hand, a smear of cake frosting across her cheek. But the old images were flimsy, and easily replaced by modern apparitions of my mother struggling to walk from the bed to the dresser, trying unsuccessfully to keep food down, and fighting a juggernaut of pain just to fill her lungs with air. Was anyone with her now? Would anyone be at her bedside when she slipped away? My fingertips traced the soft skin around the base of my thumb where the ring used to sit. The shadow beneath my hand was formless and weak behind the tinted glass of the commissary. I struggled to convince myself that I wasn't listing to the side, that this feeling of vertigo was in my imagination.

Orville was staring at me as if it was my turn to do something. I could hear the echo of his lecture, but I had lost the thread entirely. "Don't you want to know what happens if you break the Rules at Disney?" he said with a gravedigger's sobriety.

My mouth was dry, so I just nodded.

He cleared his throat. "Punishments for disobeying the Rules are handled immediately. For most offenses, we have a system of 'reprimands,' whereby a Cast Member may accrue five points within any twelve-month period before being let go. Reprimands range from one point for a wardrobe violation to two points for unauthorized food tasting."

"Food tasting?"

Orville sighed. "No eating onstage, remember?"

"So that's it? No matter what I do, I get a slap on the wrist?"

"I'm not finished," Orville wiped the corner of his mouth on a napkin before delivering Disney's three supreme evils. "Number one: using, being in possession of, or being under the influence of, narcotics, drugs, or hallucinatory agents during working hours or reporting for work under such conditions. Number two: conviction, plea of guilty, plea of no contest, or acceptance of pretrial diversion to a felony or serious misdemeanor, such as but not limited to child abuse, lewd and lascivious behavior, or sale/distribution of controlled substances. And number three: violation of operating rules and procedures that may result in damage to Company property. Any Cast Member caught with a hand in one of those cookie jars would be terminated immediately.

"Termination," he continued, "isn't always a simple matter of being let go from Disney. If a Cast Member gets fired from the Kingdom, there's a chance she or he may never be allowed to visit the park again. Disney reserves the right to prosecute that person to the full extent of the law as a trespasser. In other words, you could be banished from Eden."

I've never been a fan of team sports—the sweaty male bonding, the common goal of victory over another group in different color jerseys, or the locker rooms. Which is not to say I didn't try: Little League, AYSO, flag football, Red Rover. I participated in everything, dutifully lining up on one desiccated field after another with a bunch of kids in the same color shirt. That's what I hated first about team activities—the ridiculous costumes that defined the tribes. But I quickly learned to despise the Rules of the Game even more. That was what first attracted me to skating: the total lack of structure meant I could participate any way I wanted. From the moment I got out of bed, I could be on my skates: out the front door and down the steps, up the driveway and onto the street. When the street got boring, I could move to the sidewalk with its never-ending obstacle course of pedestrians and baby strollers and dog shit. I made my own Rules. I wore my own uniform. It was the same feeling with surfing and skiing and later snowboarding—activities that empowered a person to blaze a unique trail through a constantly evolving landscape.

When I graduated high school, my brother Michael gave me a

copy of Ayn Rand's *Atlas Shrugged*. It was like a fuel dump beneath my teenage bonfire. Here, at last, was adult justification for my rebellious angst, an ethos that celebrated my individuality as a philosophical given (as opposed to organized religion that subjugated the individual impulses using tools like sing-alongs and vigils and, yes, even costumes). *Atlas Shrugged*, in general, and John Galt, in particular, was all the justification I needed to devote my life to the one thing I truly cared about: skating.

This decision was not popular with my father, a principled man of sensibility and reason who grew up during the Depression. But my mom made a successful appeal on my behalf to allow me to pursue my dream with the compromise that it would not disrupt my education. By my sophomore year in college, I had my first skate sponsor. By the time I could legally drink in the States, I had traveled to sixteen different countries on four continents as a pro rider.

My first tag was GALT. I'd paint it on walls in every city I visited, customized with a Celtic *T* and four circles that represented the wheels beneath my feet. I was fiercely loyal to the principles of individuality, vigilant against the comforts of polite society and anything that could be summed up with "-ism." When I was twenty-two, I bought my first camera and started a skate zine. This was back when print was still relevant, and it thrilled me to get letters from places I'd never heard of, to know that there was a global community of individuals devoted to the same principles I advocated. I imagined a secret society just like the one in *Atlas Shrugged*, made up of people who eschewed the Rules in favor of something better. This invisible web of independent thinkers replaced the Disney Dream as my idealistic vision of the future.

I left the park that day feeling as if I'd just finished cramming for a final exam. What had, at first, seemed like a whole lot of inane regulations was, in fact, a corporate lifestyle that bordered on autocratic fascism. It's no secret that the most restrictive societies in the world germinate the most vituperative rebellion. The despotic regions of the Middle and Far East produce the choicest heroin; an abnormally high percentage of diagnosed sociopaths have a military history; and everybody knows Catholic schoolgirls are the most mischievous adolescents on the planet.

The Disney Rule Book was a manifesto of totalitarianism, a recipe for deviance as certain as the countdown of a live hand grenade. It was everything I had fought against, all the principles that opposed my John Galt ideal of freethinking and counterculture individuality. But there was something glorious about it too, the genetic code of a seed that had been dormant inside me since my teenage rebellion. Accepting Disney in my heart meant surrendering myself to a beautiful truth that was far more seductive than my philosophy of earnest insurgency. Like the supernatural suck of an undertow or gravity's insistent tug, I could sense an irresistible comfort in Disney's unyielding order. The holy spirit of Walt was offering me a big, furry bear hug, and I was rushing to his bosom.

I Wan'na Be Like You

The most memorable Disney stories involve an ordinary person becoming part of a magical world. This is usually achieved through the assistance of a "magic broker" of sorts, a being who identifies the regular girl or boy as special, and somehow worthy of something more, and so blesses her or him with magical ability. Pinnochio had the Blue Fairy. Cinderella had her Fairy Godmother. Aladdin rubbed a lamp and brought forth the Genie. In *The Little Mermaid*, Disney reversed the formula and introduced a magical creature to the real world using an evil squid queen as the broker. The concept of a magic broker is a marvelous one, but ultimately dangerous. Anyone who believes a puppet can become a freethinking boy with the wave of a wand or a girl can find her prince if only she has the right accessories will have no problem marching off to fight an unwinnable war or going under the knife for questionable cosmetic surgery or toasting a glass of cyanide-laced Flavor Aid and stretching out to wait.

The night was still young and I wanted to test-drive my new look, so I drove over to Pleasure Island where, Orville had assured me with Red Bull–edged enthusiasm, I'd have a *sizzling* time. "You'll love it," had been his exact words. "Jazz, comedy, live bands, beautiful girls . . . or alternative lifestyle. There's a little something for everyone."

Pleasure Island turned out to be a series of bars, a theme park for adults where every drinking hole had its own identity. In addition to Orville's suggestions, there was Technoland, Discoland, and Two-Guys-Singing-Funny-Songs-on-a-Pianoland, each theme reinforced by interior design and costumed bartenders. The best part was, you didn't have to commit to any one theme. For a simple cover charge, you were allowed access to every dance floor on the property.

I couldn't believe the indecency: pop music, racy dancers, and wide screens projecting Ricky Martin videos. Bright colors smeared across the horizon: electric Midori shots sparkling down glowing blue ice blocks, dark Brazilian girls in raspberry miniskirts with warm butterscotch eyes. I wove through a carnival of sensations, anticipation crackling in the air around me like a Rice Krispie Treat. Pleasure Island was naughty and tantalizing, but somehow still came off as steadfastly wholesome. How did Disney achieve such a sexually charged atmosphere and still maintain a G rating?

Walking into this social atmosphere without my jewelry and hair felt awkward, like window-shopping in scuba gear. As I wandered from bar to bar, I struggled to understand how I could fit in at Disney World. Back in LA, I had been certain of my identity: a counterculture, atheist anarchist who sat in the VIP room sneering at how affected everyone around me was. It may not have been entirely *consistent*, but it was comfortable. At Disney however, I had no frame of reference. I was an animated wooden boy caught between two realities, not quite the creature I had been, but nowhere near the one I would become.

Eventually, I settled on the Beach Club, a live music venue decorated with surfboards and beach paraphernalia. The place was packed with groups of tourists: college grads in mall brand T-shirts, convention attendees drinking imported beer and slam dancing as if it were still relevant, and a retinue of goths, sipping pink cocktails. I scanned the cliques, hoping for some kind of connection, an anchor point to make myself less irrelevant among the throng of drunk strangers, then gave up and went to the bar. I bought a Corona and sat down on a stool where I could watch the chino-clad convention groups mosh to the band's rendition of "Mony Mony."

"I hate it when they change the lyrics!" the guy next to me shouted over the music. "Don't you?"

"I never understood the lyrics in the first place," I shouted back.

He was a rumpled Columbo-looking man, somewhere in his thirties. He smelled like gin. "They're supposed to hold out the microphone so the audience can sing, 'Hey Motherfucker! Get laid! Get fucked!' But since this is Disney property, they're not allowed."

So that explained it. Pleasure Island was sexy, but not *sexual*. Provocative, but not so much that it could be considered lewd or lascivious. It was just another variation on a classic Disney theme. They took you up to a certain point and then left the rest up to your imagination.

"Name's Brady," he slurred, extending a hand. "Do me a favor and watch my drink while I go take a piss." He fell off his barstool, picked himself up, and then stumbled to the bathroom. Sipping my Corona, I tried to relax into the atmosphere. I was a Cast Member now. I had the haircut and a nametag; I knew how to point with two fingers and smile on cue (sort of). All I had to do was catch the Magic and ride it in. But something wasn't clicking.

Brady returned with a new drink in his hand, which he set down behind his original cocktail with enormous concentration. As he maneuvered back onto the stool, I noticed he was favoring one leg.

"You okay?" I asked.

"What, you mean my pimp walk? That's nothing. Old battle scar, that's all." He tossed back his first drink and picked up the second. "To tell the truth, it makes for some real authentic show, if you know what I mean, a nice nuance for the performance."

I stifled a yawn, and scanned the room. "So you're in production." In LA, this line was the basic starter of any bar conversation; either you were in the Industry or you were aspiring. There were six versions of the Hollywood dream, and I'd heard them all.

Brady looked over his shoulder like he was checking for spies, then leaned close. "I'm a friend of fur," he whispered. "Mike Wazowski and I are fuckin' inseparable. Pooh and Roger Rabbit too."

"I see." For the first time, I considered the very real possibility that my new drinking buddy was certifiable.

"What about you?" he said, sizing me up. "You're, what, five eleven, six foot? I bet you know Tigger, or—I know." He snapped his fingers. "Aladdin!"

"Yeah, we play hold 'em on Fridays." I reached for my beer and stood up. "Well, I guess I'll see you."

"Oh!" Brady snagged my arm. "Shit, I'm sorry. I thought you were . . . You have the haircut so, you know, I just assumed you worked at Mouschwitz."

"Actually I do," I said. "As of this morning, I am an Animal Kingdom photographer."

"No shit!" said Brady, holding up his glass for a toast. "Welcome to the Greatest Fucking Job on Earth." I waited for him to laugh or crack a smile, but as far as I could tell, he was serious.

"Thanks." I returned his toast and sipped my drink. "Why did you ask if I was friends with Aladdin?"

He screwed up his face in what I assumed was supposed to be a conspiratorial smile. "It's *code*," he said. "When you work in the character department, you say you're *friends* with your characters."

"I get it. So you dress up as Pooh and Roger Rabbit, and what's his name." I tried to sound sincere when I added, "That's cool."

"It is." He nodded solemnly. "The character department is very cool." His reverential tone reminded me of the way surfers talk about Tavarua Island. I didn't see the attraction to dressing up as a cartoon character, but I could appreciate his passion. The guy loved his job the way I had loved mine. He drained his glass and slammed it on the bar. "Hey, you want to go to a party? It's Cast Members only. Should be a blast!"

Something about Brady reminded me of Tas Pappas, a skateboarder friend with a big heart and a chemical imbalance. He had a not-so-quiet insanity behind his eyes that made him seem capable of anything, as if crime was fun, but punishment was the real adventure. It was a quality I could relate to.

"Sure," I said. "Why not?"

I offered to drive after watching Brady pull a hip flask out of his pocket and drain it in one pull. Sitting in my passenger seat, he immediately lit up a joint and started slurring out random nonsense.

"I'm flying blind on a rocket cycle," he announced. "You gotta go up to get down." He rolled his window down at a stoplight. "I like your tits," he told the drag queen in the Jetta next to us.

"Thanks, honey," she rasped. There was lipstick smeared across her teeth.

Brady handed her a card. "Call me," he told her as she pulled away.

"Disney gives you business cards?" I asked. "What does it say? Friend of Roger Rabbit?"

"Wouldn't that be somethin'?" he chortled. "I don't have a business card. But my manager does, and sometimes his cards fall into my pocket. The bastard. Won't he be surprised when he gets a call from Tits McGee. . . . Pull in here and park wherever you can."

The building was an anonymous block of apartments that went on as far as I could see. Brady explained that we were in "the Disney ghetto," a low-income, high-density suburbia where Cast Members came and went at random. "It's depressing as fuck, but it's close to the parks, and there's plenty of . . ." He shot me a sideways look. "Well, whatever you're into, there's plenty of it."

As drunk as he was, Brady negotiated a maze of hallways that brought us to the front door of an apartment, behind which there could be no doubt a party was raging. A pair of boys dressed like fairy princesses crashed out of one door and into another, squealing as they groped and snapped each other's bras. Brady grabbed the door before it slammed shut.

I put a hand on his shoulder. "What kind of party is this?"

"Do me a favor," he said, turning back to face me. "Reserve your judgment. If there's one thing I can't tolerate, it's intolerance."

Whatever I thought I was going to see in the apartment—smiling Cast Members with identical haircuts, sipping spiked punch and crooning about how *waaaay-sted* they were—I wasn't prepared for the scene that was unfolding on the other side of that door. There were dozens, maybe hundreds of people swirling through the living room. As far as I could see, they were all young, beautiful, and seminude, abandoning themselves to a reggaeton soundtrack. Couples were paired off without regard to race, gender, or even exclusivity. One group was using tubes of cake frosting to paint an underwater mural, featuring Nemo, on the living room wall, licking off mistakes, and reapplying. As I watched, two girls disentangled themselves from each other to take turns making out with a muscular guy wearing what looked like a Ninja Turtle costume. The room smelled like rubbing alcohol, hash smoke, and something I once smelled in a Vietnamese flea market but never cared to identify.

A cute blond girl rushed the door when she spotted us. "Brady," she squealed, "you're totally late. We almost started without you."

Brady whispered something to her, and she darted back into the chaos of the apartment. I followed the friend of fur into the living room, careful not to step in a suspicious puddle in the foyer. I tried to assess the madness, but there was no epicenter. Sweaty Cast Members swirled around the room giggling, brushing against me before being sucked away. I tried to make eye contact. I smiled in a way that I hoped looked natural, but I couldn't make a connection. Cast Members looked at me through bloodshot eyes, and I would see the lack of recognition pass over their faces like a storm cloud before they turned their backs and walked away. In no time, I was an awkward junior high version of myself, eating Cheetos out of a salad bowl on the kitchen counter, wondering where the bathroom was.

Suddenly the music stopped and somebody cleared his throat. "Ladies and gentlemen," Brady announced. "Almost all of us know why we're here tonight." His announcement was met with cheers and suggestions of *to get fucked up* and *screw our brains out*. "All true," Brady continued. "All true. But tonight we have a higher purpose—a mission of Truth, if you will, because as Galileo said,

'All truths are easy to understand once discovered; the point is to discover them.'" Here, he paused for effect, but the crowd of on-lookers just blinked in expectation.

"We've gathered here to honor one of our dearest friends in the world, a young man who has shown great potential ever since he came to the Tragic Kingdom two years ago. He has been a friend to all, a booty call to many, and until this day, he has rested easy in the belief that we all think he is straight. Tonight however, we dispel all illusions in outing the newest queen in the Kingdom. Ladies and gentlemen, I present to you, everybody's favorite stunt monkey, Nick Elliot!"

At Brady's announcement, a cheer went up that rocked the walls of the apartment, and from the back of the room emerged the slight form of the Orlando rollerblader I had interviewed four months before.

Nick walked over to stand next to Brady, who raised a hand to silence the crowd's chant for a speech. "Um," Nick blushed. "Thanks. I guess this is an honor." He looked up at all the smiling faces in the crowd, and there was something like relief in his eyes. Then he saw me, and the color drained out of his face. "Uh, thanks," he said quickly and bolted in the other direction.

"Ladies and gentlemen," Brady announced. "Nick Elliot! In honor of our new 'mo, I have party favors for the first five people who can finish this sentence: 'Bright covered packages tied up with string . . .'" A dozen people rushed him.

I pushed through the crowd and eventually found Nick in one of the bedrooms. He was sitting in a corner texting on his Sidekick.

"Hey."

"Oh hey," he said, pretending to see me for the first time. "I saw your Myspace post about moving to Orlando. I didn't know when you were coming or I would've . . ." He closed his Sidekick, opened it, closed it again. "I didn't recognize you with your Disney Look. Nice haircut, by the way. You look like a constipated CNN stock analyst."

"Thanks."

"When I need my taxes done, I know where to turn."

"Very clever."

"Don't worry, Mr. Parker, I'll have Debby home by midnight."

"Are you finished?" I allowed him a couple more zingy one-liners before I cut him off. "How's it going?"

"What? You mean the outing thing? That's bullshit, bro. I just let him say all that stuff so we could get on with the party." Nick wiped his nose on a rainbow wristband. "I'm not gay, you know."

"I know," I said.

"Not that I have a problem with it. I mean most of the guys here are, and they like totally hook me up with their girlfriends, so I get pussy like all the effing time!"

"That must be fun."

"It is, bro. Believe me." Nick gulped his drink. "Besides, it doesn't even matter. I'm leaving in three weeks anyway. There's this new Cirque show opening in Vegas and they want rollerbladers."

"Vegas? What happened to life everlasting in Disney World?"

"Oh yeah," Nick snorted. "Well, Cirque pays better. Hey, what are you doing here anyway?"

I didn't feel like rehashing the events of the last few months, so I summarized. "I just needed a change of scenery, you know? LA was getting stale."

A group of Cast Members ran past us giggling. As they disappeared into the bathroom, a cute brunette grabbed Nick's hand. "Come with me," she said to him. "I want you to try something."

"Cool." When she turned around, Nick mimed an "O" face for my benefit. "Just so you know, dude, you're only seeing Alice's antechamber here. This rabbit hole goes all the way down."

"How deep?"

He let the brunette pull him to his feet and smiled at me. "You're staying in Orlando for a while, right?"

I shrugged. "Sure."

He put his hand on my shoulder. "Even candy apples can be rotten, but you have to take a bite to know for sure."

I Just Can't Wait to Be King

"**D**isney World!" Considering it was just after midnight in LA, Michael sounded surprisingly awake. "What kind of Peter Pan bullshit is this? What did Mom and Dad say?"

"I haven't told them yet." The lights were dim in the parking lot of the Budget Lodge. A family of opossums scrambled for the shrubbery when I pulled in. "And who cares what they say? I'm twenty-nine."

"Just so I'm clear on the plan," he growled. "What exactly are you *doing* out there?"

"Hurricane relief." I said it with a martyr's pathos because I knew it would piss him off.

I could hear him rubbing his temples, breathing through his nose. It was something he did when he was frustrated. "This is about Mom, isn't it?"

"No." I was twelve again, and an authority figure was asking if I *wanted* to stay after school. I cut my engine and slammed my Jeep door. It felt good.

"Really."

I tried to slam the hotel door too, but the lightweight particleboard made an unsatisfying swoosh. "Why did I even call you?"

"Because you thought I wouldn't answer."

"You're an ass."

"Are you finished?" There was a long silence before he spoke again. "She starts on chemotherapy next week. It's a long road and it won't be easy on her. The body reacts in unpredictable ways when you introduce these kinds of chemicals into the bloodstream."

"What do you mean?"

"Chemo works," he explained, "because it destroys rapidly dividing cancer cells. The problem is that it can't distinguish between healthy and malignant cells, so it affects all tissue. Her hair is going to fall out. Her nails will break. And that's just the beginning." He continued with a description so vivid I had to put the phone down and take a deep breath. The next time I heard him talking, he sounded angry. "Are you listening to me?" he said.

"A ten percent chance she'll end up with cardiomyopathy," I parroted.

"Let me tell you something," he continued. "I told you the real diagnosis because I thought you were mature enough to handle it. I thought Mom and Dad were underestimating you." His beeper went off and he stopped talking. When he spoke again, he sounded exhausted, like he'd just paddled through an undertow. "I have to go. Call me when you're ready to grow up."

My early memories of Disney were no different from those of any kid on the playground. I cried when Bambi's mom died and clapped my hands to bring Tinker Bell back to life. For Halloween, I dressed in character costumes. My favorite was Peter Pan—his wanton disregard for authority, his steadfast refusal to grow up. Peter had principles I could really get behind. If I could have found a way to get to Never Land, I never would have come home. I would have left family, friends, and everything that was familiar and wonderfully mundane for the opportunity to eat at a table with a real gang of Lost Boys.

Michael was in junior high at the time, but he was something of a prodigy at being an asshole. "Grow up," he'd say. "There are no such things as pirates or Peter Pan or Fantasyland. When are you going to learn that Disney is not life? Life—" Here, he would indicate the gridlocked traffic or a dog shitting on the sidewalk or some other meaningful symbol. "Life is happening all around you all the time. Deal with it!"

My mother was quick to shush him. "Tch, Michael. Let him have Fantasyland."

As the youngest child, it was my privilege and my curse to be allowed to live in a world of wonder. Now, however, it seemed my brother had a point. My first week at Animal Kingdom was anything but magical. I woke up before sunrise every morning and clocked in at the lab where I developed and filed pictures until noon. The photographers, who worked on commission, would breeze into the lab, dump their spent rolls in my inbox, and bolt back into the park without a word. At lunch, I sat alone at long tables packed with merch vendors and stilt walkers, in clusters of wardrobe-themed familiarity, like galaxies of planets made from related elements. Other than Orville's endless lectures on Disney etiquette, it was a socially successful day when I exchanged ten words with anyone before the sun went down.

Orville didn't trust me to interact with park guests, so he lined up chores that kept me backstage, away from the critical eyes of guests and park management. I relished my time outside the confines of the little lab, when I could enjoy the warm Florida sun on my face and the scent of orange blossoms and honeysuckle on the gentle breeze. Every break I got, I would wander around the park, trying to make sense of a world filled with life-sized stuffed animals and roller coasters scored with a soundtrack.

Animal Kingdom was Tarzan's park, and Simba's. Any Disney character that existed in a jungle-themed story found a home there alongside the real creatures of the wilds. It had a soundtrack of jungle rhythms and prerecorded animal sounds scientifically developed to make tourists feel as though they were on a fantastic safari of tame, brightly colored creatures. Timon and Rafiki welcomed park guests in front of the anteater habitat. Baloo and King Louie signed autographs near the kangaroos' domain. And every day, Mickey and Minnie dressed in safari outfits and posed for photos in kiosks along the greeting trails with families who reeked of frustration and chili fries.

I spent hours exploring the backstage of Animal Kingdom where the exotic animals had their nighttime dormitories, and vets and trainers scuttled between habitats in electric Pullman carts. I skipped lunch to ride the complimentary blue Schwinn bicycles around the dirt paths backstage. When I clocked out from the photo lab, I would roam around the backstage areas of Disney's other theme properties: Epcot and Hollywood Studios, Disney's Contemporary Hotel, the Wilderness Lodge, and Pleasure Island. Anywhere guests weren't allowed to visit. Backstage entrances were marked with helpful signs announcing CAST MEMBERS ONLY. I liked to go in one Cast Members Only door and out another, relishing the feeling of *privilege*. Backstage was an exclusive VIP club, and I was on the list.

I was especially intrigued by the backstage area of the Magic Kingdom, a system of tunnels known as Utilidors beneath the park where Cast Members could travel from one land to any other without ever seeing the light of day, ascending color-coded staircases to emerge behind a fake storefront or a theater lobby.* Rows of fluorescent lights illuminated the tunnels from above, highlighting the walls with a yellowish hue. Thick, insulated pipes of high-voltage cable and chilled water striped the walls of the corridor to form parallel lines along one entire side. Overhead, the AVAC waste disposal system rumbled every time a load of turkey legs was sent from Adventureland to the central garbage-processing plant.** I would get

---

*Technically, although they appear to be underground, and Cast Members refer to them as "tunnels," they are not in fact under the ground. The system of Utilidors and rooms that can only be accessed by Disney Cast Members was built at ground level, and the "onstage" area was built on top of it, making the theme park itself the second story of a massive structure.

**Designed in Sweden, the Automated Vacuum Assisted Collection (AVAC) system uses a structure of compressed air and vacuums to move trash through

lost following the twists and turns of the thick pipes of the futuristic trash chute, spelunking the labyrinth of corridors, filled with unmarked doors and unexplored passageways.

Smaller corridors shot off from the main tunnel like a web of veins coursing beneath the surface of the Magic Kingdom. Painted signs on the walls pointed the way to Frontierland and Main Street USA. Most of the tunnels, it turned out, were there for maintenance, air-conditioning equipment, or concessions overstock, but the center of the maze, just beneath Main Street USA, had a branch of Disney's bank, a cavernous locker room, and a café called the Mousketeria, which featured Spaghetti-Os in motor oil, innocuously labeled "chicken noodle soup."

It was here in these tunnels that I became fascinated with the beau monde sect of Cast Members known as character performers.

One afternoon, I was sitting at a table in the Mousketeria when Brady and a girl dropped into the seats across from me. "What's up, shutterbug?" he said, chewing on a straw. "Didn't think I'd see you at the Queendom."

"I come for the food," I said, "but I stay for the ambiance."

"He works over at DAK [Disney's Animal Kingdom]," Brady said to his friend. Then to me, "This is Jessie. She's friends with Pooh and the chipmunks."

"Charmed," she said with a coquettish smile. She had a cute face

---

pipes from all the dumping points in the Magic Kingdom to a central processing plant behind the park. The motor runs every fifteen minutes, pushing compressed garbage at speeds of up to sixty miles an hour through the pipes along the ceiling of the corridors. Most of the time, this noisy system is noninvasive; however, there is a legend: One afternoon, on the hottest day of the summer in 2000, the pipes ruptured over the central tunnel, dumping a load of half-eaten turkey legs and discarded ice cream cones right into the hub of underground activity. According to rumor, the hot garbage fell squarely on the head of a Sleeping Beauty who, sick of getting passed over for promotion to Disney management, was about to turn in her resignation papers and start a career in real estate. The AVAC incident bumped her status to "potential litigant," and she was handed a management position within minutes of stepping out of the shower.

and a solid body, like a gymnast's. She was wearing a Tinker Bell tank top that showed off well-defined shoulders sprinkled with freckles. "I think I remember seeing you at Nick's outing party. . . . Was that you? I was pretty lit. Anyway, it's good to see a DAK CM [Cast Member] slumming with us tunnel tramps!"

Brady dropped his jaw in mock exasperation. "Jessie, do you *have* to whore out to everybody you meet? Give the new guy a break."

Jessie punched Brady in the arm, then looked me over like she was appraising a mogul run—top to bottom and back. "Let's see. You're prince height. You're an athlete—I'm a contemporary dancer, so I can tell. I bet you do the Lion King show, right? Or Tarzan. I'd say Aladdin, but he doesn't live at DAK—just here and Epcot, right?"

Brady gave her a shove. "That's what I thought too! Turns out he's a photographer."

I wasn't certain, but I could have sworn a cloud of disappointment passed over her face. "That's the theory," I explained. "But I'm mostly doing lab work right now."

"Ohhh." Jessie scanned the tables behind me, then turned to Brady. "I *loathe* the thought of leaving, but I have to get over to the Studios for Fantasmic. Track 2 tonight. Fun, fun, fun!" The two air kissed and Jessie bolted without saying good-bye.

"That was weird," I said to Brady after she left.

"What was?"

"I've never felt embarrassed to be a photographer before."

He waved it off. "Don't mind Jessie. She's a star fucker, but she's cool once you get to know her."

"You and Jessie . . ."

"What?" he said. "Are you crazy? She's a Piglet."

"Yeah."

"I'm a Pooh." He registered my blank look with the serenity of a Buddha. "Same story: relationships never last. I make it a strict rule never to date anybody who's been approved in my characters. . . . Damn, I forgot how green you are. Come on, I'll give you the nickel tour."

Brady walked me down the main corridor to the Hub where the walls were lined with rack after wheeled rack of character costumes. Sweaty Cast Members in gray shorts and white T-shirts flung colorful outfits at wardrobe assistants who wheeled the racks through a doorway into a room that Brady referred to as the Zoo.

Just inside the door, three rows of ceiling-high racks were filled with character heads. A sneering Hook leered sideways at Geppetto who gazed serenely at Brady and me. Tigger and the Queen of Hearts rubbed noses on one rack while Goofy and Dale kissed on another. Roger Rabbit, Baloo, Tweedledum, Formal Minnie, Safari Minnie, and Minnie Goes Golfing. There were Six Mickeys, three Donalds, and all seven dwarfs. They sat on wooden racks like decapitated cartoons warning other animated creatures not to enter this kingdom.

We stood in the doorway of the Zoo while Brady pointed to the different character costumes. "Basically," he explained, "there are two different types of characters: fur and face. Fur includes any character whose costume covers the performer from head to toe. Obviously, fuzzy characters like Winnie the Pooh, Terk, Chip and Dale are considered fur, but so is Buzz Lightyear and Geppetto because they have masks that cover their heads. Face characters include the princess roles and some of the more human characters. Tarzan, Maleficent, and the Mad Hatter are face roles, although performers spend so much time getting into makeup, the up-close result is more Kabuki than reality."

"Why did Jessie call me 'prince height'?"

Brady nodded. "All character roles are organized by height. Mickey stands between four feet ten and five feet. The Queen of Hearts is six feet to six feet three. For that reason, most Mickeys are girls, whereas the Queen is almost always a guy. Disney is very strict about these height restrictions. Do you know why?"

"Actually, I do," I said, proud to show that I wasn't a total rube. "Guest Service Guideline 6: preserving the Magical Experience."

"That's right," Brady said. "A character set lasts thirty minutes with a thirty-minute break between sets, but during the summer, when the heat is unbearable, these sets get shortened to twenty minutes with forty-minute breaks. During the course of the hour that guests are waiting in line, they might see three to four different Plutos, so Disney made an easy-to-follow rule: to be 'approved in' Pluto, a performer has to be between five feet six and five feet eight."

A grinning Captain Hook head wielded by a flustered wardrobe assistant pushed its way through the door, and Brady nudged me back into the hall. "Some fur characters have further physical requirements. Woody's girlfriend, Jessie from *Toy Story*, for instance, has to be extremely skinny—and flat-chested—to fit into her shirt. The Tinker Bell who starts the Fantasy in the Sky fireworks show has to weigh exactly 115 pounds to make it down the zip line at a safe speed. It's pretty standard for Cast Members to classify people by their character range, so Jessie, who's five feet seven and reasonably slender, is said to be "Pluto height." You're about six feet tall, so that means you'll never be Donald or Pooh, but you're in the right range for Genie, Captain Hook, or one of the princes; therefore, you're 'prince height.'"

Brady guided me down a tunnel and into a room filled with wigs on Styrofoam heads. Two women were perched on stools, brushing the wigs. They barely noticed us standing in the doorway. "Face roles," Brady continued, "are more specific, and for that reason, they're more highly coveted. Hair color and style are incidental as every performer wears a meticulously maintained wig. This is non-negotiable. Disney doesn't care if your stylist sculpts your mane into a perfect Snow White bob. You will be wearing an even more perfect Snow White hairpiece. To an extent, race doesn't matter. Most of the Pocahontas girls are Puerto Rican or Dominican, while the Chinese princess, Mulan, might be anything from Brazilian to Vietnamese. But to be a face character, you have to exhibit an explicit list of facial features. Alice, for instance, has a soft, roundish face, while Jasmine has angles reminiscent of her Middle Eastern ethnicity. Tarzan is lean, Jane a little more filled out. Meg has Mediterranean eyes. Snow White has big round eyes. Eye color itself doesn't matter, thanks to the invention of colored contact lenses, but a smile always has to be natural."

Brady looked at his watch. "I'm afraid that's the end of the line," he quipped with the twang of a Wild West prospector. "Until next time, keep your hands in your pants and reach for the stars!"

Confined as I was to the Animal Kingdom photo lab, I didn't have many more opportunities to interact with the character performers. Still, I had plenty of time to meet my teammates on the Disney photo squad, and I could see Orville hadn't been exaggerating about their skills. Of the fifteen men and women in the department, only two had any photo experience whatsoever, and I was one of them. Most of the shots that passed through my hands were underexposed, blurry, or off center, a condition that never escaped Orville's watchful eye.

Eventually, I was promoted to film runner. My duties consisted of muling rolls of film from the photographers in Camp Minnie-Mickey to the lab and 5″ × 7″ prints from the lab to the sales desk. It was a minimum-wage duty that was usually reserved for the mentally challenged Cast Members, but I was working my way up, "earning my ears" as Orville would remind me. I didn't mind running the film though. It got me out of the lab and backstage where I could finally interact with my fellow Mouseketeers.

The Cast Members who worked in Food & Beverage were the most talkative. They would ask to bum a smoke and then chat about anything. The souvenir salespeople were equally friendly, as were the maintenance staff and anybody who carried a broom and dustpan around the outskirts of the park. The performers in the character department, however, were impossible to crack. They would survey my wardrobe and inquire politely about my job. Then, they would drift away. It was like pulling up to a Hollywood party in a Kia.

For all outward appearances, there was no single feature that united Disney Cast Members. They didn't have perfect skin or straight teeth. They didn't have to be beautiful or striking in appearance with Cinderella blue eyes or Charming high cheekbones.

Some came straight out of high school, their hearts filled with innocent altruism, whereas others were working through their retirement years. Men and women joined up in even numbers being myopic, bald, buxom, disabled, or wearing braces. There was no one representative race, religion, or hairstyle. In fact, if it weren't for the stringent appearance guidelines outlined in the *The Disney Look* book, there would be no way to pick a Disney character performer out of a crowd.

I wanted to believe that being a Cast Member was like being part of a kibbutz, everybody collectively working toward the same goal. But I couldn't fool myself for long. Eventually, I had to face the fact that I was part of a theme park class structure, and I wasn't at the top.

The bottom of the pyramid was composed of Cast Members who never got to interact with guests: gardeners and maintenance workers, janitors and ride operators—personnel who spent their time in the dark or behind the scenes, keeping the wheels of Disney's mechanism in motion.

The middle class was made up of workers in the service sector. This included souvenir salespeople, food and beverage handlers, and anybody who stood behind a counter in a silly costume. These Cast Members performed basic Disney functions like smiling and directing people to the bathroom.

But the ruling class at Disney was the character department. Characters were the reason people came to the park in the first place, and they were the reason people returned year after year. The people who were hired to be a part of the character program were considered the most elite group on property. Character performers weren't just Cast Members doing a job; they were pillars holding up the House of Mouse.

Even within the character department, there was a subtle hierarchy based on popularity. More obscure characters like Gideon (the cat from *Pinocchio*) or Meeko (the raccoon from *Pocahontas*) ranked lower than Disney's superstars like Goofy or Captain Jack Sparrow. And fur characters ranked lower than face. But the absolute pinnacle of the Disney Cast Member caste was the most romantic group of all: the princesses.

For three generations, little girls dreamed of being Snow White, Cinderella, or Sleeping Beauty. These princesses embodied a kind of Old World femininity, which dictated that a woman's worth was to be measured by the elegance of her gown and the grace of her curtsey. Then, in the 1980s, Disney introduced a new princess, a heroine who was resilient and strong and utterly lovable—the Little Mermaid, Ariel. She was, hands down, the sexiest character ever produced by Disney, and the character quickly became the most coveted role on property. Only the most beautiful girls could play Ariel, the ones with slender figures, natural C cup breasts, and perfect, white smiles. The antics of the animated character made her a favorite among little girls. The seashell bikini top made her a hit with chaperoning daddies.

It was widely understood that princesses didn't date below their status, which, in Ariel's case, meant Prince Charming or, at the very least, a mid-level manager—men who could afford to keep a princess in the lush trappings that her elevated status demanded. Somebody like me would never be able to score a princess. As a photographer, I was firmly embedded in the bottom of the class pyramid, somewhere between landscaper and hot dog vendor, not that I had taken a single photo yet.

My big career break came after a couple of weeks in the lab. One of the photographers called in sick, and Orville shoved a camera into my hand. "I don't have time to explain. Just go out to Camp Minnie-Mickey and shoot guests with the mice, then come straight back here. Do you think you can do that?" Within five minutes of developing my first roll of film, Orville called a meeting.

"Look at the way he sets up the shot with a balanced background." He used a Winnie the Pooh coffee stick to indicate different parts of my photos for a group of Cast Members in the lab. "The parents aren't trying to throttle their little brats. Nobody's blinking. This is how I want to see all your shots come in."

It made me uncomfortable. It made somebody else uncomfortable too.

"This photo is underexposed." The guy speaking was Pluto height, with dark, crispy hair and eyelids that looked like they were tattooed with permanent makeup. His voice had the serrated edge of a feisty Latin woman, thick with a lisping Puerto Rican accent. "Their faces are dark. He should have pushed it a third of a stop."

Orville squinted at the print. "Good eye, Marco. These Anniversary Celebrators are wearing white, so the camera's automatic meter function overcompensated for the brightness. We can all learn something from this. When there is a lot of white in the photo subject, remember to open the aperture a little more. One or two thirds of a stop should do the trick. Can everyone remember that?"

Everybody in the room nodded, their eyes like buttons on stuffed animal faces. Slowly, they grabbed their cameras and wandered back out into the park. Marco approached me, beaming.

"Hola, chico. I hope you don't mind if I point out the flaws in your photography." His words were draped in false sincerity.

"I don't mind," I shrugged. "I really didn't think the photo was that great."

"An artist has to be open for constructive criticism," he said, fluttering his Maybelline lashes. "It makes his work better."

"I don't know if this qualifies as art," I said.

He put his hand on my arm and smiled. "What *you* do is not art." Then, with an effeminate head flick, he did a little pirouette and walked out.

I recognized the type immediately. In polite beach society, we called him a kook, but there were plenty of other names for guys like Marco: ass-kisser, backstabber, liar. Kooks talked a big game. They tried to work their way into the tribe with fast talk and stories about twenty-stair handrails that nobody ever witnessed, but they were always undone by their actions. I hated kooks.

"Your alpha dog just pissed on my leg," I said when Orville appeared at my shoulder.

Orville had the plastic smile of a game show host who didn't care which contestant won, just as long as the camera stayed focused on him. "He'll get over it. Now, get back to Camp."

One of the perks of being a Disney photographer was getting to spend time in the air-conditioned character break rooms where performers changed out of their costumes, rested, and prepared for the next set. The Camp Minnie-Mickey break room was located right behind the kiosks, hidden from sight by hibiscus bushes through Cast Members Only gates. Unlike the underground tunnels of Magic Kingdom, the backstage at Animal Kingdom was outdoors at ground level. It was a world without landscaping budgets or background music; the barely contained swamp of Central Florida where crabgrass and creeping vines struggled for space between mobile trailers, aluminum-sided office warehouses, and cracked concrete patios; and a place where Cast Members could sit down, eat, and point with one finger and frown. Of all the frowning people backstage, the most morose were the ones in the character costumes. Sprawled out in lounge chairs, wearing fractions of sweaty animal costumes, they swore and smoked and looked genuinely miserable.

At first, it was disturbing—these big, furry animals with sweaty human heads, but eventually, I grew comfortable with the foul-mouthed hybrids. At that point, it didn't seem so strange when, one morning, checking under the stall walls for a free toilet, I found a lineup of big colorful feet: Rafiki, Goofy, Brer Rabbit, just doing what comes natur'lly.

After a week or so in the kiosks of Camp Minnie-Mickey, I got to know some of the character performers. There was a Pluto named Alan, a Goofy named Rusty, and some guy doing Tigger who changed his nickname every few days and would only respond to the proper moniker. It didn't take me long to cross the line.

Some kid had just punched Mickey in the nuts and run off, trailed by profusely apologizing parents. The woman in Mickey was a sweet-natured, bespectacled woman in her fifties named Sunny, who always brought her own vegan lunch in a brown paper bag.

She was doubled over when I reached her side, white, four-fingered gloves clutching at her mouse belly and the Mickey head grinning amiably.

"Holy shit, Sunny," I whispered, low enough that no guest could hear. "Are you okay?"

The Mickey head jerked up and the white glove slashed across its throat in the universal symbol of "Cut!" then wagged back and forth in my face. Without a sound, Sunny straightened up and finished her set. Later, she pulled me aside by the bathrooms.

"You can't talk to Mickey like that."

"I was afraid you were hurt," I said. "Nobody heard me."

"I'm fine. Thank you," she added. "But don't ever talk like that to a character again."

I didn't do much better with the others. As the days passed, I spent hours in the kiosks, punctuated by ten-minute intervals backstage, where I recharged on Powerade and tried to stay out of everyone's way. In the break rooms, some Cast Members read books. Some listened to music. For the most part, however, break room activities included those things you might do if you were, say, sitting around a campfire or attending a slumber party: telling stories, singing songs, 7 Minutes in Heaven—pretty much anything that killed time.

Disney performers had their own language, a combination of institutional jargon and backstage shorthand. Some of these were basic acronyms. Disney's Animal Kingdom was referred to simply as DAK. The Festival of the Lion King show was FOLK. Cast Member was CM. Property-wide, the soundtrack that played over the loudspeakers was called Background Music, or BGM. If a Cast Member was part of the college program, she or he was a CP.

Characters had nicknames. Cinderella was known as Cindy. Gideon was called Shitty Kitty. When the original animated crew, composed of Mickey, Minnie, Donald, Goofy, and Pluto, appeared together, they were referred to as The Fab Five.

Some expressions, outlined in Employee Manual, were used by Cast Members to conceal those less Magical aspects of a family vacation. Janitors referred to a pile of puke as a "protein spill." Should a guest encounter serious physical problems that required outside medical attention, security would call for an "alpha unit" rather than that decidedly unmagical vehicle known as an ambulance.

Then, there was the lexicon of the entertainer, the terms that allowed character performers to speak in codes that even the administration wouldn't understand. The one-minute visit, composed of a hug and kiss, an autograph, and a photo, was affectionately referred to as a "love and shove." Children who came to the park because of the efforts of the Make-A-Wish Foundation were simply "Wish kids."

If a performer got in trouble, she or he got a reprimand. If the performer got injured, she or he might get an early release, or an ER, to go home or to the doctor. If the injury persisted, the performer might get restrictions, basically a low-impact job that allowed the Cast Member time to heal. Restrictions could be anything from greeter duty to trash detail, depending on the nature of the affliction and the disposition of the coordinator.

Everybody wore a set of basics beneath their costume, a pair of gray shorts and a white T-shirt, issued every morning in quantities of three by the Zoo. Basics served the dual purpose of absorbing sweat on a sticky day while allowing male and female Cast Members to share a single break room. Each performer got her or his own fur and, at least theoretically, every costume was washed daily.

A typical break room conversation went like this:

"I just did two back-to-back Shitty Kitty sets. My back is killing me."

"Why don't you get ER'd and take restrictions?"

"No way! They'll stick me in the Zoo, or I'll get stuck cleaning up protein spills all day."

"It's better than another day in Cindy doing love and shoves for Brazilian Tour Groups. I tell you, that BGM is driving me crazy!"

Like any language, it felt a little unnatural at first, but within a few days time, I was speaking like a natural-born friend of fur.

Within the walls of the break room, performers could relax and be themselves. There were sofas and easy chairs, bathrooms, towels, TV, and, of course, plenty of Powerade. At their most fundamental level, break rooms were a rest area for the performers, a place to re-hydrate and recharge between sets. But they were also the social hub of the character program.

"Hey, you guys! Question time!" Alan stood on a chair to ad-dress the room. "Suppose you were stranded on a desert island. What three items would you want to have with you?"

"That's easy," the Tigger said who, this week, was calling himself Shayde. "A flare gun, a tent, and one of those satellite phones with a GPS system that lets you call from anywhere on the planet. That way, I could get *the fuck* off the island before some cannibal finds me."

"Girl," Rusty called everyone girl, but he pronounced it "gr," like a growl without the rumble. "Girl, that's too sensible. This is a *fan-tasy* desert island."

Alan held up his hand. "That's okay. What's his name is entitled to his choices."

"Wanna know my three things?" Rusty asked "First, I'd have a beautiful catamaran to sail around my island. Second, I'd want one of those see-through airplanes like Wonder Woman has so I could look at everything from above. And third, a computer so I could e-mail all my friends to tell them what a great time they're missing."

"I'd want three of my friends with me," Sunny piped.

Alan nodded his head at me. "What about you, camera guy? What would you take to your desert island?"

"My longboard," I said. "Assuming there's a good break there. Or maybe a skimboard. I suppose it's no good to ask for a boat and a wakeboard, since I'd have to drive it myself, and then what fun is that, right?" Crickets. "A speargun would be useful too."

There was a moment of silence while everyone in the room tried to translate whatever I just said. "Well, I know exactly what I'd take." Alan dropped down into the chair, crossed his legs, and looked in-tently around the room to make sure everybody was listening before he continued. "I'd lay my Fendi towel across my Chanel lounge chair and wait for Johnny Depp to serve me mimosas!"

As a rule, serious conversations were avoided in the break room. Philosophical discussion topics ran the gamut from sexy celebrities to desert island fantasies, abjectly avoiding all serious news. The 2000 presidential election, for example, while hotly contested in the courthouses of Central Florida and obsessed over by record numbers of concerned citizens around the nation, went largely unnoticed in the break rooms under the Magic Kingdom. At the time the final count was made official, ushering in George W. Bush as the forty-third president of the United States, the break room behind Camp Minnie-Mickey had divided into two passionate factions: one that proclaimed *The Sound of Music* to be Julie Andrews' greatest role, and the other, which steadfastly argued for *Mary Poppins*.

Since I had no opinion whatsoever of grand issues like this one, I was quickly marginalized from the rest of the character performers. I didn't get hazed or excommunicated or anything. I just wasn't let into the inner circle. If characters were talking about something scandalous when I walked into the break room, they would suddenly drop their voices to a conspiratorial whisper or change the subject. As someone who was accustomed to being part of the cool clique, I found it a little disconcerting to be on the outside.

To preserve my self-respect, I decided I needed a place of my own. The dubious charms of the World Famous Budget Lodge were wearing thin, and I wanted with increasing urgency to integrate myself into the Disney community. And so, when I saw a note on the DAK character bulletin board advertising a room for rent, I called.

Johnny was a soft-spoken good 'ol boy who used a lot of exclamation marks in his text messages. His avatar was a smiling image of a NASCAR driver, waving from the top of a champion's podium. His ringtone was Justin Timberlake. He claimed to be a nonsmoker with no pets, looking for a nice guy to share his two-bed, two-bath apartment, located in the Disney Ghetto. He wanted $400 a month.

"Ah'm just a regular kinda guy," he told me, his phone voice thick with Southern drawl. "I put in mah nine to five and wind down mah day with a Scotch and some NASCAR." He paused, and I could hear the sounds of ice clinking against a glass. "It doesn't bother you that ah drink, does it?"

"I'm not into Scotch," I said, "but I'll join you for a beer."

Johnny was in his late thirties, Geppetto height. His smiling eyes and flushed cheeks gave him the appearance of a frat boy on spring break. He was grilling steaks on the patio when I first pulled up in front of his apartment. Offering me a beer, he flashed a big smile.

"Welcome to Orlando, roomie," he said. "Ah hope you're hungry."

I'd been living off mouse-shaped burgers and Slurpees for the last week, so the smell of steak was making my mouth water. "I'm starving."

He wore the pleasant expression of someone who had just re-membered the punch line to an amusing joke. "Your bedroom is on the left. Dinner should be ready in thirty minutes."

His apartment was clean and well organized, decorated with black leather and Jeff Gordon memorabilia. He had a better-than-decent home theater system and a well-stocked wet bar. Everything gleamed as if it had been bought right off the showroom floor.

My room was standard, big enough to fit a queen-sized bed and a couple pieces of furniture. The walls and carpet, which smelled brand new, were identical shades of Eeyore gray. I had a window overlooking a little garden, and my own bathroom.

Johnny was setting the table when I emerged, showered and changed, half an hour later. "Ah hope you don't mind," he nodded at the TV, which was showing NASCAR. "Normally, ah wouldn't be so rude as to watch TV during dinner, but Jeff Gordon's racing tonight. In my humble opinion, there's nobody better. You a fan?"

"Not really," I said. In *my* humble opinion, watching NASCAR was about as thrilling as watching snow melt, but the food smelled so good, I wouldn't have cared if we were at a NASCAR museum.

"Ah'm recording it anyway." Johnny flicked the remote and the screen went dark. "Ah record everything. It's a habit ah just can't seem to break. Photography is it?"

"Sort of. Right now, it's more point-and-shoot than art."

"Ah'm sure you'll do great," he enthused. "Ah'm proud to say ah had a hand in making the Disney system. You know those photo machines on the dark rides? The ones that take your picture right when the track drops out from under you. Ah used to manage the sales booth on Splash Mountain. Maybe five, ten times a day, some girl would get the idea to flash her titties for the camera. Well, ah couldn't sell those ones. In fact, ah couldn't even show them. So ah created a policy: if a guest was riding in the same log with a flasher, he just had to explain the situation to me, and ah would personally escort him to the front of the ride so he could have his Magical Moment *complete* with souvenir photo. Ah shit you not. Ah told my nephew about it, and he has never waited in line since!"

I offered to help with dinner, but Johnny had already taken care of everything. In addition to steaks, he had also prepared garlic bread and a salad, all of which was served on black plates with black handled flatware.

"This looks amazing," I said. "You have no idea how much I needed a home-cooked meal after five days of junk food."

"Well, don't be shy," he said, handing me the salad bowl. "If we're going to live together, we have to learn to trust each other." The salad was one of those spring mixes, made up of difficult-to-pronounce lettuce. "Ah have a confession to make." Johnny flashed a devious smile, looking about as dangerous as a dolphin. "Ah'm not like the other tenants here in the Disney Ghetto. Ah'm kind of an anah-maly."

"What do you mean?"

"Most everybody here works in entertainment," he said. "But not me. Ah work in public relations. Pepper mill?"

"No thanks. What do you promote?"

"Mostly ah work with the Disney Vacation Club and Cruise Lines. Everybody told me ah should be the cruise director, but at my age, ah thought PR would be more respectable."

"How old are you?"

"Thirty-seven, but they say you're only as old as the ones you feel, and ah been feeling pretty youthful lately. . . ." Here he paused, so I could bond with him over the pleasures of young flesh. "Bit of a Peter Pan complex maybe."

Right away, I liked Johnny. He was relaxed and easy to talk to. He didn't have many hard opinions, preferring instead to see how I felt about things, then nodding and smiling as if I had just said the most sensible thing in the world. He was reassuring in a psychiatric sort of way, and he made one hell of a steak. All through dinner, he told stories of couples he would catch necking on Splash Mountain. He used baseball terms to explain how far he'd let them get before embarrassing them with a warning announcement.

"So," he said through a mouthful of steak, "have you met anybody in Orlando yet?"

"I haven't really settled in yet," I said. "I got my heart broken in LA, so I'm just a little cautious. And rusty. What about you?"

"Not interested in settling down." Johnny smiled. "Orlando's got too many opportunities. Ah used to do most of my dating through the *Sentinel*, but then ah discovered Craigslist."

"Personal ads? Does that really work?"

"Does it ever!" he laughed. "Ah can get a date with anybody ah want within six e-mails."

"Trolls or hotties?"

"Beauty is in the eye," he said, swallowing a bite of salad. "Ah tell you what, the next time you see somebody coming out of mah room on Saturday morning, you can be the judge. But do me a favor, if you're not sure you recognize him, just call him 'Dude' or something. It'll save me a lot of embarrassment later on!"

I went to the kitchen for another beer so I could consider this new twist. My roommate was gay. So was my boss. And if my instincts were correct, most of the people in the character program. In principle, I didn't have a problem with that. Growing up in LA, I knew lots of gay men and women. I had just never lived with any of them.

When I sat back down at the table, Johnny cleared his throat. "You don't have a problem with me being gay, do you?"

"No problem," I said. "As long as you don't mind that I like girls."

"How do you say it in California?" He pretended to search for the right words. "Ah'm totally cool with that."

"Great," I said. Sensing that we had just crossed our first roommate hurdle, I held up my fresh beer for another toast. "So, do you have a lot of one-night stands?"

"Not too many." He shook his head, smiling the whole time. "But ah don't let guys stick around too long either. Ah have a tendency to get mah heart broken too, you know. And not just by guys who look like Jeff Gordon."

"Turn and burn," I said, thinking about my ex-girlfriend, who, according to rumor, had already moved in with my ex-best friend. "You let people in too deep, and they just end up hurting you."

"You'll get over her," he waved it off, the peaceful smile never wavering from his lips. "Ah learned from mah mistakes. Now, ah just date guys who are emotionally unavailable, and ah don't get too attached to anyone or anything." He pointed his fork at me. "That's the lesson ah learned. No commitment, no disappointment. Life's a lot safer that way."

Johnny sipped his wine, smiling happily, and cut himself another bite. When he ate, he switched his fork from left to right hand in that way that suggested a quaint, practiced Southern charm. He chewed with purpose, listened thoughtfully, and responded with positive affirmations that made me feel like I was a good person doing smart things. His eyes were calm and glassy like the back side of a wave when you punch through, just as it's about to crash.

That night, I lay on the carpet of my new bedroom, wrapped in a blanket, contemplating my situation. I had a decent apartment and a fun job in the Sunshine State. Romance and friendships would come in time, as would furniture and probably a whole lot of heatstroke. But I was, I felt sure, on the right path.

Whistle While You Work

Legend has it that Walt Disney wasn't much of an artist. He didn't know how to draw the modern versions of Mickey or Donald and had to consult his illustrators in order to duplicate his own famous signature.* Once he turned a project over to his stable of illustrators, the folklore goes, it became a product of the Brand. But what he may have lacked in artistic skill, he made up for in entrepreneurial acumen. He knew the value of packaging and presentation, that the tiniest details could mean the difference between success and failure. His adoration of the Disneyland theme park (the only park that was completed in his lifetime) was fanatical in its entirety, and he went to great pains to make sure each of his projects bore a perfect facade. He constantly fussed over its appearance and the presentation of its attractions, assigning hundreds of chores that cost thousands of dollars in overtime hours.**

---

*Naturally, this point is denounced by Disniacs as a muckraking conspiracy theory. Not coincidentally, these are the same people who swear that Walt's head is cryogenically frozen, waiting for technological advances in the field of human reanimation.

**For example, every night, after the park closed, custodians were assigned to repaint the dulled targets in the shooting gallery. It has been estimated that every year, landscapers replaced 800,000 plants in the park because Walt believed

He was a man of great principles. Sometimes heralded as a creative genius, sometimes denounced as an obsessive-compulsive narcissist, but everyone agreed that he was a man of puritanical diligence. A product of Midwest values and Industrial Revolution savvy, he learned how to make money the old-fashioned way: from children.

Apparently, word had leaked that I was "talking inappropriately" to Mickey, because Orville felt it necessary to give me another round of lectures. As he led me through the backstage pathways of Camp Minnie-Mickey, his booming voice commanded the attention of every spider monkey between the park entrance and Africa.

"Mickey Mouse is the most important person at this park." His tone was designed to convey enormous responsibility. "People save up their entire lives. They work overtime in third-world sweatshops. They travel thousands of miles just to shake hands with Mickey Mouse. And they are counting on you to capture that memory on film. Cheerfully," he added. "Wordlessly."

I struggled to keep up with his enormous strides as we approached the character kiosk, basically a gazebo with an entrance gate, an exit gate, and a backstage access gate marked with a CAST MEMBERS ONLY! sign. "I get it," I said. "Mickey's a unique snowflake. Walt Disney's the messiah. Guests rule."

"What did I say about cynicism?" Orville asked rhetorically. "Your job is to stand here, in this kiosk, for ninety minutes, and take photos of the guests with Mickey and Minnie. As soon as the next photographer relieves you, you are to go over to that kiosk where you will take photos of guests with Pooh and Tigger for another ninety minutes. After that, you may take a break. Do you have any questions?"

"Put me in, Coach."

The whole first week, I felt self-conscious standing in that kiosk

---

KEEP OUT signs to be the antithesis of Magic. He refused to sell chewing gum on property because he anticipated its inevitable terminus on the bottom of a guest's shoe. To this day, it is impossible to buy gum at a Disney park.

with a pair of rodents the size of short skis. I hid behind my camera and smiled at anybody who looked my way. Eventually, though, I started getting the hang of it. "Smile," I'd call out. "Say Mickey!" When the mice went backstage, I'd announce that they were going for a short "cheese break." When Pooh disappeared, I'd say he was going to get some "Hunny." If the character performers found my behavior more appropriate, they didn't show it. As long as I wasn't publicly defacing the Magic, I avoided embarrassing lectures.

Disney had rules for every situation from a hostage crisis to on-stage childbirth. One day, while I was shooting with Mickey and Minnie, a couple came forward for what I assumed was a regular autograph signing. There were hugs and smiles, and suddenly, the guy dropped to his knee and proposed to his girlfriend.

My first instinct was to shoot the whole process from beginning to end, but the mice stopped me. According to the Rules, a Cast Member had to stand aside and patiently wait until the girl either accepted or declined the proposal. If she accepted, we were allowed to gush and congratulate the happy couple. If she declined, we were meant to fade away into the background. As in all things Disney, negative imagery wasn't allowed to taint the Magic.

The way Mickey and Minnie kept the guests moving was a ballet of efficiency. A hug, an autograph, a photo, then send them on their way. To help keep everything flowing, the characters had assistants, called greeters, who stood in the kiosk and helped orchestrate the process. On average, they cranked through one family per minute, sometimes more. But it never appeared rushed. Everybody left with a smile.

Up close, I got a real sense of just how difficult it was to be a good character. A performer could only see out of fine black screens that covered the nose and mouth of the character head, so there was no peripheral vision. Since every kid who approached a character came in below the performer's sight line, Tigger, for example, had to move slowly and carefully, a characteristic that was difficult to maintain when you were trying to be a bouncy, fun-loving tiger.

Signing autographs in costumes like Tigger was especially difficult because the performer had to make it look natural as if the character was really looking at what was being written when actually the book was resting on the tiger's nose, on top of the performer's head. You had to hope the pen was facing the right way and the book was turned to a blank page or else Tigger looked like an ass.

For other characters, like Donald and Pluto, performers could see out of the eyes as well, but no fur was equipped with ideal visual range. Visibility was so limited in some heads that performers were forced to adapt to do their jobs. In Goofy, for instance, a Cast Member could only see out of the mouth, giving him a perfect view of the guest's feet and some very small children. But in order to see a bigger child or an adult, he had to tip the head back, giving the impression that Goofy was gazing up at the sky—believable for a moment, but not for any extended length of time. Pooh faced a similar conundrum. The performer could see out of the mouth and a little bit through the nose, but between the two, there was a huge blind spot. The performer got a perfect view of the guest's feet and face, but nothing in the middle. Somebody could hand Pooh an autograph book or a carrot or a stick of dynamite, but the performer had no way of knowing what the item was until the guest put it up to the bear's nose.*

To overcome these problems, the entertainment department developed character-specific movements to enhance the visual range.

---

*In 1981, the parents of a nine-year-old girl sued Disneyland, claiming that their daughter had received a beating from Winnie the Pooh. Robert Hill, the Cast Member in question, was called in to testify. If any part of the Pooh suit struck the little girl, he swore, it was an accident. Hill's lawyer then asked for a recess, during which Hill changed into the Pooh costume and remounted the stand. As Pooh, he answered questions by nodding his head and stomping his feet. When asked, "What do you do at Disneyland?" he responded by dancing around the courtroom. Everyone laughed. "Have the record show," the judge said, "he's doing a two-step." At his lawyer's urging, Hill demonstrated how difficult it was to maneuver inside the bulky suit. Within twenty-one minutes, the bear was acquitted on all charges.

Goofy bobbed his head up and down like an autistic dog. Pooh swayed back and forth like a blind musician keeping rhythm with a song in his head. Baloo jitterbugged, Mushu did tai chi, Rafiki invoked the elements with his voodoo staff, and so on through the roster. These actions provided a sweeping motion that eventually summed up every guest interaction.

As a side effect of character blindness, the performer's other senses became keenly acute. Inside a head, a performer could hear people talking from halfway across the park. Thick accents were easily identifiable. A child's scream was earsplitting. I used to think the characters were immune to the smells of the outside world, but, in fact, it was exactly the opposite. Any scent that drifted into the head stayed in the head: cigarette smoke, perfume, garlic breath. Passing gas inside a costume was to be avoided at all costs. The stench was trapped inside the body until the character bent down to hug a child, then blew out the only opening in the suit—the mouth. Within a week, I'd lost count of the number of times I heard a child turn to his parents and say, "Eew, Pluto has doggie breath!"

Every day, I spent ninety minutes with the mice, followed by an hour and a half with Tigger and Pooh, then Pluto and Goofy, and back to the mice. By three o'clock in the afternoon, I had the routine down. My pockets bulged with extra rolls of film. I smiled at everybody, determined to take the best family portraits they had ever seen. I was becoming, if not the best Cast Member Disney had ever employed, at least not the most egregious. The afternoon mouse greeter, on the other hand, sucked. He was an elderly gentleman with an uncultivated thicket of nose hair, who had a habit of forgetting where he was. Every so often, he'd wander to the back of the kiosk to hum little tunes and admire the hibiscus flowers, leaving the characters alone to entertain the guests and keep the line moving. By Rule Book standards, that behavior warranted at least two reprimands, but he'd been around so long, he had earned himself a teamster's right to be clueless. Still, he should've sensed something was up long before the South American mob arrived.

I was one roll away from wrapping up in the kiosk. The shadows were starting to lengthen again, and the moisture in the air around the hibiscus bushes had settled into a gentle simmer. Two Japanese women were jumping up and down, unabashedly giggling with Mickey and Minnie when I first heard the chant. It didn't sound like much, a rhythmic rumble like a marching band was coming our way. I posed the Japanese pair between the mice, took two photos (one for certain, one for safety) and handed out the claim ticket so they could find their photos later in the day. The old greeter was studiously picking his nose in the back of the kiosk, so I did his job, ushering the women to the exit gate, still giggling and gushing and waving to Minnie.

That's when I saw them. There must have been twenty people in the group, a small, efficient army in green and yellow T-shirts, rolling up the exit ramp like a tidal wave. They were singing as they came, dancing to the lyrics of a homemade Portuguese war song, and taking no notice of anything in their way. There was no mistaking it; they were hooligans.

The Japanese women dove over the railing into the hibiscus bushes just seconds before the mob crashed through the exit gate. Minnie, who recognized the signals right away, was already halfway up the Cast Members Only pathway, running as fast as her little legs would carry her. But Mickey was distracted, dancing a little jig for a family of Indonesians. The poor mouse never even saw it coming.

Pinned to the back of the kiosk by the advancing horde, I shot an entire roll of film as the mob swallowed the smiling mouse. Six or seven of them grabbed Mickey by all four limbs and hoisted him over their heads. As they passed him into the middle of the circle, they spun him around until his head was sideways, his arm twisted at an unnatural angle. One of his shoes bounced on the ground at my feet, before being quickly snatched up by a young boy with the face of a cherub. "Obrigado," he said and smiled. And then he was gone, consumed by the group, already retreating down the exit ramp, their hostage held high above their heads. I watched until they disappeared around the corner and their song faded away, leaving only BGM and crying children.

"That was incredible," I said to the greeter who appeared, finally, to have noticed something amiss. "What just happened?"

"Damn Brazilians," he muttered. "They think they can get away with anything."

I teetered on the knife-edge of adrenaline. "They took Mickey!" More than anything I wanted to follow them, just leave the camera and my nametag, and join the Brazilians for whatever adventure they planned next.

"Don't blame yourself." The old greeter mistook my excitement for self-reproach. "These tour groups are all made up of assholes. All of them! And they're only half as bad as the Family Reunions." He stabbed my chest with a bony finger and lowered his voice. "Know what I say? Screw 'em."

"Brazilians?"

"Guests. Screw 'em all." And with that, he angled himself up the Cast Members Only pathway and disappeared among the hibiscus.

It was my indoctrination to the Us vs. Them relationship between Cast Members and guests, and it came as something of a shock. I had spent my entire life in opposition to the institution, fiercely loyal to the principles of individuality and independence. In the world of California beach culture, antiestablishment behavior was the norm: punk rock, illicit sex, a healthy rivalry between sports that occasionally expressed itself in a bar fight or a territorial tagging. Anything counterculture was fair game.

My first reaction to the Mousenapping was empathy with the mob. Disney was a place where dreams could come true. Whether you were looking for a holiday from death or a five-foot-tall mouse grinning like a huffer, Disney was the destination. The Brazilians were just having fun, grabbing a souvenir that a thousand other Cariocas hadn't already brought back to Rio. Who could blame them for rising up against the Disney regime with their zero-tolerance policy for nonconformist behavior? No jewelry. No frowning. No ironic realism to temper the sticky sweet Goodness. Everybody dressed alike, wore the same haircut, and spoke in Disney code. Cast Members were clones of an Americana that never existed before *The Disney Look* book was published. But now that I was a card-carrying member of Mouse Inc., I was expected to squeeze myself into that very same mold.

For the first time since moving to Orlando, I felt a vast, oppressive loneliness crushing my confidence. I was nobody here; worse than that, I was the new kid at school, cliqueless, trying not to get beaten up before lunch. I had no point of reference for a corporate lifestyle. No network of friends to watch my back. Shortly after his coming-out party at Brady's house, Nick had packed up and moved to Vegas. Other than him, I didn't know a single person in Florida. I was alone in the middle of an ocean, treading water, and I was drowning.

After I clocked out, I sat on a bench under the Tree of Life for a while, dialing numbers of friends in LA and leaving messages. I had become so used to my costume that I didn't realize I was still in it until a security guard kicked me out for sitting and talking on the phone onstage. I drove around the property aimlessly for a while, eventually ending up at the Magic Kingdom Cast Member parking lot. It was the same dilapidated theme as all Cast Member gateways. Tall weeds were pushing their way through fissures in the crumbling asphalt obscuring faded signs. Men and women with Disney haircuts leaned against Nissans smoking and swearing and bitching into their Bluetooth headsets. It was about as Magical as diarrhea, but it made me feel better, somehow, that beneath the Rule Book patina, people—even Disney Cast Members—were, after all, people.

I followed a group of colorful Cast Members—attraction greeters in striped jerseys and Outdoor Foods girls in bright pleated skirts—onto a tram, which dumped us in front of the underground entrance to the Kingdom. The cement floor inside the Utilidors was slick with humidity and a layer of vending cart grease. Entertainers on break between autograph sets chatted idly in wardrobe doorways, enunciating clearly to be heard over the hum of the air-conditioning machinery. I had to step aside for a Pargo loaded with cleaning supplies, a glum duet of janitors in the front seat chewing beef jerky side by side, as silent as salt and pepper shakers.

Radio Disney was playing at full volume from speakers hidden behind the pipes and insulated ducts overhead. A little boy from Toronto was trying to answer the day's quiz. "What letter comes between R and T in the alphabet? Here's a clue: it begins words like 'spaghetti' and 'Snow White.' " There was a pause and then the little boy took a wild guess. "Is it an S?" The DJ went wild, as did Mickey, Minnie, Goofy, and at least one chipmunk.

I kept going, nodding at Cast Members along the way. Baloo and Dale turned down a corridor toward Toontown, temporarily leaving Minnie to struggle with an immaculate four-fingered white glove. Belle rolled up her sleeve to place a Nicoderm patch on her arm, smoothing it with one hand before carefully replacing the sleeve and pulling her underwear out of her butt.

Just ahead, Mary Poppins was pacing in her Jolly Holiday outfit, holding a cell phone in one delicate white-gloved hand. Prim red lipstick accented the ribbons in her white summer dress. Her pink parasol leaned against the wall beside her. "And they have no clue," she was saying. "Those motherfuckers. If they try to stick me in Pluto again tonight, I'm walking out. I'm serious. Fuck that! I haven't done fur in two years, and I'm not starting now." It was a miracle that she could get service down here. I made a note to set myself up on her phone plan.

There was nobody interesting in the Mouseketeria, and only a handful of people loitering in the hub by the Zoo, so I kept walking toward Frontierland. I was just about to climb one of the stairways into the park when I saw Pooh shuffling down the hallway with a familiar limp. I caught up with him at the break room door.

"This is *not* a good day," Brady moaned. "I am *not* feeling the sparkle."

"Forest fire in the Hundred Acre Wood?" I quipped.

He tossed the bear head into a corner and slumped down into an armchair. "I was supposed to be in Mike Wazowski all week," he said. "Instead I got screwed into doing Pooh sets."

"I see."

He pointed a threatening yellow mitten at me. "I'm not just being a diva. This suit is heavy. No performer does a whole week of Pooh without a break. Or restrictions. Normally, I wouldn't complain, but I specifically requested—"

Suddenly the door opened, and a grim-faced manager entered the room. He was Jafar height with thin lips and a crooked nose. He had the complexion of a pallid autumn squash. "I was told you wanted to talk to me," he growled at Brady.

Brady spread his furry paws. "Why did my schedule change?"

"Schedule's not written in stone. Sometimes it changes." The way he said it reminded me of my brother Michael telling me to stop playing make-believe.

"I understand that, Sam, but couldn't you just run it by me first?"

Sam sighed as if the question was causing him great pain. "Why?"

"It's my schedule."

"Actually," Sam said, glancing at his watch, "it's *my* schedule. It's your job." As he was about to walk out, he noticed me. "Who are you?"

I didn't like his tone. He sounded like a security guard on a power trip. "Name's Travis." I figured he wouldn't know the Motocross Champion. "Travis Pastrana."

"Well Travis, you're not supposed to be here."

I drifted across the room and sat down on the edge of the sofa. "How about here?" I said.

Sam blanched. "Give me your Cast Member ID."

I made a big show of patting my pockets. "Shit. Left it in the carriage with my glass slippers. Will you take a Dave & Buster's gift card?"

A bead of spittle was frothing at the corner of Sam's mouth. He drew himself up to his full stature and leveled a finger at Brady. "One reprimand."

"What!" we said in unison.

"And you're in Pooh until June." He turned to me. "You have a choice. You can leave now, or I can have security escort you out. Your choice."

"I'll wait here," I said. "I hate leaving a building without an escort."

The manager narrowed his watery eyes at me, then turned on his heel, and stormed out.

"Cunt," Brady said under his breath.

"That was totally my bad," I said. "I didn't mean to get you in trouble."

"Don't worry. I'll get out of it." He struggled against the tight neck of his costume. "You always carry that chip on your shoulder?"

"I have issues with power trippers."

With great effort, Brady pushed himself out of the armchair. "Well, get used to it. It's, like, the official psychosis at Disney. Here." He offered his back. "Can you rip this open for me?" I undid the Velcro at the back of the Pooh suit, then sat down on the sofa while Brady stripped down to his basics. "Since you're in such a dogmatic mood, how would you feel about helping me with a little project tomorrow night?" he asked.

"I owe you one. What do I have to do?"

"It's nothing dangerous. It just requires a certain—finesse. I need someone who's willing to color outside the lines a little."

"Is it illegal?"

"Possibly, but it's not unethical. Is that a problem?"

For the first time in weeks, I felt a natural, nonregulation smile tug the corners of my mouth. "That's my favorite combination."

"I'll pick you up tomorrow night at seven. Wear something dark and bring a pair of construction gloves."

The next day was one of those rare, perfect days like you only get after a spring snowstorm in Banff or a sunrise session in Malibu. The air tasted as clean as a blown glass ornament, ripe with ripples of fragrant blossoms that you could almost see on the soft breeze. A little crop of clouds hung in the blue sky, inert like a perfect, painted backdrop. The parks were packed with crowds, every ride decorated with a line that coiled around itself like a conch shell, but still the guests smiled with neighborly joy.

It was my day off. My body was on a sunrise schedule, so when I woke at dawn, I jumped into my Jeep and drove to New Smyrna Beach. There were shark warnings posted on wooden signs in the sand. I rented a board from a Rastafarian in a hut and paddled out to where a handful of surfers were bobbing on shortboards. It felt good to do something familiar, to connect with nature again, and to contemplate the direction my life was headed. Since moving to Florida, I hadn't spent a single hour at a skate park. I hadn't even thought about doing a guerrilla art project. No stencils. No spray paint. For some reason, I was no longer considering the world in an expressive or artistic framework. Was this Disneyfication?

As I often did in the water, I thought about Michael. My brother and I had never been close. He was born eight years before me, so I got the "benefit" of his counsel more than his fraternal love. Some of his sage bits of wisdom: grow up; get a life; you're too young to understand. Still, it didn't stop me from worshipping him.

When I was twelve, Michael gave me my first surfboard. It was an eight-foot Robbie Dick gun with triple thruster fins, signed by the man himself. I woke up one morning, and there it was at the foot of my bed, wrapped in toilet paper, with a note: "Happy birthday little brother. Michael." It didn't matter that it was a hand-me-down or that it wasn't my birthday. I loved it. While Michael warmed up the Volvo, I attached a leash and put a Peter Pan sticker on the deck where I'd be able to see it as I paddled out.

I usually stayed inside where the waves were smaller, but I figured, now that I had a gun, I deserved to ride with the older guys.

The waves were big that day—in later stories they would grow to be double overhead—but on this special unbirthday, Michael was urging me to catch the sets on the outside, and I was determined not to let him down.

It took me about fifteen minutes to paddle out, but I wouldn't have stopped if it took me all morning. When I finally set up on my board, at my brother's side, I felt like I'd achieved Nirvana. On the outside, the water sparkled like a bottomless wishing well. Pelicans skimmed the glassy surface, patrolling for leftovers from the preening seals. Michael put his finger to his lips and pointed to a pod of dolphins playing in the swell around us. Following his lead, I dipped my hand into the water and one of the sleek creatures brushed against my fingertips. It was the first time I can remember feeling the physical pain of beauty.

He caught the first wave of a big set. I watched him ride in and paddle back out to me. "Don't turn your back on the ocean," he admonished, pushing my nose so that I faced Catalina Island. "Turn your board around and keep your eyes open for the next set." But there's something about a thing as big and beautiful as the ocean. You get charmed by it, dazzled, and you kind of lose your self-awareness. Another wave came and again Michael took it. I couldn't take my eyes off him as he rode all the way in.

I felt the suck before I saw the wave, and suddenly, I was inside the washing machine, my face being dragged across the sandy bottom. I struggled to stay calm, but I was running out of breath fast. Just as the panic started, the wave released me and I clawed my way to the top, gasping for air. My leash was still attached to my ankle, but the board had been snapped in half, severed just beneath the Peter Pan sticker. The nose was twenty feet away, skating along the shore, taunting sandpipers as they hunted sand crabs beneath the foam.

"What did I tell you?" Michael shouted, more angry than was necessary. "Never ever turn your back on the ocean!"

As Michael and I got older, we grew more and more distant. He went to college and medical school and settled down with his own family, whereas I fell in love with the beach, the skate park, and any place that nurtured a Lost Boys lifestyle. I was a fast learner, and I had a natural gift for finding shortcuts that would reduce the stress factor in my life and allow me to chill. We quickly learned to ignore each other.

Now that I had moved across the country, it seemed that I had become a priority to him again. I spent a minute questioning his motives, then gave up and let myself get lost in the moment. I was out of shape from a month without surfing; just paddling out made me winded, and by the time I caught the first wave, I felt my shoulders burning. I spent the morning chasing a decent left, then found a burger place and slept on the beach for a while. It was exactly what I needed to bring balance and perspective back into my life. By the time I was back in my Jeep, crossing the swampy marshes of Central Florida, I was recharged and determined to fight the process that was sapping my individuality. Johnny handed me a beer the moment I walked in the door.

"Ah got two steaks on the grill," he announced. "And ah Tivo'd Talladega. What do you say?"

"I hate to eat and run," I said. "But . . ." I gave him the short version of the last couple of day's events, wrapping up with Brady's invitation. He took the Mousenapping in stride, and my misgivings about allegiance to the Corporation. But when I got to the part about my acquaintance in the Pooh suit, his expression froze, and he didn't say anything for the rest of the story.

"How well do you know this guy?" Johnny said when I finished. He was still wearing his trademark pleasant expression, but it looked forced. He poked at the steaks with uncharacteristic violence.

"I wouldn't call it a friendship," I backpedaled. "I met him at PI. He works in the character program."

He nodded, his Disney smile pinned securely in place. "Ah see. So you don't really *know* him." He continued to nod, while he sipped his whiskey. "You know, ah'm not one to judge, and people are people, God knows, but . . . Sometimes, people aren't exactly who they appear to be."

Johnny never uttered a critical word about anyone, so this tepid ambiguity rang out as a resounding warning bell. "What do you mean?"

"One hears stories about certain Cast Members. Especially the ones in the character program. Especially if they've been around a while."

"Okay." I waited for something more, and then when nothing came, "Am I supposed to distrust every Cast Member with a retirement plan?"

"Now, you have to understand, Disney's a small community . . . like a family. And like any tight-knit family, we have skeletons." Johnny's smile was slipping. He drained his glass, and went to the bar. When he reappeared, he seemed to have regained his composure. "You've worked here long enough to know how it works. People in the character program are just . . . how do ah say this? Wired differently than you and me."

"What do you mean?"

"Ah've heard a lot of stories about CMs in the character program," he said.

"True stories?"

He shrugged. "Ah've never worked in characters so it's hard to know for sure, but everybody tells the same stories . . ."

"Tell me one."

Johnny swirled the ice in his glass, then his face lit up. "There was this one guy who must have been working there for ten years. He was the pride of the character department: Chip, Dale, and Quasimodo. He brought Roger Rabbit to life in a way that no one else could match. But, by far, his favorite was Winnie the Pooh with his bashful smile and his honey-colored fur and his potbelly that was just big enough to jack off inside."

"Excuse me?"

"This was the late nineties, when Pooh wore a honey pot on his head with bees flying around it. A performer could pull his arms inside the costume to wiggle the bear's nose and then push them back into the paws to sign autographs. Or, at least that was the costume designer's original plan. This guy liked to pull his underwear down around his thighs and have at it."

"But–"

"How could he?" Johnny interrupted, now at full speed with his story. "Is that what you were going to ask? 'How could he masturbate *and* sign autographs *and* pose for photos without losing focus or breaking character? Surely, that kind of multitasking requires supernatural concentration.' Simple. He could do it because he was, above all, a professional. He knew the choreography by heart and was able to do the dance steps in his sleep. He could sign souvenir books with one hand, grab his pecker with the other, and wiggle Pooh's nose with his elbow. Since Pooh is a right-handed character, he just had to learn how to jerk it with his left. After all, it wasn't like there was a whole lot else for him to do inside that suit for thirty minutes straight.

"You said this was an old costume. So it's not still going on, right?"

Johnny shook his head. "The new design has arms that the performer can't get out of. Rumor has it this guy was sorely disappointed when they unveiled the new Pooh wardrobe. He dragged his feet through character sets until the *Monsters Inc.* costumes came out."

"I don't get it."

"One of the stars of *Monsters Inc.*, Mike Wazowski, is the same height range as Pooh. Basically, a giant eyeball with stick legs, Mike Wazowski is shaped in such a way that the performer has to keep his arms inside the costume at all times. He could eat a burrito in there if he wanted to, or check his voice mail, or, yes, even jack off!"

"So he still works at Disney?"

Johnny sipped his Scotch. "Like ah said, ah have no idea if it's even true. It's just something that ah heard around the proverbial water cooler."

It seemed a little off-color, but Johnny certainly had a lot of details. For the first time, I was beginning to understand Nick's warning that night at the party. *Even candy apples can be rotten, but you have to take a bite to know for sure.* I had a mouthful of candy apple, and I was looking at a mighty suspicious piece of fruit.

Cruella de Vil

Disney villains are easy to spot because they're storyboarded to be bad. They make sweeping entrances on discordant swells. They have fingers like daggers, chins that jut at obscene angles, and goatees dripping from sneering mouths like pubic stalactites. They have names with sounds that make you frown: Maleficent, Jafar, Shere Khan, Scar. Disney cinema contains no subterfuge, no twist in the plot where an honest, trustworthy character is suddenly revealed as a malicious antagonist. Unlike the real world, where people—even the most wicked ones—believe they're doing the right thing and struggle constantly with shifting conceptions of good and evil, Disney villains wear their black, twisted souls on their sleeves. They're archetypes of evil, and they fascinate us.

At seven o'clock that night, I met Brady in the parking lot. He pulled up in a Range Rover that smelled as if it was about three hours old. "Nice whip," I said, sliding into the seat next to him. The backseats were down, and there was a heavy tarp spread across the carpet.

"Thanks," he said, lighting a joint and passing it over. "I like to be comfortable." As he pulled out of the parking lot and onto the long stretch of highway that leads to the East Coast through the Everglades, he demonstrated some of the Rover's features: paddle shifting and a top-of-the-line navigation system. I didn't know much about English cars, but I knew this kind of ride didn't come cheap. Johnny was right—a character contract was unlikely to afford such luxury.

What did I really know about Brady? He had been at Disney long enough to be approved in every character in his range. He flaunted achievements and defects alike as badges of pride, but kept secret the source of his information. He was socially connected and tech savvy (surprising since most of Central Florida seemed to be about five years behind the technology curve). His avatar was Che Guevara. His ringtone was Shostakovich.

And what did he know about me that made him think I'd be willing to finesse a midnight mystery adventure? I gave him a ride once. I helped him out of his Pooh suit, and I mouthed off to his manager. It seemed unlikely that our limited interaction would cement a thieves' bond between us. It occurred to me that I fit the profile for one of those swampy dismemberment victims: alone in a new city, no friend of the law. I was already pretty sure Brady was a certifiable sociopath; just how far could he go?

"So," I said in a voice designed to set serial killers at ease. "What's the plan?"

He looked at me as if he was trying to decide if I was responsible enough to borrow his *good* board. "How do you feel about premeditated domestic neglect?"

His tone suggested it was the kind of thing I should be against. "I'm against it."

"Good, because tonight we're going to do something about it." We passed a building that looked like it had been turned upside down, a two-story teddy bear. "Not too far from here, just on the outskirts of Orlando, there's a pit bull being patently neglected by her caretaker."

"A what?"

"We're going to liberate the beautiful creature and set her up in a safe house."

"Did you say 'pit bull'?"

He took the last drag off the joint and threw it out the window. "Does that frighten you?"

"It's my understanding that neglected pit bulls can be hazardous."

"That's quite possible," he agreed. "And there's a good chance she won't want to be rescued."

In my distinguished career as a juvenile delinquent, I emancipated many items: Watchamacallit candy bars, king-sized Ralph Lauren sheet sets, and patio furniture. I spent many happy afternoons in the Sherman Oaks Galleria moving items from store to store, thrilling as much from the restocking of inventory as I did from the original shoplifting. But I'd never stolen anything alive, and there was something unsettling about the thought. *Things* didn't care where they existed; a sweater was just as happy tied around my waist as it was folded on an Old Navy shelf. But a dog had a home and a caretaker and needs.

We drove past a souvenir shop shaped like an orange, an ice cream stand shaped like a swirly cone, a funhouse, a hedge maze, and a medieval dinner show set in a fiberglass castle. The sidewalks were filled with tourists buying bootleg Mickey beach towels, waiting for tables at Outback Steakhouse. An old man in a wide-brimmed hat sat in a nylon beach chair in the middle of a dirt parking lot. A sign at his feet advertised his trade: Genyuwine Florida navels. $3 a bag.

"Why me?" I asked.

Brady rolled down his window, and I could smell the wilderness of the Everglades closing in on the car as we moved away from the city lights. "Don't take this the wrong way, but you seem like the kind of guy with a certain moral, um, flexibility."

"How should I take that?"

"As running commentary."

"Just to make sure I have this right: we're stealing somebody's dog?"

"Not stealing. *Rescuing.*" Brady's face relaxed into a comforting smile. "Try to think of it as 'salvation.' While this dog might not, at first, realize that she is being saved and might even put up a struggle to defend her substandard lifestyle, she will ultimately come to realize that she can benefit from our intercession. We are going to give her a better life."

I surveyed the tarp in the back of the Rover. "And what is this better life?"

"I have a contact at Animal Kingdom, a trainer who takes care of strays. She'll make sure the dog gets all her shots and gets into a loving home. If that makes you feel better."

"If I don't have rabies by the end of the night," I said, "I'll feel better."

I probably should have been more worried, driving into the dark Florida swamp on a dognapping mission, but it felt good to be doing something illicit again. Illicit, yet oddly humane. We drove for another twenty miles on a two-lane highway through dense swamp, the only light coming from the dull glow of the Rover's dashboard.

"I heard Sunny got snatched from the Minnie-Mickey kiosk," Brady said.

"Was that Sunny?" I pictured Mickey's twisted body, high above the Brazilian mob, and felt a sudden pang of empathy for the woman. "I watched them take her."

Brady shook his head. "She came out of it okay. Couple of bruises I think. They'll give her some cushy restrictions for a while, and she'll be back in the saddle." He glanced sideways at me. "Speaking of which, you met anybody yet? A nice photographer or a dancer? DAK's got a smoking Poca."

I played with the tilt of my seat. "It hasn't been as easy as I thought to break the ice. Especially characters."

"You have to understand something," Brady said. "Character performers are like members of a country club. They seem intimidating from the outside, but once you're in, bam! You're part of the family. And you know what they say: if you can't keep it in your pants, keep it in the family!"

"So how do I get in?"

"Ah, the eternal question. How does the outsider get *inside*. And once inside, what will he do so they don't think he's a fraud." Brady dropped his voice to a whisper. "You have to earn their trust."

"How do I do that?"

He turned down the radio and cleared his throat. "Cast Members in the character program are—how do I say this tactfully? They're not normal. They're deviant and diabolical. For the record, I don't recommend it, but if you really want to join our club, you simply have to do something to prove that you're cut from the same cloth."

"Like jacking off in a costume?"

He looked at me sideways. "That rumor's still circulating, huh? I thought it died out when they changed the Pooh body."

"Word on the street is Mike Wazowski works the same way."

Brady laughed out loud. "I have no doubt you'll figure out a way into the inner circle. Just don't get caught. The character manager you met yesterday, Sam. He's one of the more pleasant authority figures roaming the tunnels." He stopped and his face went dark. "Here we are."

To me, it looked like the rest of the swamp. There was no sign, no light, no pavement—just a worn dirt track off the highway. Brady barely hit the brakes as he turned off the highway and bounced the Rover to a stop under the low-hanging branches of a cypress tree where the Spanish moss hung down just past the license plate. A hundred yards away, an Airstream trailer glowed like polished ammunition, nestled in the swamp. By nomad standards, it was nice, lined with Malibu lights, and a garden gnome.

"Alright," Brady said. "It's 8 p.m. The owner of this fine specimen of '70s Americana should have just clocked in at his low-pay, medium-risk security job. Due to his inability to maintain a meaningful relationship, the dog will be alone. You brought the gloves?"

"On sale at Home Depot."

"Bangarang." Brady smiled. "Let's make some mischief."

The cypress trees cast shadows like crooked hands along the gravel and scrub, the Spanish moss glowing like tinsel in the moonlight. I followed Brady as he limped along the edge of the shadows, approaching the trailer from the side. About twenty feet away, he stopped and crouched down. The trailer was silent; the only movement was the spooky Spanish moss swaying around us.

I crouched next to him. "Where's the pooch?"

"She's right there." From under the tree, I could barely make her out, a sleepy mongrel with fur the color of dirt, snoozing by the rear tire. She was tethered to the axle of the Airstream with a piece of rope. "We need to move as quickly as possible, so here's what we do. You grab the dog while I untie the rope."

"How come I have to do the grabbing?"

"Because you have the gloves."

"They're one size fits all," I said, holding out the gloves.

"Are you gonna help me with this or not?"

There was a wild desperation in Brady's eyes. I was pretty sure he could go postal without much buildup. "Fine."

"Okay." From a jacket pocket, Brady pulled a small package. In the shadows, I could just make out the gleam of his teeth. "Every negotiation requires incentive, and this situation will certainly call for negotiation." He opened the package and unfolded a layer of wax paper to reveal chunks of roast beef. "If she shies away, offer her some of this. She probably hasn't eaten in a while, so she should warm right up to you."

The smell reminded me that I hadn't eaten dinner yet. "Hope she doesn't mind sharing," I said.

"I wouldn't." He handed me a fist-sized chunk. "They've been marinated in muscle relaxant. One bite will knock you out for the rest of the night."

I took the meat in one leather-cased hand and followed Brady into the open, crouch jogging like PlayStation soldiers toward the Airstream. Immediately, the dog woke up and began to lose it, straining against the weave of the rope, teeth flashing in a haunting chorus of howls and growls. We stopped within feet of her dripping snout.

Brady hissed. "Negotiate!"

I tossed a piece of meat in front of the dog and, right away, the barking stopped. She kept her eyes on us while she lowered her nose to the offering. Up close I could see that she was way too thin, shaking with fear. Her fur was missing in patches where she had chewed herself down to the skin and beyond. Gingerly, she nibbled at the edge of the roast beef, then snapped it up and devoured the whole thing. Immediately, she began to growl at us again.

"What do we do now?" I asked.

"Now, we wait."

Brady sat down in the dirt and dusted off the head of the garden gnome, humming the J. Geils Band 1980s chart topper, "My Angel Is a Centerfold." We were two hundred feet away from the road, far enough that I could just barely hear the passing traffic over the hum of the trailer's generator, but I couldn't see any headlights.

Within a couple of minutes, the dog lowered herself to a crouch and put her snout down on her paws. She continued to growl, but by this time, her eyes were getting heavy, her breathing slower. Eventually, she stopped growling and started snoring.

"Good girl," Brady said. He pulled a knife out of a pocket and cut the rope, then lifted the dog into his arms and carried her to the back of the Rover. After firing up the engine, Brady lit another joint and offered it to me, but I waved it away. I wanted to relish the high of successful adventure. As I watched the Everglades slip past my window, a thought crossed my mind.

"You and I both know you could have pulled this off alone."

"Probably," he said, the joint dangling from his lower lip. "But it wouldn't have been as much fun. And besides, I thought a secret mission might do you some good. You've been looking so fucking forlorn lately."

"What are you talking about?" I protested. "I've been smiling like my life depended on it."

"Your Disney smile looks like you're one parking ticket away from a killing spree—Now, don't get offended. You're new, and God knows you'll get plenty of practice." His features softened as he glanced back and forth between the road and me. "Anything you want to talk about?"

It was the first time anyone in Orlando had expressed genuine concern for me. After nearly a month of preserving the Magical experience for strangers, it was something of a shock to find someone who cared what I was feeling. Still, opening up to Brady would have meant admitting some ugly truths to myself, and I wasn't ready to do that yet. "I'm good," I said.

He took another toke, his face momentarily illuminated in a car's passing headlights. "What drove you to Disney anyway?"

"You make it sound like it's a bad thing. I thought this was the 'greatest fucking job on Earth.'"

"It is, but you didn't come here for career opportunity. And I don't think you're on a spiritual journey; taking photos in a mouse kiosk is not exactly the pinnacle of the human condition."

I used my stock response. "I like photography."

Brady jabbed his finger in the air. "Not good enough." The contemplative twist of his mouth made him look like the subject of a Baroque oil painting. "There's something more for you here."

"Alright, Descartes," I said, trying not to sound more amused than offended. "What's my higher purpose?"

"You, sir"—Brady enunciated each word with melodramatic flair—"have got the makings of a Guerilla Philanthropist in you."

"Nope," I said. "Means nothing."

He dragged the last smoke out of the roach and flicked it out the window. "Being a Cast Member is like getting your foot in the door to a place where you really can make a difference. Take this dog for instance. Look at her fur. She is not what you would call healthy. What you did just now—what you helped me do—we just saved her life. And we're going to use our connections at DAK to keep her alive. That, my friend, is philanthropy. Think of it as underground altruism. You're doing good deeds under the radar."

Guerilla Philanthropy—the concept appealed to me in a Robin Hood kind of way. Saving a dog was certainly noble, and doing it ourselves rather than calling in the SPCA had an attractive vigilante quality, but I had my doubts about Brady's motivation. There was madness in him, and genius as well, but what really made me nervous was his ability to rationalize misdemeanor. It was one thing to call a crime a crime and accept your role as a miscreant, but it took a special breed of sociopath to sanctify it. In action sports, the sociopath was a well-represented breed of individual, and it was my observation that all sociopathic types had one quality in common: unpredictability. They went from life of the party to gunman in the belfry in less time than it took a wave to wall up and close out, and if you were standing too close when it happened, they'd take you down too. Still, I was glad for the companionship. The night's activities had been fun, and they constituted the foundation for what was shaping up to be my first Florida friendship.

I couldn't see it then of course, but that trip into the Everglades marked the end of my Age of Innocence in Orlando. It was like BASE jumping off a bridge in Colorado and landing in Never Land. From that point on, I was on my way to becoming a part of the demented world of Disney, and my involvement was only going to make it worse.

We're Your Friends 'Til the Bitter End

There is a rumor that Walt Disney created "Snow White" as the representation of his drug of choice, cocaine, and the Seven Dwarfs were meant to depict the seven levels of coke addiction. This, I am happy to say, is balderdash. First of all, Uncle Walt didn't create the story. *Snow White and the Seven Dwarfs* was based on a European fairy tale that was collected by the Brothers Grimm over a century earlier. Second, all records show that Walt stood firmly against drug use of any kind. So while the original storyteller may have had symbolism in mind when he wrote the story, it is certain that Walt would never have condoned it. Plagiarism is one thing, but drug use? Never.

I spent as much time as possible in the air-conditioned break room, lingering between sets in the deep sofas, drinking Powerade. For the most part, I was ignored by the other CMs, but I got to know them through observation.

After a couple of weeks on restrictions, Sunny returned to Mickey, brighter and cheerier than ever. Her ringtone was "Walking on Sunshine." Her avatar was a dancing happy face. She was never happier than when she received Guest Appreciation Letters or crayon-scrawled notes from guests. Her favorite food was *actually* cheese. One time, a Lebanese girl gave her a handmade Mickey

Mouse figurine, carved from a cedar root, and she cried over it for her entire forty-minute break.

Rusty, the Goofy, came from somewhere in the Midwest where being a gay African American was more or less against the law. His dad wanted him to be a pro ballplayer, but after getting rave reviews as Angel in a Minneapolis production of *Rent*, Rusty was convinced that theater was his calling. "You may come visit me on the Upper West Side," he would say if he liked you, or "you are off my island," if he didn't. His avatar was a picture of himself in drag (as the always lovely "Amber Alert"). His ringtone was techno.

Alan, the Pluto, was a skinny white guy in his twenties. His thin hair and weak chin gave him the appearance of a competitive gamer. He kept his phone on vibrate. His avatar was Salvador Dali. He was the smartest guy in the group, often leading group discussions or taking counterpoint in backstage debates. He was always imagining romantic interludes, but never acting them out. As they said in characters, he had a face for fur.

Apparently, Alan and Rusty were dating. I learned about this when I saw the two of them kissing one afternoon by the fire-breathing rocks. I must have startled them because Alan blushed intensely, and Rusty looked as menacing as I'd ever seen him. "Oh no, you didn't!" he snarled. "Girl, you need to back your little tugboat ass off my island. Go on." When they returned to the break room later, they acted as if nothing had happened, and neither of them ever said a word about it again.

On that particular day, the discussion topic was Disney porn titles. *Pornocchio* suggested the hip-hop Tigger. "The story of a real boy who lies when he gets horny."

"I like that," Alan said. "Stromboli already looks like he was modeled after Ron Jeremy, so casting's a no-brainer."

Tigger beamed. "*Pornochio and G-Spotto!* Costarring me as the G!"

The Tigger was a wannabe hip-hop gangsta. He wore his basics with the fashion sense of a break-dancer: black shorts below his hips,

XXXL T-shirt hanging down past his thighs. He never got tired of high-fiving Pluto and shouting, "What up, dog?" I still had no idea what his real name was: one week he called himself Toxik; the next he was DJ Shrinky Dink. Not surprisingly, his ringtone changed almost every day, but it was always hip-hop. His avatar was a picture of himself on Spring Break, shirtless.

Rusty offered *Blowjobs and Black Dicks*, but Alan shot it down, saying the movie had to include at least one character he was approved in. "How about *Booty Full of Beast*, starring yours truly as Beast."

Sunny clapped her hands together. "You made Beast? Congratulations, Rusty! I tried out for Blue Fairy, but I was too short."

Brady's friend Jessie sat on the edge of an armchair playing with Rusty's hair. She wore her Pooh feet like slippers. I'd been shooting her all morning in the Hundred Acre Woods kiosk, but she hadn't acknowledged me. *Who Rogered the Rabbit?* she said, as a suggestion.

Rusty looked up at her, appalled. "That's disgusting!"

"It's a love story," she said, nonplussed, "between a young man and his imaginary friend."

"I like that," Alan nodded. "It's a fantasy *coming*-of-age tale. How about *Alice in Anal Land* featuring the Queen of Tarts and the Mad Nutter?"

"That's where I know you from!" Jessie exclaimed. "Parades! It's been driving me crazy all morning."

I knew it was risky, but I wanted to play, and I thought if I came up with something clever, it might earn me some points. "*The Little-Sperm Maid*," I ventured.

Jessie's face lit up. Rusty glared at me. "Girl, you have to choose a film with a character you're approved in." He leaned in and lowered his voice. "If you're not in the character program, YOU CAN'T PLAY!"

Just then, the door opened and Marco walked in. Everyone cheered and there were kisses all around. It was like the second fucking coming. "I'm here to pick up your pictures," he said to me after making his rounds. I pulled the film out of my cargo pocket and dropped it into his outstretched hand. He raised a waxed eyebrow. "Only three rolls?"

I tasted blood, but I couldn't tell where it was coming from. "It was raining all morning."

An Eeyore I'd never met whispered something in Marco's ear, and they both laughed. Then, he spun around to leave. As he opened the door, the beautiful Pocahontas walked in, her turquoise jewelry sparkling against her dark skin. She gave Marco a hug. "You're coming tonight, right?" she said.

Alan called out. "Hey Nikki, we're playing Disney porno . . . . Go!"

"*Poke a Hot Ass*," she said, without missing a beat. Everyone applauded. Marco gave her a spank, and I managed to slip out without anyone noticing.

In the entertainment industry, a weekend is an arbitrary circumstance, a holiday is something that you're expected to provide for other people, and days with names like "Sunday" and "Christmas" are rhetorical.

When Cast Members talk about the "weekend," they might be talking about Monday/Tuesday or Thursday/Friday or even just Wednesday, depending on the time of year and the whims of a questionably medicated Coordinator. Free days occur at random intervals. You might work a three-day week, then get a day off, and then come back for twelve days in a row. And you can forget about holidays: that's rush hour in the Mouse Kingdom, and nobody rides free. The unpredictability is one of the things that makes a Disney job more interesting than a career in the real world, but it can be disorienting for the more traditional Cast Members. If, for instance, you celebrate Hanukkah, chances are you'll be spinning dreidels on Teacup flywheels.

Because of our patchwork schedules, I barely saw Johnny. Sometimes, our paths would cross in the deep blue moments before dawn, when he was coming home from a date and I was going to work. But most of the time, our communication was limited to scrawled messages on a little pad of Princess paper on the kitchen counter.

Johnny's walls were lined with dozens of glossy framed photos, paparazzi plunder of my roommate posing with various handsome young men at red-carpet affairs. In every picture, Johnny wore the same cherubic smile, his cheeks flushed with Scotch and his eyelids heavy.

That night, I was lingering in the hallway, looking at the pictures, when Johnny walked in the door. He put on his worn Jeff Gordon cap and poured himself a drink from his gleaming wet bar. "Admirin' mah friends?" he asked.

"What's with the red carpet?" I asked. "Are you a celebrity?"

"The PR biz has its perks," he said happily. "Here, ah'll show you."

He led me into the living room and presented a series of photo art on the wall. "This"—he indicated an autographed *Rolling Stone* cover featuring five boys in their underwear—"is The Backstreet Boys, Nick, Brian, A. J., Kevin, and Howie. They got nominated for five Grammys in 2000. Five. Can you believe Nick is only twenty?"

He pointed to another framed photo. "This is me and Howie at the '97 tornado relief concert right here in Orlando. The boys got the keys to the city from the mayor for that one."

He walked me around the room, describing every image. There were promotional shots of 'N Sync, Westlife, Take That, New Kids on the Block—even the Spice Girls. His favorites were the candid pictures of himself, pleather clad and giddy, with his arms wrapped around this or that band member. This was Johnny's Never Land, the musicians his gang of Lost Boys.

Finally, he stopped at a photo that was hanging alone, in a gilded frame, lit by a single halogen light. Johnny was nestled in the armpit of a sneering behemoth with thin hair and spectacles. He had a grease stain on the front of his shirt, which he had attempted, unsuccessfully, to cover with his tie.

Johnny's voice was a whisper. "And that's the fairy godmother of them all, the man who made their dreams come true: Lou Pearlman."

"The producer." It wasn't a guess. I had recently read a story about how he fled the country after being charged with tax evasion.

Johnny nodded solemnly. "He launched the boy band as a genre. Would you believe he started out as a simple dreamer with an airplane chartering business? One day, the New Kids on the Block chartered his jet, and he got the idea to start up his own boy band. He put an ad in the *Orlando Sentinel* for singers and put together The Backstreet Boys."

"How about that."

"After their success, he started 'N Sync and, of course, you know how big *they* got." He heaved a heartbreaking sigh. "Of course, these days it seems like ev'rybody's trying to sully his good name, but that's what happens when you're number one. Folks come gunnin' for you!" He raised a glass to the picture and finished it in one swallow. "Here's to the man who started the whole thing."

"To exploiting the talents of others," I said, but Johnny didn't seem to hear.

"So, what are you doing tonight?"

"No plans," I said. "Tomorrow's my weekend, so I can stay out past curfew."

His eyes sparkled like a fireworks show. "You should come with me to a party."

"What kind of party?"

"Just a little soiree right here in the Ghetto," he said, picking at something in his teeth. "Casual dress. Finger foods. I think the host is a Fantasmic Maleficent. Or is he a Merlin? Anyway, he's tall. Ah'll be ready in twenty minutes."

An hour and a half later, Johnny was ready. We walked through acres of identical hallways until, eventually, we came to a door like all the others, behind which I could hear the high hat snare of the newest boy band sensation and an avalanche of giggling. Johnny opened it without knocking and we walked in.

All around me, a Cast Member bacchanal writhed and bloomed, surging, cackling into the light, and then retreating into the shadows. Illuminated by scented candles and the occasional flare of a bong lighter, fur and face fumbled for common ground: two groping Tumble Monkeys, a Brer Fox and his greeter, an Eeyore feeling up a roofied Cinderella. Shadow puppets danced on slender fingers, celebrating dark corners filled with patchouli incense. Pottery Barn furniture had been tipped on its side and stacked around the living room to create a labyrinthine path that linked hiding places like hedge-maze grottos, lit with festive strands of lights: Chinese lanterns in the kitchen, twinkly Christmas lights in the bathroom, chili peppers in the bedrooms.

Within moments, Johnny had fallen into a debate with somebody about the most recent episode of *American Idol*, so I headed out on my own. I made my way through the furniture maze to the bar and pulled a beer out of the ice chest. Uncapping it, I came face-to-face with Marco.

"Hola, chico," he lowed. "What are *you* doing here?" His tone was condescending as if I'd just rolled into the Burnside Bowls with Rollerblades.

"My roommate knows a guy," I said, as cordially as possible, considering I'd had a few beers while I was waiting for Johnny. "Are you wearing makeup?"

Marco patted his cheek, pleased that I had noticed. "It's just a little foundation to keep away the shine. Maybe you should use some."

"No thanks." I moved down the bar to a bowl of tortilla chips. Marco followed me.

"A little advice," he hissed like the valve on an empty can of spray paint. "If somebody offers you concealer, it's because they can see something that you can't."

"I'll keep that in mind."

Marco hovered at my elbow, finger stirring his cocktail. "I've been looking at your photos," he said. "Your yellows are too saturated. Winnie the Pooh looks like a big fat banana."

I pretended to study a jar of salsa, then turned my full attention to the guacamole.

"Also," he continued, "you should do manual focus. Auto focus is too unreliable. Oh my God, you're not going to eat that guacamole, are you?"

I couldn't ignore him any longer. "Yes."

"But you could be so handsome if you just lost a little weight—like, say twenty pounds."

"What are you talking about?"

"Or maybe chubby is your thing. I'm just saying, if somebody gives you diet tips—"

"Marco," I cut him off. "Let's get a couple things straight. I don't wear makeup; I don't take photo advice from Disney kooks, and I'm not overweight. What's your problem anyway? Why are you such a dick?"

"I'm not a dick," he sniffed. "I'm a perfectionist."

"You're annoying."

Marco pushed his lower lip out in a petulant pout. "If you don't want my help, just say so."

"I. DON'T. WANT. YOUR HELP."

He couldn't have looked more insulted if I'd just smeared his lens. "Your negative attitude does not make you popular," he huffed. "You are bitter and you don't belong here." Then he spun around and disappeared into the labyrinth.

A Minnie and a Donald were standing close, mixing cocktails, pretending not to eavesdrop. When we made eye contact, they glared at me and drifted back into the party. I wandered through the furniture maze for a while, looking for friendly faces that weren't buried in somebody's crotch. After about twenty minutes, in one of the bedrooms, somebody offered me a spliff. He was a drowsy-eyed Baloo, stocky and disheveled. Most of his beer was soaked into his Pluto sweatshirt. It was low-grade schwag, cardboard dry, but I thanked him and passed it to the girl next to me, who took it without looking at me.

"Whose place is this anyway?" I asked the Baloo.

He jerked his head at the girl at my side.

"I thought it was some tall guy's place," I said.

"That's my roommate." She blew smoke into my face. "Oh no, it's you again. What are you doing here?"

I waved the smoke away and took a closer look. She was exotic and beautiful like the barrel of a Kalashnikov. She had skin the color of coconut husk; dark, wavy hair; and lips like plump oysters. "Do I know you?"

"You're the asshole photographer who thinks children are idiots." It clicked. Usually, when I saw her, she was wearing turquoise jewelry and a wig of straight black hair, but sure enough, it was Pocahontas.

"That was a joke," I laughed. "Kids are great when they're not destroying public property with their skatey boards and listening to punk rock music."

"Oh, I get it." She was glaring at me with a full metal jacket of hatred. "You're trying to impress me with your witty detachment because you think I'll soften with icy, sardonic realism, right? Or maybe you're communicating how 'above it all' you are so I'll think you're *cool*. Or maybe you're one of those perverts who wants to work *real closely* with children. . . . That's it, isn't it? You're a pervert. You make me sick."

Without waiting for a response, she got up and stormed back into the living room, brushing past Johnny on her way.

"Wow," he sat down next to me, cross-legged, his mouth slack. "How did you piss off the sweetest girl in the world?"

"You know that harpy?"

"Everybody knows Nikki. She's done every character in her height range. She was Poca when they broke ground at DAK."

"Well, she's got a serious Madonna thing going." The Baloo was slumped against the wall by this time, a bead of drool rapelling down his chin. "I made a bad joke about kids being dumb when I first met her, and she won't let it go."

Johnny made a face like he was watching a high-speed car wreck in slow motion. "Tell me you're kidding."

I shook my head.

It was the only time I saw Johnny look genuinely sad. "Nikki can't have kids of her own," he explained. "She came to Disney to be close to children, and to collect miracles. She and her partner have been on the list for South American adoption for years, but so far, nothing."

I wandered around the party for a while longer, but my heart wasn't in it anymore. Nobody noticed when I left.

The next morning, I woke up to the shrill screech of my phone.

"Hi, honey, how's Florida? Are you enjoying Disneyland?" My mom's voice was so quiet I could barely hear her over the phone.

"They call it Disney World out here, Mom," I said. "But it's good. I got a job at one of the theme parks."

"That sounds nice." She chugged a mouthful of air into her lungs. "I have to say your father and I were very surprised when Michael told us you moved. You didn't even come for dinner."

"Yeah," I said. "It was kind of a last-minute decision."

"Well Florida's nice."

"You sound tired, Mom. Are you feeling okay?"

"Oh, I'm fine, I'm fine. I just woke up so I'm a little groggy. That's all." She quickly changed the subject. "Are you eating enough? Do you have multivitamins?"

I started to rub my temples, then stopped when I realized how much I probably looked like Michael. "I have plenty of food. Don't worry so much about me."

"I can't help it," she said softly. "You're my little boy."

After we hung up, I sat there for a while and tried to imagine what she might be feeling. She was exhausted—probably drained from the chemo—and a little delirious as well. When I left LA, I had bolted with the jet fire ferocity of a motorcycle launch, putting as much distance between myself and the specter of death as possible, arcing high and long over the country to land in the Sunshine State. Three thousand miles away and what had I really achieved? Was I safer now? More insulated?

I was heartbroken by her breathless words and the image of

her face, which by now was surely growing more gaunt and pallid from the treatments. But if I felt guilty, I buried it beneath layers of ugly indignation. I felt eviscerated by her secrecy, like her silence was meant deliberately to malign me, and worse, I was learning to justify my own stubborn reticence with a coward's rationale: if she wanted to exclude me from her world, I would create my own. The more I retracted into the Disney reality, the more my life became a reality TV show, where I was my own panel of judges rewarding my most puerile tantrums with fireworks shows and holiday parades. My emotional outbursts, I rationalized, were justified. It was rebellion as *growth*, an insurgence against a spiteful conspiracy that discriminated only against me. I suppose that on some level I was aware of the retarded psychology behind my behavior, but fuck me if I was going to admit it.

The smell of bacon lured me out of bed. I pulled on a pair of sweats and walked down the hallway, lined with boy band photos. "I hope you made enough for two," I announced.

"You mean three." Johnny was sitting at the table, fingering an unlit cigarette while a boy who couldn't have been older than nineteen cleared the table. "I'd like you to meet Ricky."

It was the first time I had ever met one of Johnny's overnight visitors. "Nice to meet you."

"Charmed," he said. He was prince height with long eyelashes and bleached teeth. His fair cheeks were dotted with red pimples. When he walked, he loped as if he had just gone through a terrific growth spurt and wasn't quite sure what to do with his extra frame. "Johnny tells me you're a skater. That is *so* killer. When I was younger, I *totally* wanted to be a pro-skater. I have, like, the *hugest* crush on Tony Hawk."

"Is that a fact," I managed.

Ricky flashed Johnny a smile. "BRB," he said.

Johnny laughed as his guest disappeared into his bedroom. "Try the lavender soap!" he announced. "It's like being in Lyon!" He sipped his coffee thoughtfully, then looked over at me. "What?"

"I didn't say anything."

"He's not as young as he looks, you know."

"He seems very mature for his age."

"He is. And he's smart too." Johnny tapped one end of the unlit cigarette on the table. "Look, Lord knows ah have mah fair share of issues. But ah'm not gonna apologize for what ah like, and right now, this just feels right."

Ricky emerged from Johnny's bedroom, wearing a Jeff Gordon racing cap. "This hat is the sickest!" he said. "I *have* to have it!"

"You know ah can't resist those lashes." Johnny stood up from the table. "Want to take the Firebird for a spin?"

His young ingenue gasped. "Serious? I can drive it?"

Johnny jingled the keys seductively. "Show daddy your license."

Ricky opened a Quiksilver wallet. "I've never even had a parking ticket." He handed his ID to Johnny, who passed it to me without looking at it.

"What do you think?" said Johnny. "Is he okay?"

It was a Washington state license with an accurate photo. The birthday made him twenty years old, not old enough to drink, but certainly mature enough to make his own decisions.

"He checks out, boss," I said, handing the card back.

Ricky squealed and snatched the keys, and the two disappeared out the front door. I sat down to gorge on bacon and consider my situation. Apparently, my roommate was a chicken hawk, a September dude who lured May boys back to the roost with muscle cars and candy. I had no ethical problem with either the age difference or the promiscuity. At least Johnny was putting it all on the table.

It was one of the more endearing qualities of Disney World, the way people lived out loud without a patina of shame or self-censorship. If Pocahontas didn't like you, she told you so. If Winnie the Pooh had skeletons in his closet, he threw the door wide open and displayed them for your approval or scorn. Nobody danced around cancer or dated your friends. Disney life was honest and true. Happily ever after.

I resolved to integrate myself into the Orlando experience. LA had nothing left for me, but Disney was offering the full lifestyle experience, a community of 53,000 residents, arranged over forty-three square miles, with events to keep me entertained from sunrise until 2 A.M. For Cast Members, there were housing projects like my own apartment complex and Celebration, Walt's original utopian view of the community of tomorrow with its pristine elementary school, fire station, and homeowner's association. There were bars and restaurants hosting dedicated nights for every special interest group you could imagine. For anybody with a Disney ID, there was always an industry appreciation night somewhere. Anyone who believed in fairies could work, live, eat, drink, and date entirely within the Disney matrix without ever leaving Disney property. And from what I could tell, it wasn't uncommon.

They were called lifers, the ones who came to Orlando to escape the drudgery of their daily lives and never left. They didn't make a lot of money (even among the top level of management, Disney doesn't pay that well), and they didn't have fancy houses, but damn it, they were happy. They lived in a *nice* place. And I was starting to see the attraction.

Yo Ho! Yo Ho! A Pirate's Life for Me

About two thirds of the way through *The Lion King*, there's a scene where Simba, Pumbaa, and Timon are lying on their backs, looking up at the stars. Simba gets up, walks to the edge of a cliff, and flops down. A dust cloud flies up and dissipates in the air, and, for a moment, the letters s-e-x appear in the swirl.

The original incarnation of the 1998 film, *Who Framed Roger Rabbit*, featured Jessica Rabbit flashing her crotch; Baby Herman giving the middle finger before disappearing under a woman's skirt and reappearing with drool on his upper lip; and in a scene where Bob Hoskins goes into a Toontown men's room, rumor has it Michael Eisner's home phone number appeared under the graffitied phrase, "For a good time, call Allyson Wonderland."

In 1999, Disney recalled 3.4 million copies of the home video version of their 1977 animated feature, *The Rescuers*, because it contained the photographic image of a topless woman. It happened approximately thirty-eight minutes into the film while Bianca and Bernard were flying through the city in a sardine box strapped to the back of the albatross, Orville. She only appeared in two frames, but anybody with a remote control could stop the action and clearly see the picture.

The 1989 film, *The Little Mermaid*, gained a certain notoriety when it was discovered that there was an enormous phallus adorning the cover of the original home video. According to rumor, a disgruntled artist drew one of the spires of King Triton's castle to resemble a penis. After a slew of complaints, Disney reissued a new cover without the offending spire; however, they did not remove the erection of the minister who presides over the first wedding scene between Prince Eric and Ursula. This controversy led to a short-lived lawsuit by an Arkansas woman named Janet Gilmer who tried to sue Disney over the offending images (Gilmer v. Disney also included a complaint about the S-E-X message in *The Lion King*). The lawsuit was dropped within two months.

Freudian theory would explain these associations as an unconscious expression of repressed sexuality—the anarchic Pinocchio id in conflict with a Jiminy Cricket superego. In all things scandalous, Disney's standard explanation is a plea of insanity—not on their part, but on the part of the viewer. . . . The audience is simply imagining things.

The more I learned about my fellow Cast Members, the more I started to understand what Nick had been talking about when I interviewed him in my previous incarnation. Disney people were deviant. It seemed like every Cast Member in Orlando was leading a double life: Disney by day, alter ego by night. An acrophobic Tarzan in the stage show had to take valium every night to calm his nerves before his soaring web routine. The cutest stilt walker in the Jammin' Jungle Parade was filming adult videos on her days off. It seemed to me all the Cast Members had been high onstage at least once in their career, and they all had had sex on property.

I thought about what Brady had said that night in the car, about what I had to do to gain their trust. Listening to the awe in Cast Members' voices as they narrated these Disney legends, I finally understood that the only behavior to earn any lasting respect around Disney World was *getting away with "it."* It didn't even matter what it was. If a Cast Member could pull it off without getting caught, she or he gained entrance into a club with an exclusive guest list and no paper trail.

For me, it started with a piece of gum. It was a blustery after-noon, and I was riding a blue Schwinn to Camp Minnie-Mickey for a photo assignment in the character kiosks. Lunch had been an Ital-ian affair—pasta with spicy sausage and garlic sauce—and I nearly knocked Orville over when I clocked back in. "This is a photo lab, not a morgue," he said, holding his nose. "You'd better do some-thing about that breath." So I did. I popped a piece of Trident into my mouth and went onstage.

It was the first time I had deliberately broken a Rule. If I had been caught, I could have been reprimanded anywhere up to two points for eating onstage, but I didn't care. Breaking the Rules was invigorating. I flaunted my petty crime to Mickey when the kiosk was empty, and he gave me a silent thumbs-up. When the gum lost its flavor, I ate another piece and showed off to Minnie by asking if she wanted one too. I hoped that nobody wielding any type of con-sequence would catch me, and to my surprise, nobody did.

The next day, I snuck a bag of M&Ms onstage in my pocket and ate them between guests; the day after that, beef jerky. It was shock-ing to me how quickly I had assimilated to the totalitarian regime of the Magic Kingdom. My whole life, I had been a grade-A hooligan, following my shadow into questionable situations, but one month at Disney had restructured me into an upstanding citizen who actually felt *guilt* at the idea of eating in front of strangers.

The situation escalated on its own. Once the Cast Members knew that I was the kind of photographer who snuck snacks, character performers began approaching me about a new kind of illicit activ-ity: "out of character" photos.

Disney is very protective about the image of its characters. Nobody should ever see Winnie the Pooh doing something he shouldn't do, wearing something he doesn't wear, or, God forbid, spending time with another Winnie the Pooh. Not even backstage.* Of course, that

---

*Rumor had it that Disney maintained a relationship with all the film process-ing labs in Orlando and received first word if one of these "illegal" photos turned up anywhere in the city. And it was probably true. In 1989, Disney threatened

didn't stop the performers from horsing around in wardrobe and taking snapshots for their own personal photo albums.

"Hey girl." Rusty was lounging on the patio, enjoying a cigarette between sets. "You got any shots left in that thing?"

"One or two," I told him.

"Do me a favor," he said, inhaling an enormous drag off his cigarette. "Get a shot of this."

He put on the Goofy head and struck a standard pose, then he exhaled a mouthful of smoke through Goofy's mouth, just as I fired the shot.

"Oops," I said.

"Didja get that?" He pulled off the head, grinning wider than the character itself. "With the smoke and everything?"

The Smoking Goofy photo became notorious around the Animal Kingdom break room. Soon, I was getting requests to shoot Smoking Minnie, Smoking Chip, and Smoking Baloo. It was fun, shooting those illegal pictures, and it allowed me a level of creativity that I hadn't enjoyed since the old days of skate photography. In no time at all, I was shooting performers in all kinds of nontraditional poses.

Using the break room as my photography studio, I created such favorites as "Mickey Picking Minnie's Nose," "Dale's Head on Pooh's Body," "Terk and Rafiki," "Monkey Style," and, my masterpiece, "Three Tiggers," an action shot involving a series of strobe flashes and a trampoline. It became the highlight of my day, that last roll of film when I would be able to fill in the last shots with character tomfoolery.

Since Disney's character continuity policy was so strict, I had to be very careful about the photographic process. I would wait until my last roll of film and then shoot no more than three or four illegal

to sue three Hallandale, Florida, daycare centers if they did not remove murals that included Mickey, Minnie, and Goofy. When Universal caught wind of the impending lawsuit, they stepped forward and offered use of their own characters like Scooby Doo, Yogi Bear, the Flintstones, and the Jetsons. The Disney images came down, the Universal images went up, and life went on in Hallandale.

pictures. To keep from being caught, I had to time the development to finish when Orville was out of the lab, on lunch or working at the sales desk. It wasn't that big a deal; most of the time I had my run of the office anyway, but still, I didn't want to push it.

As the "out of character" photographer, I began to enjoy my new status as the coolest guy in the break room. No longer was I treated like an outsider. Performers stopped me on the way to the bathroom to fill me in on the daily gossip. They stood up to let me sit down on the most comfortable sofas. They invited me to play desert island fantasy and Disney porno. I was in the club.

Even Nikki softened. At first, she just glared at me less. Then, she started sitting at my table in the cafeteria. Next thing I knew, we were having conversations.

"I knew you'd come around," she said to me one day over lasagna.

Up close, her teeth were impossibly white. "Me?" I protested. "I'm the same jaded cynic you met two months ago."

"You think you are." She blotted her lips on a napkin before sipping her Diet Coke. "But I can see you've changed. There's a light inside you now. You're beginning to get it. Don't roll your eyes! It's true."

"You don't have to get all Burning Man. I already promised to do your headshots."

She smiled, brushing her fingertips against her cheeks. "You can get rid of these laugh lines, right?"

Outside the break room, Alan would hand me a cup of Powerade, and show me the features on his new phone or MP3 player or game console. He was a tech weenie. He wanted to learn about cameras, but he couldn't afford to take up a new hobby until he made the jump to management.

"I just picked up a shift at Universal," he told me one morning. We were standing on the patio by the cooler. He was wearing basics, drying his hair with a crisp, white towel. "Wardrobe work right now, but I'm thinking of trying out in Beetle Bailey."

I crumpled my cup and tossed it in the trash. "Won't Disney find out?"

Alan's eyes drifted across the cracked parking lot to where Rusty was standing with an athletic FOLK tumbler, warming up for his show. "They don't care. Universal pays better, and I'm trying to make enough money to buy tickets for the Madonna show next month. I want to surprise Rusty." Across the dusty lot, the FOLK tumbler put his arm around Rusty, and Rusty pushed him away, laughing. "Maybe a limo too," Alan said.

"Sounds like fun," I said.

Alan turned his back on the parking lot. "Yeah, well, Madonna hasn't been relevant since *Confessions*, so who knows. Maybe, just like, fuck it, you know? Hey, there's a Tarzan party tonight. Are you coming?"

"I dunno. I've been out every night this week."

"Yeah?" Alan's eyes drifted back to the parking lot. Rusty was now holding the tumbler's muscular leg, helping him stretch. "I heard that Toy Story party was fun. I wanted to go. I had this incredible Slinky costume, but Rusty couldn't get his GI Joe makeup together, so we just stayed home and fell asleep on the couch." Alan pulled his T-shirt up to dry his pudgy belly, then yanked it down. "Well, I should go get ready for my next set. See you onstage."

Bolstered by my new popularity, my taste for transgression grew beyond the scope of voyeurism. I wanted to do something more, something that would seal my reputation as a bad boy and maybe even earn me a position among the ranks of the Disney legends. I had an idea, but I needed help.

Brady's friend, Jessie, was becoming more and more flirtatious with every incident of misbehavior. After "Chip Groping Dale," she said hi. "After Brer Rabbit Goes to Rehab," she gave me her number. By the time I got to "Naughty, Naughty Eeyore," she was like Silly Putty on my comic strip. Jessie was well acquainted with stories of Cast Members having sex on property, and she was eager to tell me all about it. "There's even an informal club for Cast Members who pull it off," she said. "Like the Mile High Club."

"Are you a member?" I asked.

She lowered her eyes, blushing. "Not yet," she said. The liar.

Jessie was princess height with red hair and pretty blue eyes, which she used for high-performance flirting. We started making out in break rooms in the tunnels beneath Fantasyland and another time in the attic of the UK pavilion at Epcot. The bathrooms of Camp Minnie-Mickey were usually crammed with other Cast Members going at it, so we engaged in light petting in the animal pens behind the Pocahontas stage. One night, as the Magic Kingdom was closing, she went down on me in Ariel's Grotto, our bodies pressed against the bright orange and green starfish so that the security cameras wouldn't spot us. I was gearing up for the inevitable climax, but in the end, Jessie was the one who set up the encounter.

Epcot Center is composed of a dozen international pavilions arranged around a lagoon: Canada, Morocco, France, Japan—each pavilion is like a little country, showcasing regional food, drink, and entertainment.* The sun was low as I walked through the turnstile into Epcot, but still the park was packed. I had thirty minutes until I was supposed to meet up with the pretty Pooh, so I wandered from arcade to souvenir shop to sweltering kiosk until, eventually, I got distracted by a group of characters out in the park gallivanting around a fountain. Mickey, Minnie, Goofy, Chip, and Dale were dancing, signing autographs, and posing for photos with a rambunctious tour group of kids who were all screaming to be noticed. I walked to the edge of the fountain and sat down, watching the performers as they expertly worked their way through the children. I tried to imagine what it would be like to be inside one of those costumes: hot, sticky, uncomfortable. The upside must have been pretty good to counter all the negatives.

Next thing I knew, there were paws on my shoulders and brown

*The governments of these countries pay exorbitant rent to Disney, and in exchange, Disney is responsible for the landscaping, maintaining, and staffing of the international pavilions of Epcot with expat Cast Members. These "temps" are housed in one of the college program ghettos, located in nearby Kissimmee. Parties at the CP ghetto are world-class free-for-alls with guest rosters that include Justin Timberlake, Paris Hilton, and, at any given time, half the adolescent population of Sweden.

fur in my face. "Easy, Dale," I said, careful to preserve the Magical experience for the kids around me. Someone yelled, "You're my favorite chipmunk!" A crowd gathered around us, and Dale turned to sign somebody's autograph book, wagging his little fuzzy tail across my legs the whole time.

I stepped out of the way, but Dale backed up, pushing me against the edge of the fountain. He had me pinned so effectively, in fact, that his butt was now grazing my crotch with every wag. It was a little disconcerting, to be wedged between that fountain and Dale, feeling the stirrings of an erection. At five foot one, I was pretty sure that Dale was a girl, but it brought up some bizarre bestiality issues I preferred to ignore. I extracted myself as gracefully as possible and ducked back into a camera store to cool off. When I finally met up with Jessie twenty minutes later, I didn't mention the Dale encounter.

"So how was your day?" She pulled her hair back into a ponytail and batted her eyelashes at me. "Did you have any Magical Moments?"

"No Magic," I told her. "No Moments."

"Well, I have a whole hour before my next set," she said. "Let's see if I can take care of that."

Her eyes sparkled with friskiness. Her basics smelled like Downey fabric softener. When she kissed me, she sunk her teeth into my cheek and left marks and a wet smudge. She led me around the Mexico pavilion and past Norway. We wandered through China and Germany and an area that represented the entire continent of Africa. When we got to Italy, she pulled me into an alcove with a grim face carved in bas-relief on a wall. The carving had an open mouth, big enough to fit a small pizza.

"This is La Boca de Verita," she said. "The Mouth of Truth. You put your hand in it and say something, and if you're lying, it bites off your hand."

"That's morbid," I said.

"No, it's really fun! Try it."

I put my fingertips inside the mouth and thought for a moment. "I am telling the truth," I said.

"There! You see. Nothing bad happened. Now me." Her entire hand disappeared up to the wrist, and she looked me dead in the eyes and said, "I want you."

Her smirk was so cute and she smelled so good that before I knew what was happening, we were all over each other.

"Stop." She pushed me away, gasping.

"What. You said you wanted me."

"Not here." She took my hand and led me to a wall with a cleverly concealed gate. "If anybody asks, we got lost looking for the parking lot, got it?" I nodded and followed her through the secret door.

It was like passing from a vivid color movie into a black-and-white photograph. Behind us, in Italy, children were scampering around beds of blooming flowers and twinkling fountains. Jugglers and rhythmic gymnasts danced around a gazebo of Renaissance musicians. And everywhere you could see the fantastic bright red and blue and green of painted murals, blown glass, and gondolas on the lagoon.

But on the other side, everything was a subdued shade of earth. Dirt pathways wound shortcuts through worn strips of grass. Stucco walls, grimy with rough patchwork and cobwebs, displayed a collage of dead leaves like dull mosaics. The air-conditioning machinery hummed so loud, I could hardly hear myself think. Even though I had never worked at Epcot, the passage from onstage to backstage was unmistakable.

She led me up the steps of a nondescript brown building that looked like a strip of low-income classrooms. She tried the first door, but it was locked. Same with the second. The third door opened, and as she pulled me inside, I caught her nervous glance over my shoulder, checking to make sure we hadn't been seen.

The only light in the room came through the crack around the door and around the set of closed window shades. I could just make out a line of shelves along the perimeter of the room, stacked to the ceiling with bags and boxes.

"Where are we?" I said

She put my hand on her breast. "Fuck me," she whispered.

I kissed her hard and pushed her back against a pile of boxes, which collapsed under our weight. There was something soft inside: T-shirts and sweatshirts with Disney graphics.

I tugged at her T-shirt, but ended up with a Chip and Dale tank top instead. She undid my belt.

"Did you like that back there?" she panted as a box of snow globes upended around us.

"Oh yeah." I was half concentrating, struggling with the drawstring on her shorts. "La Boca de Verita," I mumbled. "Very cool."

"Not that." She lifted her hips and pulled her shorts down. "I mean before, with Dale. Did you like that?"

"How did you know?" But I knew how she knew.

She kicked away a box of Tinker Bell pens, which exploded around the little room, and got on her hands and knees. "That's how I want it."

When we finished, we lay there, sweating into the spring line of children-sized Little Mermaid T-shirts.

"Welcome to the SOP Club," she purred.

"We're official members now, huh?"

She wiped her hands on a Goofy beanie and smiled.

I poked through the pile of merchandise, looking for my original clothes. "Standard Operating Procedures?" I guessed.

"Sex on Property."

I kissed Jessie good-bye and stumbled back to my Jeep. I had done it! I had committed the Original Disney Sin. It was a crowning moment and I should have been ecstatic. But something didn't feel right, like a cricket voice in my ear chiding me for bad behavior. It was as if I could almost see the spirit of Walt shaking his head, sorely disappointed.

Something There That Wasn't There Before

When Disney Imagineers and artists create rides, movies, and structures, they sometimes hide Mickey silhouettes in the background. They build these "Hidden Mickeys" right into the design, three familiar intersecting circles in a seemingly random background pattern: a place setting in the Haunted House dining hall, a pair of mouse ears on a skeleton in the Indiana Jones ride, a Mickey doll in the Tower of Terror pre-show movie. It started as an inside joke between artists, but quickly became an obsession for thousands of guests who enjoyed searching for hidden symbolism within the Disney architecture. For the average guest, the symbolism of the image ends at the discovery itself; just knowing there is a Hidden Mickey in the rock wall in Toontown is enough to check it off their all-inclusive been-there-done-that list, but a select few find deeper meaning in the discovery. For them, each Hidden Mickey is a holy symbol, the emblem of the Templars of the Order of Disney, and can only truly be appreciated by other Disney scholars. Like an archaeologist discovering a prehistoric cave drawing or an Egyptian hieroglyphic, unearthing a fresh Hidden Mickey is the closest a real Disney fanatic will ever come to God.

In the weeks that followed my induction into the SOP Club, I enjoyed all the perks of the popular clique: I ate lunch with beloved face characters; I was on the guest list for every Ghetto party; and Nubile FOLK tumblers and stilt walkers invited me into break room bathrooms for hand jobs and one hits. (For the record, the canoe behind the Tarzan stage is painfully uncomfortable, and the FOLK elephant puppet is better than a twin bed at the World Famous Budget Lodge.) In less than a month, I had gone from backstage pariah to DAK royalty, and then suddenly and inexplicably, I became the de facto Cast Member therapist.

Maybe something about the photographer/Cast Member relationship carried more intimacy than it ever had on, say, the X Games Mega Ramp, but characters began baring their souls, whether I wanted to hear what they had to say or not. It always started with a photo request—"How about Chip and Dale in a 69? Tigger with a riding crop? Goofy in a Louis Vuitton bra?"—and ended with a tearful confession.

Jason, a Magic Kingdom Prince Charming, expressed his devastation over a full hour of spaghetti Bolognese (me) and Ripped Fuel (him). Apparently, his girlfriend of five years had dumped him ("A Prince Charming! Is she, like, a lunatic or something?") for a dancing chef in the Parade of Dreams. He was already three weeks into his retaliation, a draconian itinerary of alcoholic blackouts and homosexual one-night stands.

Brenda, a Midwest debutante, had dropped out of college after her first year in the college program to devote herself to a full schedule of Mickey. She was a "furry," a woman who fetishized the anthropomorphic features of Disney's fuzzy characters, who enjoyed a fulfilling relationship with her partner, a girl who had been approved in, perhaps not so ironically, Minnie. The two girls were gifted kleptomaniacs, and at least once a week, they would smuggle a new piece of fur home in their gym bags and hide the pieces in their closet. Whenever the mood struck them—as it often did after stealing a bottle of expensive wine from Epcot—they would slip into their costumes and consummate the mice's relationship in ways that Uncle Walt probably never imagined.

"It's Storytime," Sunny announced one day. She held her finger up to her lips to indicate that this was a *big* secret, and not a word of it was allowed to leave the break room. "You know the DAK Character Coordinator, Bobby?" she began. "Well, listen to what I just heard. . . ."

Someday My Prince Will Come

After his daughter was born, Bobby decided to make a few changes. He ordered a new Disney nametag that said Robert because it sounded more grown-up. He gave up his regular boxer shorts for more formfitting boxer briefs because he liked the fit better. And he started working out. Everybody in his life seemed to appreciate the changes: his manager, his wife, and especially his boyfriend.

Before he met the mother of his children, Bobby had been an honor roll student, a letterman, and the leading role in all the high school theater productions. He had been accepted to his top three colleges (including Oxford) based on his SAT scores alone, but his girlfriend had cried for almost a week straight at the prospect of his moving away, and nothing short of a marriage proposal would calm her down.

Being dutiful Christian Fundamentalists, Bobby's parents advised prayer on the difficult issue of his future, so Bobby got down on his knees and prayed. He needed guidance, a sign from above that would help him decide what to do. But he couldn't concentrate with the phone ringing and his girlfriend wailing, and weren't all his friends getting married and having kids anyway?

And so it came to pass that they graduated high school, got married, and within three years, had a beautiful baby girl. With a family to support, Bobby had to work hard to make ends meet. He took as many hours as he could get in concessions, and when he couldn't get scheduled for more, he took a second job as a character greeter. This exhausting schedule demanded almost seventy hours a week, but he didn't mind the work. His affable good looks and diligent work ethic made him something of a hero among his fellow Cast Members, and what was more, praise God, he was almost certain he'd discovered his true calling.

Being a character greeter was an ever-evolving tapestry in which the schedule was never the same and obstacles had to be negotiated with on-the-spot finesse. It was a dramatic role that ignited Bobby's long-forgotten passion for theater. And best of all, the Cast Members in the entertainment department shared his passion—like Scott.

Scott was an Aladdin who performed his role with significance. He trimmed the hair on his arms and plucked his eyebrows into perfect high-arched loop-de-loops around his eyes. He learned the Prince Ali choreography for all the parades, whether he was in them or not. He had dark features and dimples that made him appear simultaneously shy and unconscionably flirtatious whenever he smiled—which he did constantly, whenever Bobby was around.

"Robert, you are too handsome to be a greeter," Scott said one day. "You should try out for Prince."

Bobby blushed at the compliment. "I don't know," he said. "It's been a long time since I did any acting."

Now, it was Scott's turn to blush. Very few people recognized the theatrical skills it took to be a face character. "Don't worry," he said. "I will teach you everything you need to know."

And so, when face auditions were announced, Scott drove Bobby to the casting call—and to the callback. And when Bobby made Prince Charming, Scott was the first one to congratulate him with a big hug and a warm kiss on the cheek.

His wife frowned when he told her the good news. "A Prince? Why would anybody want to do that?"

The coordinators began casting Bobby immediately, not just as Charming, but as Prince Phillip and Prince Eric, as well. Soon, the two boys were doing sets together at all four parks.

Bobby taped pictures of Scott to the inside of his locker, next to the photos of his two daughters. He kept a stack of notes and letters addressed in Scott's handwriting. In no time, the rumors began flying.

"Me? Gay?" Bobby blanched when he heard the gossip. His forced laugh was convincing enough. "What would I tell my wife and kids?"

The rituals of Bobby's life put him under a tremendous amount of stress. He woke up at dawn and got home after dinner. He rarely saw his wife and never had enough time for his daughters. Soon, migraines and anxiety became a regular event in his life. Witnesses recounted an episode with a lunch tray one day when the salad bar ran out of croutons.

One afternoon, on break between sets, Bobby's zipper jammed and he found himself stuck inside his Prince costume. Panic rose in his throat until he could hardly breathe.

"Robert, are you okay?" Scott was at his side in an instant.

"Get it off!" was all he could manage. "Get it off!"

Scott easily unhooked the fastener and pulled down the zipper, and, in a moment, Bobby had clawed the costume off his body and thrown it against a wall.

"Fuck!" he screamed. "Fuck fuck fuck!" until his voice was hoarse and tears were rolling down his cheeks.

Scott put his hand on Bobby's bare shoulder. "It's okay," he whispered.

Bobby sobbed into his hands. "I'm so tired, so, so fucking tired."

"It's okay."

"I've been on the schedule for, like, nineteen fucking days in a row."

"I know," Scott said in a soothing voice. "You amaze me."

"I need . . . I need a . . . I just . . . I don't know what."

"Come here." Scott put his arms around Bobby's broad shoulders and stroked his hair. "You are so important to me."

Bobby buried his face in Scott's neck, wiping his tears on the Aladdin tunic. If Scott wasn't holding him, his knees would've buckled. And then, he was kissing Scott's neck and ears and face. And then, his tongue was in his mouth.

Scott pulled back. "Robert?"

Bobby could only nod. He pulled Scott closer and slipped his hands into the Aladdin pantaloons. It was the first time he had ever felt another man's dick, and it was perfect. He felt Scott's breath on his mouth, his hand against his stomach. And he thought that if it could just be like this forever, then everything would be fine. . . .

Now, five years later, Bobby is a coordinator. He has a cubicle, a swivel chair, and a personal phone extension of his own. On his desk is a collection of photos, the most important people in his life. There are several of his family: his wife, his two daughters, and his newborn son. And in a special frame, the most expensive one on the desk, he has a black and white of his boyfriend, blowing a kiss from beneath the Aladdin wig.

As a lifestyle, I was surprised by just how gay Disney really was. Almost every guy in the character department was gay, and the ones who weren't seemed to revel in the ambiguity of their sexuality. The same was true for the women. Three out of five of the girls who worked in the photography department were gay, and the best Princess Jasmine on property, the one who appeared in all the print ads and TV commercials, was life partners with one of the more memorable Blue Fairies. It may have had something to do with the flamboyant nature of the job—the entertainment industry is notoriously fabulous and Disney offers a full range of Mac products and all the glitter dust you can apply. Or if the rumors were to be believed, there may have been a conspiratorial element in the hiring department.

According to legend, the famous antigay policies of Disney's early years (the ones that inspired numerous lawsuits in the eighties) attracted the attention of a militant gay rights group, which sought to change the policy from within. They dispatched a single agent, who took a modest position in the company and worked his way up the chain of command until he alone wielded the final say for all job interviews in the entertainment department. It wasn't long, so the story went, before homosexuality became the single, qualifying criteria for Cast Members, and the payroll began to fill with gay employees. As an alternative to the gay conspiracy theory, there was another popular notion that, at least for women, sexual preference came down to a simple lack of selection.* Possibly the simplest

*If this sounds obtuse, try spending some quality time with the straight men of Florida during Spring Break, Mardi Gras, or any of the other ostensible "mating seasons."

solution was the best: that over the years, Orlando had become a strong, stable community for "alternative" lifestyles.

After a couple of months at Disney, I was beginning to figure the place out. Guests didn't care if I had my hands in my pocket or pointed with one finger. They wanted to have fun. From the moment they handed the parking attendant their money in the morning until they bought one of my photos at night, they flowed from ride to restaurant to souvenir shop. The best I could do was stay out of their way. A smile, some polite words, and Disney Magic would do the rest.

The character performers played no small part in this magic act. No matter how much alcohol had been consumed the night before, no matter how many pills, the characters were able to pull themselves together onstage. They did this because they were professionals who genuinely loved what they did. Characters didn't earn a lot of money. An entry-level fur position made just above minimum wage and a face character, even after years of experience, made only a couple dollars more. People who were looking to get rich quick sold Florida real estate; people who loved the sound of children laughing became characters.

As one of the most coveted positions on property, people traveled around the world to become a part of the character program, and they went to extraordinary lengths to get the role they wanted. It wasn't uncommon to see a performer researching her new role by studying archived Donald Duck movies.* I knew one girl who

---

*Christians and conspiracists have long been convinced that Donald Duck is a racist, based on a snippet of dialogue between Disney's Donald and Warner's Daffy Duck during a bar scene in *Who Framed Roger Rabbit*.

DAFFY: I've worked with a lot of wisequackers, but you are dethpsicable!
DONALD: Goddamn stupid nigger! I'm gonna WAAAAAAAAGH!
DAFFY: This is the last time I work with someone with a speech impediment!

According to the subtitles on the film, Donald is actually saying "Goddurn stubborn nitwit," but then again, he is a white-feathered fowl, whereas Daffy is considerably darker.

stuffed her shoes with fresh Maxi Pads every day just to get the extra half inch she needed to be Pluto. It took a degree of pathos and emotional clarity to be a good performer and maybe something a little more Machiavellian to be an outstanding one.

Of course, the guests were unaware of the political struggles that happened behind the scenes. They were overwhelmed with their own agendas. Orville had a classification system that covered every ticket buyer who came to the Kingdom: the "Family Reunion"; the "Mouseketeer"; the "Parkhopper," who only had four days to cover six theme parks, seventeen restaurants, and a waterslide; and the "Pintrader," who couldn't pass a Cast Member without stopping to finger the little enamel buttons on the lanyard around her neck.

The most interesting guest to me was the "Disniac." Easily identifiable by their clothing (not just signature apparel, which everybody wore, but limited edition, collectable clothing from theme parks and stores around the world), the Disniacs were the only people over the age of twelve who were comfortable wearing autographed baseball caps. They had annual passes and planned long weekends to Orlando. They came to hunt for hidden Mickeys or break personal records for number of times on the Dumbo ride. The Disniac didn't ask for much. He already had Ariel's autograph. He got it in 1998, the year they opened Animal Kingdom, the year Hurricane Andrew forced the Magic Kingdom to close for the afternoon. The Disniac just wanted to talk, to let *you* know that *he* knew that Tigger's voice was originally done by a man named Paul Winchell, a ventriloquist, inventor, and genius who created, among other things, the disposable razor. Interacting with a Disniac was like being trapped with a Trekkie in the *S* aisle at Blockbuster when all you wanted was *Spaceballs.*

"The Disniacs are crazy, but they aren't the dangerous ones," Orville warned in his most ominous voice. "You gotta watch out for the Collectors."

"Collectors?" I struggled to keep a straight face. "They sound terrifying."

"Don't underestimate the Collectors! They come to the park with oversized handbags, which they fill with Tomorrowland napkins and mustard-stained hot dog wrappers, and whatever else they can pick out of your pockets for their coffee parlor scrapbooks. They wear Dalmatian fishing hats and Tinker Bell charm bracelets. You may not recognize them at first because they look like the Disniacs, but look a little closer and you'll see the materialism shining through. They're snobby. They know the birthdays of the characters and quote lines from the movies. If you don't know how many gallons of Powerade it would take to fill the 20,000 Leagues Under the Sea lagoon, they'll openly mock you. Then, they'll turn their backs and shake their heads like the whole world is going to hell."

I laughed at Orville's description, but once I knew they were out there, I saw Collectors everywhere, and they creeped me out. The Collectors were souvenir hounds. They wanted photos from every angle. They wanted the pen out of my pocket and a lock of Minnie's fur. One Collector would hand Tigger three books and request signatures. "One for me, one for my niece, and one for my poor mother, who couldn't make the trip from Albuquerque, bless her heart." A week later, two of those books would turn up on some online auction site with a minimum bid of $200.

One morning, the skies were a little more overcast than usual, so I wore my Animal Kingdom bush hat. Soon, however, the clouds had burned off, and I found myself sweating profusely. I still had another hour in the Hundred Acre Wood kiosk, so I took the hat off and set it on the railing behind me, where it wouldn't be in my shot.

It wasn't long before I was approached by an older woman, who asked if I knew the legend of the Animals That Never Were. She had a fire in her eyes, which I identified as the Disniac glow, so I indulged her, patiently sitting through her lecture. She explained that Animal Kingdom was originally supposed to have a themed section with imaginary creatures: unicorns, dragons—in fact, the popular Dueling Dragons ride at Universal's Islands of Adventure was originally supposed to find a home at Disney, but budgets had been overextended already and the project went on hold.

I thanked her for the information, waved good-bye, and returned to my photography. When I turned around again, a photograph later, the woman was gone. And so was my bush hat.

The Tigger in the kiosk clutched his belly and shook in silent laughter. He pointed his orange finger in my face and bounced up and down, the enormous grin frozen on his stupid, fuzzy face. He cornered me backstage. "Dude, you got snaked!" He was calling himself Crooze that week, wearing earphones around his neck and BluBlockers on top of his head. "You put your hat down and homegirl just snagged it, like that!"

"Yeah." I slung my camera over my shoulder and pushed it behind me, away from his enthusiastic bouncing.

He put the BluBlockers over his eyes, then pushed them down his nose. "Yo, I'm the mack in the driver's seat. Got tiger head and tiger feet," he rapped. "Make the ladies' hearts skip a beat when they see me bouncing down the street!" He pushed the glasses back up on top of his head. "Hey, I hear you're tappin' Jessie. That is ill!" He put his fist up for a bump.

"We went out a few times," I said. "Nothing serious."

He pulled off the BluBlockers and headphones and picked up the orange head. "Very cool, my man." He leaned in close and lowered his voice. "I wasn't sure which team you played for, you know?"

"Okay."

"A'ight!" He gave me another fist bump and put on the Tigger head. "Tig to the izzo!" he shouted and bounded out the door.

He was annoying, but he was a damn good Tigger, naturally animated and spry. Onstage, he was such a ham that people wanted to pose for pictures with only him, while Pooh shambled off to the side to get out of the way. Through the lens, it occurred to me that this hip-hop Cast Member was the personification of Tigger. Even without the fuzzy costume and tail, the personality was dead on.

When the pictures came through the processor, I showed Orville the Disniac who stole my hat. The hip-hop Tigger was motion blurred.

"I know him," Orville said, one sausage finger tapping the print. "I call him 'Wigger.' . . . You know, like 'White Tigger'? Get it?"

"I get it," I said.

"As a matter of fact, it's probably not an accident," he said. "A lot of people see Disney as a kind of finishing school. They feel as if they need a little polish, something to give them another dimension, so they pick a Disney character and take on his personality traits, like Tigger. What's not to love about a bouncy, good-natured tiger?"

"Allergies," I quipped.

"Other people," he continued, "come to Disney to find themselves. Teenagers and divorcees, widows, and folks who just woke up one day and realized their lives don't mean jack diddly. They look to Disney the way some people look to God. They want *meaning*, and they find it in a Wish Kid's smile or a Honeymooner's love story or the description of their favorite animated hero."

"Isn't that a little—I don't know—psycho? There's a whole world of icons out there to idolize. Why use a cartoon?"

"Don't be such a little black rain cloud." Orville narrowed his wet eyes and looked me over. "Let's see. Who did you dress up as for Halloween? If I didn't know better, I'd say you had a bit of a Peter Pan complex going on." He raised his hand to silence my retort. "When I first came here, I had a thing for Mary Poppins. It was something about her no-nonsense attitude. I imagined her wearing a whalebone corset and garter hose beneath that wool overcoat." He gave an ecstatic little shiver that shook the entire trailer. "I wanted her to spank the bejeezus out of me!"

The door opened and Marco walked into the lab. "Ay dios mio, it is so hot out there!" He slithered over to where Orville was sitting and leaned on the edge of his desk. "Can't you assign me to the water park instead. I could wear a little lifeguard swimsuit and a whistle around my neck. I would do my *baila fantastica* just for you. . . . Oh, Chico, I did not see you here."

I didn't have to turn around to sense his single arched eyebrow or his scowling lip. I changed the batteries out of my flash and tested the charge.

"I don't think so, Marco." Orville's tone was professional again. "I need you here where I can keep an eye on you."

Marco's voice twisted into a high-pitched simper. "But you have *him* here. He can shoot adequate photos for you. And I can work on my tan."

I dropped the spent batteries into a recycle bag and tested the weight. A well-placed blow to the temple with a sack of dead batteries could knock a guy out.

"Marco," I heard Orville say, "I need someone out front shooting. Why don't you show me what a good job you can do at this park, and then we'll talk about transferring you to the Lagoon—Don't give me that look. Go."

Marco heaved an enormous sigh. "If I die of heatstroke, it's your fault."

When the door closed, Orville said, "If he dies, I'll get a lot more work done around here."

After a few weeks working together, Orville had become more comfortable with me. Some days, when he was especially talkative, I felt like a sidekick or a confidante rather than just an employee. Maybe he saw me as a kind of kindred artistic spirit. Maybe he just sensed that I wasn't the type to pass judgment. Through the little window by Orville's desk, a couple of Goofys traded high fives as one went off and the other came onstage.

Orville watched them, smiling, then turned back to his computer screen and began typing. "When I die," he said, "I want my ashes spread over Cinderella's Castle."

"If only Tim Burton had created Pixie Dust . . ." I had meant the reference to the death-obsessed director as a frivolity, but it left a bad taste in my mouth. It had been weeks since I had spoken to my mom, and in that time, I had actively fought to suppress any thoughts of her condition. I pretended to make little adjustments to the film processor. "Is it true that nobody's ever died at Disney World?"

He stopped typing. "Why do you ask?"

"Just curious," I said. "It was something I overheard."

"Well, it's true," he said. "Nobody has ever died on Disney property."

I was enormously comforted by his answer, and it occurred to me that I had been dreading asking for direct confirmation ever since I moved to Florida. I picked up a set of prints just coming off the machine. "You know what I like most about photography?" I announced. "I like how, when you're taking somebody's picture, you can get right on the edge of their consciousness. You pick the exact moment you want and shoot, and just for a second, you can see inside someone else's life."

Orville nodded his head, smiling. "It's honest," he said.

"Yeah."

"Like they're opening their soul to you."

"Yeah."

He looked over the top of his spectacles. "And it's safe because you never have to give them anything in return."

"Well," I hedged. "I didn't mean that."

"Here," he said. "Let me show you some of my personal photography. The stuff I shoot outside of Animal Kingdom."

I rolled a chair over to his desk as he brought up his home page. Before my eyes, the screen filled with images of nude men. One after another, in black and white and color. Some were arranged in provocative poses while others were downright pornographic.

"What *I* like best about photography," he said, "is the camaraderie that develops between a photographer and his subject. When two people do a photo shoot, they form a bond that holds them together forever. It can be very intimate." Orville's fingers danced over the keyboard, clicking on thumbnail images to enlarge them to full screen size. Glancing over at me, he paused. "What's wrong?"

"Nothing," I said. "I'm just surprised at your, um, technique."

"I'm particularly proud of the composition in this one." He clicked on a picture of a dark-skinned guy with a shaved head, fanning his hard-on with a cowboy hat. "He was actually a lot smaller than he looks, but I used a 28 lens to make his cock look bigger without distorting the rest of his body."

"Does Disney know about your other job?" I asked.

"Let me tell you something. If I had a nickel for every lewd, perverted, illegal, immoral thing that happened right under its nose, I'd be able to buy Disney World. And besides, I'm not sure that it technically counts as another job if I'm using Cast Members as models." Orville magnified the picture so that the entire screen filled with penis. "Do you recognize him?"

"Not from this angle."

"It's Jazz." He played with the light balance in the photo, adding shading around the pubic hair. "You know, he used to be a Tarzan."

I had seen the Tarzan show dozens of times. The main character wore a wig of dreadlocks and swung from vines thirty feet above the audience. I remembered that day the summer before, when Tarzan jumped off the float to save the drowning boy.

"Jazz used to think like you," he said. "When he first came to Disney, he was straight, straitlaced, boring. He kept a safe distance without ever immersing himself in the experience. But now, well, let's just say he has a new perspective." The computer screen hummed, happily displaying the full-screen image of Tarzan's phallus while Orville adjusted the saturation levels of the photo.

"Are you suggesting I try men?" He wasn't flirting with me. He was making a recommendation. "To get more out of my Disney experience?"

"Of course not," Orville clucked. "Everybody opens up to Disney in his own way, and you clearly have the genetic disposition of a breeder. But there are many ways to achieve a happy ending. You told me once you were looking for Magic." He looked over the rim of his glasses. One two three. "Disney can help you find it, but you have to let it in."

Just then, the door flew open and another photographer walked into the lab. Quick as summer lightning, Orville closed the Web page and gave a convincingly casual stretch.

"Well," he announced, "as long as you have everything under control here, I'm going to the powder room."

I didn't want to admit it, but Orville was right. I used photography to keep my distance, like a voyeur watching other people's lives unfold through a long, long lens. Part of it was my journalism training, which urged me to keep a pen or a camera between my subject and my own opinions, but most of it was inside me; I didn't trust the charm and dazzle of Disney World. After being betrayed by everybody who was close to me, I simply wasn't ready to immerse myself in everything Orlando had to offer.

By the time June rolled around, it had been almost six months since my girlfriend had left me, and I was finally starting to shake off the awkwardness of reentering the dating scene. My new popularity had afforded me plenty of trysts with random Cast Members. For a while, I had gone out with Jessie. Then there was a delicate Tinker Bell, a stilt walker who walked around the park camouflaged as a growth of ivy, and a Scottish linguist working as a reptile handler. It had been fun and the company had kept me warm through many a night, but in all that time, I had not felt a single romantic spark. At first, I figured I just needed a little time to get comfortable with my new environment—it can be difficult finding the rhythm of a new town—but after half a year in Florida with all those beautiful college program girls, I was beginning to wonder if I had finally become too cynical to fall in love. Then I met the Little Mermaid.

In the action sports industry, nobody would have mistaken me for anything better than an average photographer, but by Disney World standards, I was Richard Avedon. The fact that I could frame an entire family of four without cutting out an appendage made me some kind of savant.

"I need you for an assignment," Orville's voice was low as I clocked in one morning. "The Disneyana Convention is coming to town, and I need a good photographer. Are you up for it?"

"Sure," I said. "What do I have to do?"

"Just show up and take some pictures," he said. "It'll be a piece of cake."

"Will there be any characters there?" I asked.

"Of course." He twisted his face into a Cheshire cat's grin. "I'm the biggest character in the Kingdom."

And he was too. He danced around the lab, singing the songs of Celine Dion and Lionel Richie. He spoke with an affected drawl as if he were the leader of a big-game hunting party rather than the manager of a photographic organization, and he fussed obsessively over his appearance. His vanity was entertaining. He maintained an air of supremacy, a blend of arrogance and feigned humility that passed for confidence with people of a certain weight.

As it turned out, Orville lived for Disneyana. Once a year, the Disneyana Convention came to Orlando and brought with it a barbarian horde of devoted Disniacs. They came like pilgrims from Amsterdam, Osaka, Cairns and Kuala Lumpur, wearing sequined Minnie Mouse sweatshirts, Goofy boxers, and outback hats so heavy with limited edition pins, they could barely keep their heads up. These people weren't just fans of Disney. They cherished it the way a magician guards his secrets. They gathered in groups at the bars to chant "Mice rule. Ducks drool!" or "Ducks forever. Mice never!" until the bartender kicked them out at closing time. They woke up at five in the morning to be the first in line to bid on a Lenox china Pinocchio or a Waterford crystal Sorcerer Mickey, and groaned when they found that somebody had already posted their treasure on eBay at 50 percent of their bid.

They traded pins, earnestly. They boasted about Kabuki Donald from Tokyo Disney or a full set of Tinker Bells with aurora borealis wings. A Pintrader would drape a lanyard of pins around his neck like papal vestments and stroll through the banquet halls staring at conventioneers' chests until he found another member of the clergy. Then, the two of them would stop and stoop over each other's lanyards, coo little admiring sounds to each other, and pick at pins like lowland gorillas in a grooming ritual. These people behaved like junkies, whispering and twitching, their hands shaking every time they reached out to finger an especially rare item. If they liked what they saw, they sat down right there on the lobby floor and began negotiations, surrounded by wary security guards.

The people who came to Disneyana came every year. They attended banquets, dressed as their favorite characters. They ran around the parks like children on recess, giggling and spritzing each other with confetti. They knew each other by name and reputation. There was the guy tattooed with every character ever created (including all 102 Dalmatians) and the mentally challenged census taker who traveled to every park to make sure all the characters had been counted. Without exception, they wore some item that labeled them as part of the club, whether it was a Mickey pendant or a pair of Pluto socks.

Every year, they told stories of their favorite convention events and tried to impress each other with recent purchases and autographs. They passed around petitions to keep Disneyana from returning to the California park, where it was disorganized and dreary and "they just don't have the pixie dust!" They critiqued the artwork that was up for auction: "Who painted that egg anyway? The Tramp looks like a Chihuahua." "And that Belle statuette! Could she *be* more cross-eyed?"

It was considered an honor to work at the Disneyana Convention because it meant I was good enough to be put on parade in front of the most acute Disney fans in the world. Orville wanted to make sure I understood the magnificence of this honor.

"I could have hired anybody for this job you know." We were setting up a photo table in the convention hall, filing the morning's photos in alphabetical order. "Any photographer would kiss my feet to get this opportunity."

"Well, don't hold your breath," I said, "but I appreciate the new environment."

"Just remember," he preached, "you're doing more than just shooting Disniacs with characters. You're creating memories."

"I know."

"Preserving the Magical Experience."

"Got it."

"And for the price, these pictures are practically a giveaway."

I pushed a box of photos down the table. "First of all, quit stressing. I'm an assassin with a camera. And second, we sell these photos for $12.95 apiece. That's, like, a two thousand percent profit!"

Orville was unfazed. "Well, there's a lot of overhead," he yawned.

It was fun to see so many characters in one place. Disniacs and Collectors were character snobs; they weren't going to be impressed with a basic Tweedle sighting, so the Disney executives used the Disneyana Convention to air out some of the more obscure character costumes in the wardrobe department: Shang (from *Mulan*), Kronk (from *The Emporer's New Groove*), and Goofy's son, Max.

But there was one drawback. Because of the long hours (Disniacs were an all-day responsibility), Orville had hired me to help him open and Marco to help him close. That meant that for four long hours a day, from noon to four, we had to work together.

It was 11:45 on the morning of the first day of Disneyana when Marco walked in. I smelled his aftershave before I caught sight of him.

"Good afternoon, Marco." Orville barely looked up from the supply boxes.

"Good *morning*, Orville." His voice was like fingers on a balloon. "I came in early just in case you needed extra help."

"Sure. Why don't you grab a camera and go get some candid shots on the floor. Just make sure you don't clock in 'til twelve."

"Hola, chico." As he turned to greet me, Marco's greasy face transformed to shock. "Oh my God. What happened?"

"What?" The word slipped out before I remembered to ignore him.

"Your eyes. They have such dark circles. You look like you haven't slept in days."

"I slept fine, Marco. I'm fine."

"Usually, you are quite handsome, but today . . ."

Orville stepped between us with an armload of film boxes. "Gentlemen," he said cautiously.

Marco put his arm around Orville's shoulder. "I was just telling your second-best photographer how handsome he is. Don't you think so?"

Orville pushed his specs up on his nose and frowned at Marco. "Didn't I just give you an assignment?"

Marco stuffed his pockets with film and took the camera out of my hands. "When I get as old as you, I hope I am just as handsome."

Watching him disappear into the crowded convention hall, I gritted my teeth together. "How do you put up with him?"

"He's got issues," Orville dismissed, handing me a camera. "But he's a good photographer. Now, listen. Ariel's about to start a set, and the Disniacs are already lined up out the door. So get in there and make some Magic."

I took the back route. I was feeling ruffled from Marco's attitude, and I didn't have the patience to battle the crowd. Navigating the convention center hallways, I made my way to the character break room and pushed open the door. I was surprised to find Brady inside, dressed in a floor-length lavender gown with furry arms. The pretty fox head of Robin Hood's Maid Marian was sitting on a table beside him. He was shouting at his manager, Sam.

"She's a *damsel*!" His face was red with rage. "She's *in distress*!"

"A damsel." Sam stepped closer, one index finger shaking like a dirty syringe at the end of his spindly arm. "Not a whore. Back off with the flirting."

Brady threw his arms up. "Now you're an expert on Robin Hood. You were a fucking dancer, Sam! A step-touch-kick-ball-change dancer. You have *no idea* how to animate Maid Marian. I do. I've studied the movie. I've been *approved*." Brady smoothed his skirt. "But this isn't about animation, is it?'

Sam ran his hand down his face. He opened his mouth. Then he noticed me. "We'll discuss this later," he said to Brady. He picked up his clipboard and headed for the door. As he walked past me, his eyes narrowed. "I know you."

His condescension was like brain freeze. "I work with your pharmacist," I said.

His scowl jumped, but he kept walking. Brady waited for the door to close before unloading a string of expletives in German, Spanish, and, I think, Farsi. He took a deep breath, held it for a moment, then expelled it as if he was filling a balloon. "We weren't always like this," he said. "Sam and I used to dance together. We were Kids in the Kingdom. Neither of us was great, but we were young and enthusiastic. We were best friends in those days. And arch rivals." He sat down on the edge of a sofa and crossed his furry legs. "Then one day, I was riding my bike to work and I got sideswiped by a city truck. Knocked me out. When I woke up, I was in a hospital bed with a cracked pelvis. The doctors told me I'd never walk again, but that just made me want it more, you know? Still, it took almost a year. I made decent money off the lawsuit, but I was done as a dancer."

"Shit."

"Whatever." His words were flimsy. They shook away from the sentences like dry autumn leaves. "I wanted to reinvent myself, so I went into characters and did pretty good. Then one day, I was at a Ghetto party and hooked up with a CP. It was a total fling— mindless. Course it turned out to be Sam's ex—well, except it wasn't his ex at the time . . . He freaked out. I apologized every way I knew how, but he couldn't hear me. That was like ten years ago. He still won't let it go." He tugged at the fur around his neck. "And I'm running out of remorse."

Brady was as vulnerable as I'd ever seen him. I fought the urge to lift the camera to my eye, to observe his melancholy reflected through glass and mirrors, to "capture" it for later observation. Instead, I put the Nikon down on the table next to the Marian head and struggled to find a word, a sound that would convey the sympathy that my head was scrambling to suppress.

"Something's gotta give." He picked up the Maid Marian head and looked into her eyes, stroked her fuzzy nose. "Something's gotta give."

I dropped into the sofa next to him. He was the one baring his soul, and yet he seemed at ease, while I sat there stumped, acutely aware of the naked space around my fingers, in front of my eyes. I was shocked at my ineptitude. I felt honest compassion for Brady, but I was completely unable to express it. Somewhere between my heart and my mouth, a line had been severed. Did my mom understand this about me? Did she keep her cancer secret because she knew I was incapable of heartfelt expression.

Just then, a cheer erupted from the character hall on the other side of the wall. "I love you, Ariel!" piped a voice, borderline hysterical.

Brady stretched his legs. "That's your cue," he said.

I stood up and grabbed my camera, my mind still grappling for something comforting. The best I could manage was a weak echo of Johnny's old standby: "I'm sure everything'll work out." Brady nodded, his arms around the lovely Maid Marian head. I pushed open the Cast Members Only door and went onstage.

I suppose I should have been ready for Ariel—after all, I had been working at the parks long enough to know that all the Little Mermaids were attractive—but I was completely unprepared for Calico.

She sat on a stone in the middle of the stage, wearing a long red wig and a seashell bikini top that exposed her shoulders and stomach. A sequined, iridescent fin, which appeared to be her lower half, flipped lazily back and forth in front of the stone.*

---

*This effect is, in fact, achieved by a system of gears, which attach to bicycle pedals hidden inside the stone. The Little Mermaid works the pedals slowly while sitting comfortably in a padded seat. It's like a slow-motion spin workout every time she does an autograph set.

She had eyes the color of fresh-cut grass and cheekbones like the high, carved peaks of the Matterhorn. Her flat stomach and well-defined feminine arms contrasted with the soft curve of her breasts like the petals of an orchid. Her smile was so sultry, even her dimples seemed naughty.

I took my position in front of her rock and tried to maintain a sense of professionalism, but every time she smiled for a picture, my head was engulfed in flames. She was the consummate performer: gorgeous, gracious, and approachable. Locked in her rock with those piercing green eyes, she simultaneously conveyed a sense of fiery purpose and delicate vulnerability. She could juggle a group of raving princess fans, disarm a slavering computer geek, and trade lipstick tips with a four-year-old minimermaid without once breaking character.

"What is this thing?" She held the pen up to her ear and shook it. "Does it ever come out of its shell?" The little girl in her audience squealed and jumped up and down, excited that she was able to impart her worldly wisdom to a celebrity like Ariel. "You have a picture of me on your arm?" Her eyes grew round like teacups as she expertly deflected the groping hands of a tattooed doofus. "If you really loved me, you'd put me on your chest! Now, begone before my dad finds you here!"

I found myself zooming in tighter and tighter on Ariel's face, until I was cropping the guests out of the frame altogether. As I photographed her, I watched her eyes through the lens, so green and deep, it was like looking into the soul of the ocean. When I lowered the camera from my face, it seemed that she was smiling a fraction of a second longer than she had to, holding my gaze for a moment before returning her attention to the guest.

I shot until I ran out of film, then waited for the line to end. When her greeter finally closed the door, I rushed to her side to help her out of the fin.

"Whew!" she breathed. Up close, I could see that she was wearing glitter dust around her eyes. She smelled like cocoa butter. "I thought that was never gonna end."

"You were great," I stammered.

She stumbled a little and put her arm around my shoulder. "Oh!" she exclaimed. "My leg fell asleep in there. Would you mind walking with me back to the break room?"

With her arm around me like that, I would have done anything. Unfortunately, Orville had other ideas.

"Ahem." He wasn't clearing his throat. He actually said it like that. "Could I borrow him for a moment, Ariel?"

She smiled and something more than simple recognition passed over her face, then disappeared. "Of course."

My palms were sweating as I handed her off to her greeter. "I guess I'll see you around."

"Definitely," she pouted. "I'm Calico. Come find me later."

Now that she was out of the fin, I could see that the rest of her body was just as beautiful. She had tan, shapely legs and a perfect butt. I also noticed that she was walking without assistance and without a limp.

"Have I mentioned," Orville said, now at my side, "what a privilege it is to work this event?"

I watched as she disappeared through the door. When she gave me one last glance, my heart skipped a beat. "Did you see that!" I said.

"Watch out for that one," he said. "She's got issues."

"That's what you said about Marco," I reminded him.

"So you can be sure I'm right."

"I know it's in the Rule Book somewhere," I said. "But remind me: how does Disney feel about relationships between Cast Members?"

Orville looked down his nose at me. "That's dangerous territory," he scolded. "Work relationships always end in disaster."

I pretended to consider his warning. "'Always' is a strong word."

He glanced at his watch. "You wanna hear a story?"

"Is it about you?"

"It's about a friend of mine," he squinted carefully through his spectacles. "Let's call him 'Norville.'"

Once Upon a Dream

It was Gay Day at the Magic Kingdom, and Norville was taking photos of same-sex couples in front of the Magic Castle.* He was having a good-hair day and feeling confident—he'd already picked up three phone numbers and a headshot from somebody who said he was a big porn star in the Dominican Republic. (He had his doubts, considering the guy looked like a terrier with a mullet, but whatever, he was on fire.) It was late in the day, and he was on his last roll of film when what to his wandering eyes should appear, but this beautiful young man—from here on known as Adonis—in a Cardinals jersey.

Norville introduced himself and Adonis let it slip that he was also a Cast Member. He was a part of Disney's college program; he had only been in Orlando for a couple of months, but already, he loved the place.

"Are you a Cardinals fan?" Norville asked carefully. The guy seemed straight, but you could never be sure. The red shirt might just have been an unhappy coincidence.

"Actually, I like the Browns," Adonis said. "But you can't wear white to a wedding."

Norville hid his excitement as he loaded the camera. He took some interesting shots where he slowed down the shutter speed and added a flash. It was, he thought, very artistic, very "wish you were here." Now, under normal circumstances, Norville would never shirk his managerial duties, but circumstances be-

---

*Gay Day is not an official holiday; Disney does nothing to promote the event, nor does it discourage its celebration. Once a year, usually some time in May, Disney World becomes *the* destination for the gay community—thousands of boys and girls—from all around the world. All you have to do, so everybody knows which team you play for, is wear a red T-shirt. This event has occurred every year since 1991, and every year, Christian groups work themselves into a lather over its implications. Martin Mawyer is the president of the Christian Action Network. "It's absolutely impossible to describe the depth of depravity we saw," Mawyer said after visiting the park during the 2003 Gay Day Event. "Not only did we see men kissing men, but these shirtless homosexuals were twisting the nipples of each other and fondling the butts and groins of their 'lovers.' And all this occurred right out in the open at a Disney theme park." What Mawyer was doing at Gay Day in the first place is still undetermined.

ing what they were—the sun was about to set, Adonis was flirting like a schoolboy, and maybe, just maybe, he was feeling *empowered*—he invited Adonis to go for a walk.

The two men walked around for a little while and made small talk. Adonis was a Scorpio. He had never been to Disney World before, and he couldn't believe how Magical everything was. He mentioned that it was his first time out of Ohio, but Norville had the distinct impression that it was his first time *out*. Something about him was so hot. Norville had always been attracted to men who were more masculine, and this guy was a quarterback. Very manly. Muscular. He didn't have any of those effeminate quirks that made Norville's eyes roll.

"That sure is an amazing sunset," Adonis said.

"Better than anything in Ohio, I'm sure." Norville bit his lip, hoping he hadn't offended his young friend.

Adonis took a deep breath that threatened to pop the buttons off his jersey. "I sure wish we could see it from the castle."

"Adonis," Norville heard himself say, "there just might be a way."

It was madness what he was considering, but there was something illicit and wonderful in the air that day, and he felt certain that he could get away with anything. He pulled out his key ring—which he possessed because he was deemed trustworthy enough to carry a manager title and all the responsibilities that went with it—and he led that Ohio boy right into the heart of the Magic Castle.*

Naturally, Adonis was dazzled. He leaped from window to window, looking at all the different angles—honestly, you would've thought they didn't have sunsets in Ohio. His excitement was a total turn-on for Norville, plus the added danger of being in the castle with a college program Cast Member. If Norville had gotten caught . . .

After they started making out, everything happened so quickly.

---

*A little history: The ground floor of the Magic Castle is a souvenir shop. On the second floor, it's a restaurant. But the third floor is Roy Disney's unfinished apartment. In 1971, while they were putting the final touches on the Magic Kingdom, Roy died. Management offered the living quarters to his widow, but she declined, so the space became a storage and dressing room. Nowadays, the bedrooms are piled high with boxes of old costumes and props used in *Kids of the Kingdom* dance revues.

Adonis had no idea what to do with his hands, so Norville did all the work. He unbuttoned the boy's pants, pushed him back in a chair, and went down on him. It wasn't the most beautiful cock, but it was the biggest Norville had ever put in his mouth.

After a few minutes, Norville looked up and saw that Adonis had found a Minnie head and put it over his own head. He had always fantasized about an encounter like this, but now that it was actually happening, it was turning into a freak show—those big round eyes, that ungodly smile. Rather than being erotic, it turned out that sucking Minnie's dick was just plain freaky.

Norville didn't even exchange numbers with his Adonis. That night, recrossing the drawbridge to Main Street, he pitched the Castle key as far as he could, nearly hitting a Mallard duck that was floating on the peaceful waters of the moat.

I smiled. "So you're in the SOP Club."

Orville's smile was demonic. "I invented the SOP Club." He nodded his head in the direction of Ariel's rock. "So I know what I'm talking about when I tell you to stay away from Calico."

You Ain't Never Had a Friend Like Me

The unfortunate science of cryonics has failed ever since its idealistic birth in the 1960s. Based on the idea that a person can be frozen within moments of death and revived years later, cryonics got off to a bumpy start in 1967 when the Cryonics Society of California first attempted to freeze people in crude capsules not far from Disney's Burbank studios. These early pioneers met their end the way God intended: decomposing in a Chatsworth cemetery, the by-product of limited funding and a failed cooling system. Recent advances in nanotechnology and bioengineering, however, have sparked a renewed interest in the field of cryonics. Currently, there are more than a hundred people frozen in a state of suspended animation and about half that many pets. These new age alchemists are the true Utopians: idealists, dreamers, visionaries who dare to put it all on black because, if Magic really does exist in the universe, Eternal Life is the ultimate rabbit in the existential hat.

The day after the Disneyana Convention, I was back at DAK. It was an exceptionally muggy day and a disaster, photographically speaking. On the whole, the guests were in a funk. Children, who could only be differentiated by the patterns of ice cream stains on their shirtfronts, screamed when the characters reached out to hug them. And parents, all of whom looked like they would gladly trade their spleens for an hour at a pool with a margarita and a Xanax, protested that they were too sweaty to have their photos taken. As a result, I had only shot three rolls of film by the time I clocked out for the day.

I had no way to reach Calico, but I had a pretty good idea where to find her. I wanted to take her a present, something to let her know that I had been preoccupied with thoughts of her all day at work. Stuffed animals were too predictable, and real animals were sure to put up a struggle. But luckily, Animal Kingdom had one other natural advantage: beautiful tropical flowers.

Calico was at the Magic Kingdom doing love and shoves in Ariel's Grotto. I finally found her at four in the afternoon, and at least fifty kids were in line ahead of me. I recognized one child, covered head to toe in rainbow sherbet, who had kicked Mickey in the shin with such resolve that the Mouse had to get ER'd. It took thirty minutes to get a private audience with the animated celebrity, but it was worth it to walk into the cavernous Grotto lit with colored lights and see her there, perched on her rock. She was radiant.

"Oh my!" she exclaimed, her hands pressed together in her sequined lap. "What a handsome prince!"

"I had to beat down a Japanese family to get in here before your break," I said.

"Are those flowers for me?"

"They're tropical," I offered.

She examined the rough edges of the stems where I had to hack through them with my car keys. "If I didn't know better, I'd say these blooms weren't acquired in the traditional manner." She took a deep breath of the bouquet. "They're beautiful."

I was impressed by the way she stayed in character throughout our exchange.

She handed the flowers off to her greeter. "Would you mind . . ." As he took the flowers, I felt a general discomfort, as if, up until that point, he had been watching me, but now, he was deliberately *not* watching me.

Calico smiled at me. "So what can I do for you?"

"You could let me take you to dinner," I said.

She clapped her hands together next to her cheek. "Oh! I am flattered, but I cannot go out with you because my heart is already promised to another."

"You have a boyfriend?"

"Soon, I will marry Prince Eric," she said dreamily. "And then I will have a husband."

"Oh, right—of course." I wiped the sweat off the back of my neck, turned the Magic Kingdom map over and over in my hands.

Her greeter cleared his throat and tapped his watch meaningfully.

"Give me your map," she said, uncapping a Sharpie. "I'll give you my autograph." She scribbled some words on the soggy paper and handed it back to me. "I would never do anything to break Eric's heart, but you can always come visit me right here at the Magic Kingdom. Bye now."

It took me a moment to adjust to the bright sky outside the Grotto. Behind me, I could hear Calico's greeter announcing that Ariel would be taking a short break, but she would be back in just a moment.

Glancing down at the map in my hands, I read Calico's autograph. "Call me in fifteen minutes!" it said, and below it, a phone number.

Half an hour later, we met at the Cast Member parking lot. She had changed into a pair of jeans and a tank top that spelled out the word *Princess* in rhinestones across her chest. Released from the red wig, her hair was dishwater blonde and streaked with sweat, pulled back into a ponytail. Without the hair and makeup, she looked older, late twenties maybe. I felt a surge of relief that she was somewhere close to my own age, not another adolescent in the college program.

"So, this is what I really look like." She shrugged. "Not so glamorous, huh?"

"You look great."

"Thanks," she said. "The funniest thing happened right before you walked in. This kid hauled back and kicked me as hard as he could."

"What? How is that funny?"

"Because it wasn't me. He could only reach the fin, and—you know. He kicked the rock so hard, he probably broke a toe. He was bawling when he left! Isn't that funny? I mean, I hope he's okay and everything, but he like, totally deserved it, right?" Her eyes were deep green, surrounded by long, spiky lashes. It was like looking at a perfect point break through razor wire.

I told her about the same kid's identical interaction with Mickey, and her jaw dropped. "I knew it!" she said, and her hand brushed my arm. "He totally deserved it!"

She could have told me squirrels grew on trees, and I would have agreed. The rhinestones on her chest flashed distracting Swarovski explosions, but I kept my eyes on her face. "Are you hungry?" I asked. "I know a place that does an amazing Cuban sandwich."

We had reached her car. She dropped her keys, and I picked them up. When I handed them back to her, my fingertips brushed against her wrist. "I'm sure it's great," she said, "but I don't eat meat." She opened her hatchback and threw her bag inside. Just before the door closed, I caught sight of a pair of roller skates.

"You skate," I babbled.

"I need to," she said. "I have an audition next week to be a roller skating Tinker Bell. I pulled my old skates out of the closet, but I haven't had time to practice."

Sensing an opportunity to make a good impression, I smiled. "How about today?" I suggested. "I have a pair of skates in my Jeep."

She only considered for a moment. "Why not?"

"This is great!" Calico put her arms out to the side and did a little twirl. "I haven't done this since I was a kid."

"What were you?" I panted. "A competitive speed skater?"

"I like to go fast," she said as she pulled ahead of me.

It was golden hour, and the sun was lighting everything with a warm honey glow. Our shadows stretched out behind us, dancing over the pavement. Calico was wearing short shorts that showed off exceptionally toned legs. There was just a hint of tan line above the waistband of her shorts. She looked over her shoulder and caught me staring at her ass. "How long have you been a Little Mermaid?" I said quickly. "You're really good."

She spun 180 so that she was skating backward, and did a little curtsy. "Thank you. I do other characters too, but Ariel is my favorite. I just love the way people respond to her."

"By kicking her?" I teased.

"That boy was an exception. Karma gave him the right punishment. I'm sure of it. Next time, he'll be more polite to the characters."

"Next time, he'll take the wheelchair shortcut to the front of the line."

"Don't say that!" She put one hand over her mouth. "Now I feel bad. You don't think he was seriously hurt, do you?"

"He got beaten by a girl," I pointed out. "And he cried in front of her. It'll hurt for the rest of his life."

She giggled at my lame chauvinism, and it was like landing a perfect trick. As we skated, we talked and, in the guise of a playful crack the whip, I held her hand. She had an adventurous spirit and wasn't afraid of anything. She liked it when I whipped her ahead of me and then raced to catch up. We watched the sun set over the tailored rooftops of Celebration where streaks of color smeared across the deepening blue sky, like a scoop of rainbow sherbet melting in an abalone dish. Every so often, a car drifted down the wide street and into the mouth of a yawning garage, leaving nothing but silence on the freshly swept streets of Disney's Tomorrowland community.

"Do it again!" she commanded with princess bravado. "Don't hold back!"

I whipped her so hard, I threw myself off the skate trail into the grass. By the time I caught up to her, she was sitting on a park bench next to a fountain, looking up at the darkening sky. The sunset colors had faded, but the fountain lights were dancing against the twilight, flickering a web of prisms against the tree branches. I was dripping sweat from the exertion of the skate. She didn't appear even to be perspiring.

"Star light, star bright, first star I see tonight. I wish I may, I wish I might, have this wish I wish tonight." Her hands were clasped together like a little girl reciting prayers before bedtime, her head tilted back to stare at the sky.

"That's Venus," I teased. "You're wishing upon a planet."

Fountain light danced across her face. "Whenever I make a wish, I wish for love. When the clock turns all the same numbers or when I blow a dandelion or find an eyelash on my cheek, I close my eyes and hope that the one I love will find me and love me back. I make my wishes on Venus because only she can bring the sweet fulfillment of my secret longing."

It sounded like a line from a movie, but I couldn't remember which one, and, at that moment, with her hair playing around her lips and the moonlight dancing on her eyelashes, it didn't matter anyway. That night, we kissed in the parking lot, under the stars, and it was electric. I couldn't wait to see her again.

The next day, I was ordering a sandwich at the DAK cafeteria when Wigger cornered me. "Dude! I heard you nailed an Ariel. Siiiick!"

The speed at which rumors circulated backstage was frightening. "How—"

"Playas gotta play. Looters gotta grab. When you fuckin' with a mermaid, you gotta watch for crabs! Oh! Snap!" Having a conversation with Wigger was like watching interactive MTV. I did a lot of listening and interjected little expletives during the appropriate pauses. *Really? Cool. No way.* Most of the time, I had no idea what he was talking about. I just nodded and smiled and punched his fist when he raised it.

"Dude, you gotta see this little hottie I'm working on right now." His sneakers were unlaced. His headphone cord hung down the sweaty front of his T-shirt, the jack banging back and forth between his knees. "She's a gazelle or some shit in the Lion King show. Bro, she *is fine!*" He raised his fist, my cue to knock knuckles with him, but then noticed that I was carrying a tray with both hands.

"Do you want onions on that?" the fry cook mumbled into the sneeze guard.

"No, thanks," I said.

"Timing, what!" Wigger bobbed his head at the cook. "I'll take one of them too."

A woman in line behind me reached around to tap Wigger on the shoulder. "Excuse me." She was dressed in manager wardrobe, nice slacks, a walkie-talkie on her hip. "There's a line," she said with amiable authority.

Wigger smiled in a way that was probably intended to be winning. "It's cool." He turned back to the fry cook who, despite my request, was lacing my chicken breast with crisp concentric circles of raw onion. "And a side of fries, my man."

The manager sidestepped me to put herself back in Wigger's frame of reference. "Actually, it's not cool." Her voice was still cordial, but a taut line of tension threatened to tear her patience like a strip of Velcro. "I only have twenty minutes for lunch and I'm next."

Wigger looked her up and down, and up. "Are you feeling lucky?" he leered.

"I beg your pardon?"

"I bet you I can guess your age within one year, plus or minus."

Behind trenches of condiments, the fry cook chuckled. "Man, I can't wait to see this."

The manager stared at Wigger as if he had just proposed a tea party on the ceiling.

The heat was unbearable, and I was standing right in the middle. "Hey Gecko." That's what he was calling himself that week. "I'm not that hungry. I'll split this one with you." I grabbed my chicken sandwich—onions and all—out of the cook's hand and retreated to the soda fountain.

Wigger was right behind me. "I totally could have had that one.

I know for a fact she's thirty-one. And a cougar. She wants the tiger bone, yo!"

I pressed a cup to the Coke spigot. "Are you trying to get reprimanded?"

"Bring it on!" he grinned. "This time next month, I'm gone anyway." He picked up my soda cup and took a gulp.

I snatched the cup out of his hand and put it back on my tray. "Where are you going?"

"Time's up." He blew a kiss at the manager. To my immense surprise, she blushed and turned away. "I'm a CP, remember? My tour of duty is done," he rapped. "And though it's been fun, when I'm flyin' first class, they'll all miss this tiger ass." Noticing that my hands were free, he made a fist. When I raised my fist near his, he punched it with such force that it knocked my whole arm behind me. "Peace, paparazzo!" He shuffled past me out of the cafeteria, standard issue sweat socks bunched down around the top of his unlaced black Reeboks.

The lady behind the soda counter clucked her tongue. "That looked like it hurt," she said. "Why'd he punch you?"

I met her look as casually as possible. "It's hip-hop," I told her like I'd been having to explain it all my life. "It doesn't hurt when you do it right."

Whether it was deliberate distraction or accidental osmosis, I found myself learning more than I ever cared to know about the characters that made up the animated films of Walt Disney. I learned Sleeping Beauty's real name (Aurora) and which prince went with which princess. Splinters of trivia stuck in my memory and refused dislodge. "Where's the bathroom?" a guest asked me one day. "Just up ahead on your right," I said, pointing naturally with two fingers. "Just past the Tree of Life, where you'll be interested to know there are 325 animals carved into the trunk and branches." Cautiously, I watched *Disney's Eyes and Ears* for reports of a guest passing at one of the parks, but that news never came. Disney World remained immune.

Maybe it was nostalgia, but one night I found myself reading over the Nick Elliot interview. "This is what utopia would look like if it were run by eight-year old architects," he had said, and at the time, I had struggled to keep a straight face. But after six months in Orlando, I understood exactly what he was talking about. Disney wasn't just a kid's Mecca or a family destination. It was a society that embraced every culture imaginable—no matter what the lifestyle. You could be a gay, Southern superfan of boy bands and you would still find happiness in Orlando. My roommate was a perfect example.

Johnny was a quiet guy and a cheerful listener who always had an extra beer on hand. He was relentlessly social, devoted to his friends, and ritualistic in his daily regime. Every morning, he would get up at 8 A.M., shower, shave, drink a protein shake, and go to work. Every afternoon, he would walk in the door at exactly 5:30, change into a T-shirt and his favorite Jeff Gordon baseball cap, and patiently prepare two fingers of Scotch in a glass over ice before settling into the task of checking voice mail and returning calls.

In principle, he did PR for Disney—his specialty was lifestyle brands: cruise ships, timeshares, honeymoon packages—but *friendship* was Johnny's real career. He was an empathetic listener and had a horoscopic knack for giving broad-stroked advice. A few selections from his all-purpose didactical stockroom: "You're a better man than me." "Sometimes you just have to go with your gut." "Who knew?" As far as I could tell, he held no opinions of his own, so he was never in danger of violating his own principles. If anybody ever noticed his inconsistencies, they didn't mention anything. He was reliable and sympathetic and people loved him for it. For all the things that Johnny was—compulsive, noncommittal, celebrity obsessed—he wasn't an asshole. He was something that I was grateful to have in my life again: a good friend.

Despite the promising pickup potential of Orlando area gyms, Johnny didn't believe in a deleterious workout regimen. For exercise, he ruthlessly cleansed every inch of his apartment. This included each of his beloved, framed boy band photos and, much to my surprise, my bathroom. Every weekend, no matter what the weather forecast, he would wash and wax his glossy black 1977 Bandit-edition Pontiac Firebird, meticulously armor all the tires and dash, and top off any low fluids in his engine.

He didn't have what anyone would term an athletic body, but he kept himself in good enough shape to claim "healthy physique" in his online personal ads and not be lying. The ads ran like this:

> 30 something GWM, 5' 9'', 180 lbs., handsome, good build,
> clean, wants to spoil a special young man. If you're cute, I'm
> rich. Let's talk!

Every Saturday morning, a new face would emerge from his room, a face that smelled of Oxy Wash and orthodontia. Twenty-four was the oldest. The youngest was barely legal. "Every man has the potential," he told me one morning after the front door closed behind the bandleader for the Dr. Phillips High Panthers. "But it takes an uncommonly honest man to embrace his true nature as a chicken hawk."

One night, I walked into the living room to find Johnny on the sofa, watching TV with a guy I didn't recognize, who looked close to my own age.

"Ah'm glad you're here." Johnny waved me into a chair. "Sit down. You have *got* to see this."

I dropped into the black leather armchair and directed my attention to the TV where a group of boys were doing a singing and dancing audition. They all had soothingly clean-cut good looks and nonthreatening ethnic characteristics. Suddenly, the face of Johnny's hero, Lou Pearlman, filled the frame, and they cut to a commercial.

"He's a genius," Johnny said. "Just when you think he's gone as far as he can go, he totally reinvents himself."

"It's like he cryonically freezes himself every few years, then comes back as another genius altogether," Johnny's friend said.

"What is this show?" I asked.

"This—" Johnny's proud face was flushed from Scotch and excitement. "This is a reality show about a boy band! Can you believe it? *The Making of the Band*, cast and filmed right here in Orlando!"

"He's inspirational," breathed Johnny's friend.

"Lou Pearlman is making another boy band?"

"They're going to be called O-Town," Johnny said.

"He's inspirational," breathed Johnny's friend again.

Seeing that Johnny wasn't going to do it, I introduced myself to his friend. "I'm Johnny's roommate," I said.

"Name's Jericho," he said. "Jazz Jericho."

Jazz Jericho had the crazed charisma of a suicide cult leader. He was wearing leather pants and a long-sleeved silk shirt unbuttoned to the shelf of his smooth chest. Thick hair flowed like dark whiskey from his head, cascading down the sides of his face to splash against his shoulders. His eyes were barely concealed behind the vivid blue lenses of a pair of trendy glasses.

"Jazz is a singer himself," Johnny offered.

"I'm not a professional or anything," Jazz said with solemn sincerity. "But I have a dream, and I intend to see it through because if there's one thing I know it's this: if I don't, then somebody else will, and it's a guarantee they'll screw it up."

Something in his eyes triggered a memory. "This might sound a little weird," I said, "but did you ever do the Magic Kingdom parade?"

He nodded. "I wasn't a regular, but I sometimes used to swing it."

"Last year, I came to visit the park, and this little boy fell into the water. I jumped in with a bunch of other people, but Tarzan was the one who pulled him out."

Johnny gasped. "Ah heard about that! Jazz? Was that you?"

Jazz lowered his eyes, smiling with rehearsed modesty. "The smile on a child's face is the most rewarding part of the job."

"Ah can't believe that was you!"

"I got two reprimands for that stunt, but it was worth it."

When he wasn't occupied with the TV, Jazz was obsessively choreographing his hair, alternately dipping his head forward to drop his bangs into his face, then tossing it back grandly like a lion shaking water from his mane. Conceal. Reveal. Drop. Flick. I got the impression that he had cast himself as the leading man in an imaginary play, which he alone was writing, directing, and producing.

Jazz turned to me. Flick. Reveal. "What about you? Johnny says you're in the entertainment department."

"Not exactly," I said. "I'm just a photographer."

"Just a photographer?" Drop. Conceal. "Did you hear that, Johnny? He's *just* a photographer." Flick. Reveal. "No Cast Member is *just* anything. You have a responsibility to be the best Cast Member you can be. The children are depending on you."

Johnny put his hand on Jericho's shoulder. "Jazz works for Universal now. I met him singing Christmas carols at CityWalk." His eyes were heavy lidded, his speech slow and purposeful. "He was singing baritone. He's amazing."

"It's nothing really." Drop. Conceal. "Oh look! It's back on!"

My conversation with Jazz had lasted one commercial break, but already I couldn't stand him. It wasn't any one thing that he did; it was more like that wary feeling you get when a boozy panhandler is schmoozing you for the dollar bus fare that'll supposedly take him home to his sick wife. He was too slick, too dishonest with his affectations.

I hoped that he'd follow the predictable course into and out of Johnny's life, lounging around the leather furniture for a couple of nights, sipping Scotch before one day vanishing for good. But Jazz didn't go away. He returned to the house week after week, and the more I saw him, the less I trusted him.

And so, while I was never able to prove conclusively that he played a pivotal role in the collapse of my Disney world, I always had my suspicions.

Can You Feel the Love Tonight?

Over the next couple of weeks, Calico and I went out on more dates. I spent time at the Magic Kingdom, where I visited her between sets, and she surprised me at DAK with cappuccinos and little flowers that she picked out of the landscape. We held hands through Adventureland, skipped across pontoon bridges, and kissed for the cameras in the dark corners of the Haunted House and the Pirates of the Caribbean.

She showed off pencil sketches of mermaids done by little girls who held notebook paper against TV screens and traced paused VCR images. Ariel fans were generous. They gave bountiful gifts: bead necklaces with silver-dipped sand dollars, hand-painted plastic combs, Dixie cups filled with shells and smooth beach stones.

She found beauty in everything. She sang out loud to the BGM no matter who was listening. When she laughed, her eyes sparkled and every child in hearing range stopped crying to see where the laughter was coming from. There was Magic inside her. I could feel it.

One day, Calico and I both clocked out early and met at Epcot. It was a typical Florida summer day that required shade, mist machines, and, as often as possible, hydration. Because of the wide variety of alcoholic beverages available at the park, Epcot was one of the most popular places for Cast Members to drink. It even inspired a game called Drinking Around the World, where it was required to consume one regional beverage at each pavilion—sake in Japan, beer in England, red wine in France. The goal was to make it all the way around without passing out.

"Are you sure you're up for this challenge?" Calico flicked a blond hair out of her face and eyed me over the salty rim of her plastic margarita glass. "The last time I played, I went all the way around and back to Africa."

"How many days did that take?"

"That's not the point." She had an adorable pout, all lower lip and flushed cheek. "The important lesson for you to get out of this is, I'm a force to be reckoned with. If you think I'm going to get all drunk and let you take advantage of me, you're mistaken."

"Drinking Around the World was your idea!"

Calico smiled, the light of the late afternoon sun warming her face like a blush. "A girl has to maintain her dignity." She was wearing a denim miniskirt and a tank top with a tiny embroidered Flounder over her heart. Her eyes sparkled like pirate treasure.

It was a beautiful afternoon. We were sitting at one of the sunny patio tables in the Mexico pavilion at Epcot, sipping tropical margaritas through clear plastic straws. In the souvenir kiosks around us, guests sifted through Mexican wares, posing in sombreros and hitting each other over the head with maracas. Everybody was in a good mood, dancing through the park, serenaded by the summer breeze. Occasionally, the wind shifted over the lagoon, bringing us an exotic musical selection from Morocco or the UK pavilion. Licking salt crystals off our lips, we finished our margaritas and moved on to Norway.

The Norway pavilion looked like a little Scandinavian village. Bat recordings swelled from inside the wooden eaves of a rural church, piercing the Nordic folk music with tiny shrieks. We ordered two Ringnes beers and sat on a bench at the foot of a waterfall to inhale the warm, sugary smells of fresh Danish from the bakery. Behind us, a store window displayed Helly Hansen jackets and

Swedish chocolate. A guest moved past us, carrying a plate of piping hot meatballs. Calico wrinkled her nose.

"Meatballs not your thing?" I said. "I think it's the shape. It puts people off."

"I don't eat meat." She tossed her hair over her shoulder. "I just think everything with a heartbeat deserves a chance to enjoy life, you know? I guess you could say I'm vegetarian. I'm trying really hard to be vegan, but I love butter—isn't that silly?" She put her hand over her heart. "I am addicted to butter. There. I said it. Go ahead and judge me."

A group of guests walked past, talking in another language. One man said something, and the rest of the group erupted in laughter. Calico laughed with them.

"You understood that?"

"My French is a little rusty, but I got the gist," she said. "It was a dirty joke. Very unladylike. I couldn't possibly repeat it. Unless we were in France. Then, I'd have to tell you."

I picked a bug out of my beer. "And I'd have to pretend not to be offended."

Calico's face lit up with nostalgia. "A couple years ago, I did a year at Disney Paris. It was amazing! Have you been? Well, take my word for it. The countryside is breathtaking and the people are so friendly. Everyone warned me about the French before I went, but I never had a single problem. In fact, I kept meeting French families who would invite me to their homes for wine and cheese and music. It was incredible! I must have gained twenty pounds eating all the desserts! I love France!"

"The *real* France? Or some Disney version?"

She threw a wadded napkin at me. "You think I'm a princess? A delicate orchid? No way. I want to see the world. I want to climb mountains and cross deserts. I want to go to Morocco."

I tilted back the last of my beer. "Lucky for you, it's just on the other side of this lagoon. If you don't pass out in the Japan pavilion, I'll show it to you."

"Come on," she said, tossing her empty cup in the trash. "I've seen enough of Norway."

By the time we got to the China pavilion, we were both feeling the effects of the first two countries. We held hands to cross the bridges, but still bumped into guests feeding caramel corn to hungry koi. We ordered two glasses of plum wine from the cafeteria and sat on a teak wood bench in the back row of the theater. Up onstage, a family of preadolescent girls was performing a gymnastic routine, bending themselves in half and balancing glasses of water on their noses.

"So," Calico whispered, "other than photography, what are you into?"

"For fun?" It had been a long time since anyone had asked me about me. "I like s'mores at the Disney Wilderness Lodge. And Tomorrowland—did you know that every plant in the garden is edible? And anteaters. I never realized it before I worked at DAK, but I really like anteaters."

She hit me, a little too hard, considering. "I'm serious."

"So am I. I want to pet one." We watched the youngest girl tie herself in a knot at the top of a pyramid of her sisters.

Between the alcohol and the shared spirit of adventure, the afternoon had become dreamy. Calico and I danced to the BGM and laughed at clouds shaped like Family Guy characters and Bratz dolls. We talked about movies and music and about which theme restaurant had the best onion rings. We knew all the same people, and I was happy to hear she didn't like Marco either. "It's like he resents Disney for not being Hollywood," she said. "If he'd just relax and stop trying so hard, he'd be a lot less annoying."

We shared a beer in Germany and sat down on one of the benches overlooking the lagoon. A janitor wheeled his cart over to the railing and began to sweep. We lifted our feet when he pushed his broom underneath our bench.

"One time," Calico took a long sip of beer, "I stole a visor from a kiosk at the Studios."

"What!"

"I had to have it. It was Ariel and it matched my outfit perfectly."

"My whole image of you is blown." My melodramatic sincerity drew her in. She put her head on my shoulder. Her hair smelled like vanilla and rhubarb.

"Come on," she pouted. "You've never stolen anything? Not even 'on accident'?"

"Sometimes I steal dogs from trailer parks, but that's more philanthropic than criminal." I considered the outfit I was wearing—skate T-shirt, shorts, flip-flops, almost none of which I'd paid for—and felt ashamed. "Actually, I used to get away with a lot of shenanigans. Before I moved to Florida, I wanted to be an art thief."

"I want to be a wedding planner." She handed me the beer and stood up, so she could dance out her words. "I'd make fantasy weddings, and never do the same one twice. Island paradise. Mountaintop hideaway. Underwater dream sequence. People would fly me around the world to design their special ceremony. And the cake would be vegan, and nobody would ever know!"

"Except the butter."

"Oh, yeah." She stopped dancing and sank down onto the bench next to me. "I forgot about that."

Why did I have to be like that? I bit down on my cheeks.

Calico's face lit up. "I'll invent vegan butter."

I was pretty sure it already existed, but this time I didn't say anything.

A little boy scampered past us, clenching something tight in his fist. He deftly climbed the lagoon guardrail and swung his feet over the top, then opened his hand. For a moment, the sun glinted off his prize, a shiny penny, hammered flat, indented with the Epcot seal. He cupped it between both hands and closed his eyes. I swear I could hear the pixie dust. A stern woman darted across the pavilion, shouting in Cantonese. The little boy braved one quick look over his shoulder, then tossed the coin into the dark lake. It flipped through the air, but didn't even hit the water before his mother snatched him away from the guardrail and scolded him all the way past the bakery.

"She was not happy," Calico whispered.

"How many languages do you speak?"

She rolled her eyes. "*That* was basic intuition."

We strolled past the miniature German village into Italy where Andrea Bocelli was pouring out of the speakers. We ordered two glasses of Italian wine and sat by the lagoon. Just beyond a bank of night-blooming jasmine, guests were staking claim to sections of railing. By this time, the sun had disappeared completely beneath the horizon and the streetlights were beginning to wink on. Around the perimeter of the lagoon, the torchieres flared with hot orange flames that reflected off the water like tangerine spills. I pulled Calico close. Her cheeks were warm and flushed. There was a crackle of excitement in the air.

"The fireworks are starting soon," I said. "Let's find a good spot to watch."

She put her hand on my leg. "If you promise to keep a secret, I'll show you the best view in the park."

What could she show me that I hadn't already seen? I began to plan the look of surprise I'd adopt when she showed me the view. "I promise."

She led me back to the main walkway. Everybody seemed more relaxed after the sunset. Happier. Flames rose high off the torchieres, warming our faces as we dodged through the crowds. We crossed the border into the America pavilion, but rather than move past the America Gardens Theatre, Calico turned and led me over a low hedge to a spiral staircase. She stepped over a barricade at the bottom of the steps and began to climb, still holding my hand.

"Calico?"

"Ssh!" She kept climbing. "Trust me."

The staircase rested in semidarkness, but there were hundreds of people just on the other side of the low hedge, jostling one another to be the next in line at the honey-roasted nut stand. I stepped over the

barricade and followed her up the spiral. The wine and the winding made my head spin with vertigo, but I focused on Calico's long,
elegant fingers pulling me forward and kept walking. Twenty feet
off the ground, the stairs let out onto a deck that measured about
ten feet square. We were in what appeared to be the sound booth,
totally hidden from the view of anybody else in the park. Calico was
resting her elbows on the railing, smiling triumphantly. Under the
light of the streetlamps, her eyes sparkled with mischief. I moved to
the railing next to her and looked out over the AmGard Theatre lit
with white twinkly lights.

"Wow."

She nodded and looked away, following my gaze around the
world.

I could see every pavilion from that height: the pagodas of Japan,
the Eiffel Tower in France, and the enormous painted totem pole of
Canada. The whole park was laid out before me like a map of the
world, and in the very center was the dark expanse of the lagoon,
as lightless and foreboding as the great ocean itself. We were above
the treetops, above the torches. Nothing stood between the open sky
and us. Calico raised an eyebrow, watching my reactions.

"How did you find this place?"

She studied my expression. "I thought you'd like it."

All at once, in each pavilion throughout the park, the lights
dimmed and the speakers crackled. Around the circle, guests jock-
eyed for position as the announcer predicted an event that would
"warm our hearts and dazzle our souls." He made a sound as though
exhaling, and as if in a sudden gust of wind, the torch fires and all
the rest of the lights in the showcase suddenly extinguished.

I had seen the Illuminations show dozens of times. The show was
meant to symbolize the creation of the universe from Big Bang to
present day. Fireworks, lasers, projected videos, and fountain ballet
were combined to create what was probably the most dramatic pyro
show ever produced. Even so, I'd never felt anything as powerful as
the first explosions above our platform. Music surrounded us. Fires

lit up the night, painting us orange, then purple, then Maleficent green.

Moving to stand behind Calico, I pressed my chest into her back and breathed her rhubarb-springtime smell. She leaned into me, smiling, and I moved my hands to envelop hers, clasping her fingers along the glossy white railing. Somewhere between the drinks and the danger and the rush and the romance of our isolated hideaway, I found myself transported beyond culpability. We had built a tree fort and nobody else knew the password. The symphony rose around us from speakers in the platform. It vibrated through the soles of my feet, into my chest. In the center of the lagoon, flames burst into the sky. Her fingers moved gently against mine, brushing against my skin like a whisper. I pressed my lips against the back of her neck, my breath in the shallow pool of her collarbone, hot and spiked with excitement.

The music rose and skyrockets launched high overhead. Bits of charred paper fell onto the surface of the lagoon where a pair of ducks scooted around the debris, hoping for something edible in the sudden gift. The night smelled like gunpowder and flowers.

Calico tilted her head, giving her throat to my kisses. Her elbows pressed against the insides of my arms, the backs of her thighs against my knees. Her skin was smooth beneath my fingertips, her breath loud and exciting when she pressed her mouth to my ear.

The music dipped and rose. The pyro was fiercer now, louder and more violent. Feather-tailed comets and double helix spirals arced over our heads. Firelight reflected off her bare shoulders, bouncing off her smooth golden hair. Yellow skyrockets climbed like pussy willows, culminating in starfish explosions overhead. White-hot sparklers screamed skyward and shattered against the night, raining down like a pixie dust cloudburst. The symphony built. The fires expanded until the skyrocket finale exploded above us. As the music faded away, I held Calico close to my body and felt her heart beat through my chest.

Around the world, people rushed to their feet. They applauded with inspired enthusiasm, screaming for the miracle of creation it-self. Pulling the long blond hair away from her face, I kissed Calico's cheeks, her ears, her eyelashes. Even with my eyes closed, I could feel her smiling. I didn't want the lights to come up. I never wanted to leave our secret hideaway high above the world.

For the next couple of weeks, I floated through my photo sets, only vaguely aware of things happening beyond the scope of my lit-tle mermaid. Rusty and Alan broke up. Wigger slept with the FOLK gazelle and then with the manager from the cafeteria. Sunny taught me how to needlepoint. Rusty and Alan got back together. At home, Johnny was drinking more than ever. When he wasn't on the phone with Jazz, the two were meeting at a café somewhere, scheming. He wouldn't tell me his plan, only that it was going to "revolutionize the music industry."

I developed a special walk that I used when I was onstage but out of costume, wandering through the park. I called it the Disney Waltz. The walk itself was casual, relaxed, yet directed, as if I knew exactly where I was going, but I was in no hurry to get there. I stepped with purposeful, evenly spaced strides, hips forward, chin in the air, and a little bounce on the balls of my feet to show that I had a spring in my step. Even when it was so hot that I would sweat just taking a deep breath, I would keep up this energy because (Guest Service Guideline 5) it projected the appropriate body language.

I turned my lips into a pleasant smile—not a grin so much as a good-natured joy that radiated from my entire face. Of course (Guideline 1), I made eye contact with all the guests and smiled at each one as they passed. When I did this, I put a little twinkle in my eye and sometimes even wiggled my eyebrows a little. I didn't want to come across as overly intimate or insane, just happy, like my face was saying, "I'm having a good time, and I know that you are too." I was confident that the guests all felt my excitement because they usually smiled back.

One time, I was walking from Tomorrowland out to Main Street when I noticed a little boy, maybe six years old, standing on the bridge, looking up at the sky. His mother was standing behind him at the water fountain trying to clean a streak of melted ice cream off her blouse. He was concentrating so hard that I just had to stop.

"Whatcha lookin' at?"

"What is that?" the boy asked, pointing to the sky.

He was looking at a safety wire, which ran from an upper spire of Cinderella's castle down into the backstage area behind the Buzz Lightyear Space Ranger Spin. At night, to kick off the fireworks show, a Tinker Bell was hooked onto that wire and zip-lined from the castle down to Tomorrowland. It was one of the most dangerous jobs at the Kingdom, and the girls who did it were paid a handsome sum to take the risk.

"Well," I said, my mind working quickly to preserve the Magical Experience (Guideline 6). "Every night, Tinker Bell has to fly from the castle up there down to the ground over there, and that signals Peter Pan to start the fireworks show. But you know how Tinker Bell gets a little distracted? Sometimes she forgets where she's going and flies off every which way and nobody knows when to start the show. So Peter Pan drew a line in the sky for her to follow, and now, she never gets lost!"

The boy's mouth dropped open and he looked at the wire again with a whole new understanding.

"What a load of bullshit!" his mom interjected, dragging her toddler away from me. "Honey, don't believe all the crap you hear about flying fairies!"

Not even a month before, that might have been my reaction too, but not anymore. Now, I understood Walt's vision. Cynicism and gloomy attitudes were things that people had to deal with in the real world; they had no place in Fantasyland.

If somebody looked lost (Guideline 3), I would stop and offer assistance. Mostly, people were just confused by the layout of one of the parks or wanted to find one of the critters to sign autographs. I learned just enough Spanish, German, French, and Japanese to address simple issues like "Where is the bathroom?" or "I need to vomit." If I saw that a guest wasn't having a good time (Guideline 4), I did my best to rectify the problem.

I changed my ringtone from Sublime's "What I Got" to "Hakuna Matata." Depending on which part of the park I was walking through, I'd hum or whistle a little tune. For instance, in Frontierland, I'd whistle the Country Bear Jamboree. In Fantasyland, I sang "It's a Small World," just softly under my breath as if it was stuck in my head but I didn't want to get it out just yet. If I was in an area without a specific theme song like, say, anywhere at the Studios, I would just hum along with the BGM. I didn't belt it out or dance or do anything that obvious. I just made myself a part of the Experience. After all, that was why I was here.

It had taken the better part of a year, but at last, I had given myself over to the culture. I had internalized Walt's system of Rules, a mantra that applied to even the most private aspects of my life. I had a never-ending supply of entertainments and distractions to fill my downtime. And best of all, I was surrounded by a group of vibrant, happy people who never slowed down or took life too seriously. *At last, I had found Disney Magic.*

"Everybody, gather 'round," Rusty commanded from the armchair. He had just wrapped a successful drag revue at The Parliament House, and he was eager to share his new gossip. "It's Storytime!"

A Queen's Fury

At six feet five, Gary was a rising star in the drag scene. As Misty Meaner and Holly Golustly at the P House, he was sassy and fabulous and always received a standing ovation. But for a real performance, girl, you hadn't seen Gary until you'd seen him as Maleficent in Disney's Fantasmic show.

For those of you who need a character refresher, Maleficent is the Queen bitch of Sleeping Beauty, who challenges Sorcerer Mickey in the second act of the Studios' Fantasmic show by turning herself into a fifty-foot-tall dragon.

This was no easy feat of Magic. To create the illusion of transformation, Maleficent had to be strapped into a hydraulic lift and hoisted fifty feet in the air. At the musical crescendo, approximately five thousand dollars' worth of pyro was detonated and Maleficent's lift descended in the dark to be replaced with a giant dragon puppet.

Fifty feet on a scissor lift was scary under normal circumstances. But when you considered how much cocaine Gary had in his system the night the lift failed . . .

When he went onstage that night, Gary was feeling, if not exactly relaxed, then at least *in control*. The music, the smells, the action—everything was familiar. He conjured his bitchiest persona—a vitriolic combination of Meaner's haughty attitude and Golustly's self-involvement—and swept through the hallways backstage.

The tech who ushered him onto the platform made his usual joke about seeing up his skirt. He fastened the safety line to the railing and snapped Maleficent's dress around Gary's waist, then gave him the thumbs-up.

When the lights found him on stage, Gary launched into his performance. He shook his fists at Mickey and openly mocked the bravery of the little mouse. As the hydraulics clicked in and the lift began to rise, Gary ground his teeth together and sniffed back the postnasal drip. Fifty feet in the air, the lights went out and he prepared for the descent. That was when the machine quit.

Explosions rocked the set and gusts of fire billowed around him. Gary was certain something bad was happening, but as coked up as he was, he couldn't quite put his finger on it. From somewhere in the back of his mind, he recalled a fire safety tip. In an emergency, Maleficent's fire-retardant dress could be used to shield the body from burns. A blast of flame shot directly at him, and he was just able to cover his face with the thick beaded sleeves.

As the pyro subsided, he breathed a short-lived sigh of relief. On the edge of his vision, a massive dragon puppet was making its way onto the stage and his heart jumped. The transformation trick required the dragon to appear right where Maleficent disappeared, which wasn't a problem when the machine was functioning normally. Now, however, he was six stories high, precariously balanced on a platform that measured no wider than his shoulders. Even as he watched, Gary could see the puppet closing in on his position, obviously unaware of the change in plan. In seconds, the contraption would collide with his narrow lift, and he knew his chances of coming out on top weren't good.

Locked onto his little platform, fifty feet in the air, he summoned all his wits about him, and girl, don't you know, he screamed like a princess!

Somehow, over the music and the explosions and the strobe lights and applause, the techs wielding the dragon heard his scream and swerved out of the way. Word spread quickly through the backstage that Maleficent was stuck in the lift, but nothing could be done about it. There were ten thousand guests in the audience, and each one demanded Magic. Gary was stuck in position for the remainder of the performance.

As the show dragged on, and the coke high shifted from paranoia to absolute fucking terror, Mickey defeated the forces of evil, and the princes and princesses surrounded the lagoon singing. Gary had no choice but to animate the lyrics that he'd never experienced onstage before that night. He moved his arms and tilted his head, too far away for the crowd to notice the tears that rolled down his cheeks. Don't look down, he reminded himself repeatedly. Keep your eyes on the audience.

It took an eternity for the lights to come up and the guests to leave the amphitheater. Three managers, six techs, and half a fire brigade turned up before somebody figured out how to release the hydraulic lift manually.

"We're going to cut the hydraulics," a voice shouted up to Gary. "We're not sure how fast this thing is going to come down, so hold on to something."

His whole body was shaking from fear and exhaustion. If it weren't for the massive amounts of cocaine in his bloodstream, he probably would have been in shock. He slipped his fingers around the guardrail and braced himself for the worst.

The hydraulic system released with a hiss and descended to the ground. Onlookers would later recall that it dropped at a normal rate, but to Gary it was a freefall. When he was finally unclipped and released, he staggered out of the cage, into the arms of his manager, who smiled at him as if the whole thing had been a grand adventure.

"Jesus," Gary's manager appraised him with a pained expression. "You look like shit."

Gary could only nod.

"Well, you better get back to the break room. The next show is in fifteen minutes, and you have *got* to do something about that makeup."

One evening, Calico invited me to dinner at her parents' house. They lived in a large house in a new development named after the orange groves that the developers had razed to create a neighborhood there. The front yard was lined with an immaculate rose garden whose colors perfectly complemented the pair of BMWs in the driveway.

Calico's father was a scowling man who attempted to break my fingers when we shook hands in the doorway. He looked me over from top to bottom, then sniffed before stepping aside with military precision. Calico's mother, on the other hand, was a charmer.

"What a handsome young man!" she exclaimed, her eyes twinkling in the reflection of the halogen lights. "Of course, after everything Calico's told us, I knew you would be."

"Thank you Mrs.—"

"Please, call me Sandra." Her teeth were perfect, like a row of Chiclets. "Calico, why don't you get us something to drink? Two Cosmopolitans I think."

The living room was camera ready, decorated with modern furniture in understated fabrics and lit in a way that looked art directed. There was a row of framed photos on the wall. Sandra was already adjusting the lights to give me a better view.

"Whatever you do," she said in a conspiratorial whisper, "don't let her know you saw these. She gets so embarrassed."

It took me awhile to realize that I was looking at photos of Calico growing up. The girl in the pictures was the kind of girl you never noticed in high school, the one who stood alone at the class reunion because she didn't have any memories to share with the rest of the group. She had unkempt brown hair and glasses and a half-hearted smile that conveyed a weak desire to be anywhere but there. Somehow, she even managed to fade into the background of her senior class portrait.

"She was such a shy girl," Sandra lamented.

"I was a late bloomer too," I offered.

Sandra was just about to say something when we were interrupted by her daughter entering the room with two drinks on a tray. "You two had better not be doing what I think you're doing."

Sandra was all innocence. "Your boyfriend was just admiring what a beautiful young woman you've become."

"Boyfriend?" I ventured.

Calico blushed, even as she dimmed the lights above the photo frames. "Mother," she said, "you are in so much trouble."

At dinner, Calico's father was predictably taciturn, scowling through salad, soup, and most of the main course. Sandra, however, knew every technique to fill the silence and employed her skills with relish. She talked about the weather and current events, then turned the conversation to California and my family.

"I can't believe," she said, dabbing the corner of her mouth with a napkin, "that you didn't want to follow in your brother's footsteps. Medicine is such a noble field."

"He's a photographer, mother," Calico interrupted. "Before he worked at Disney, he did sports photography."

"How wonderful!" Sandra exclaimed. "I just love Ansel Adams. All those beautiful black-and-white landscapes. And tell me, what do your parents do?"

"Well," I said, "my father was an engineer, but he retired, and my mom is—" It felt as if a door was opening somewhere nearby and I was being drawn into it. I hadn't spoken about my family with anyone in Orlando—not because of my promise to Michael—but because I wasn't ready. Now, however, with Sandra's question and my half-finished response hanging in the air, a hundred words rushed into my head: *wonderful, loving, dying* . . . "also retired," I finished.

"A job that takes a lifetime to master." Sandra beamed at her scowling husband. "Now, who's ready for dessert?"

It was just a small part of the evening's conversation, but it got me thinking. It had been a couple of weeks since I had phoned my parents, longer since I had e-mailed, and in all that time, I hadn't heard from them. If I was being stubborn, then what were they doing? What could be happening that they wouldn't even try to reach out to me? I shuddered to think what complications might have developed in that time.

On my way home, I dialed LA. "Hey, Dad. Is Mom there?"

"Mom?" He sounded terrible, like he hadn't slept for a few nights. "She's, uh, out right now. Running some errands."

I looked at my watch and did a few calculations. "What kind of errands?"

He cleared his throat. "Pardon?"

"It's almost eight. What kind of errands is she doing?"

"She went to the grocery store. The fabric store. Places like that."

I could tell that, even after fifty-some-odd years of marriage, my dad had no idea what my mom meant when she said she was "running errands." I could also tell that he was lying.

"How is everybody back home? Are you all, you know, healthy?" I was challenging the boundaries of my promise to Michael, but I wanted to give my dad a chance to talk about Mom. If I could just get him to open up a little, just give me some small, significant acknowledgment that he knew that I knew what was really happening, I would be happy with that.

"Healthy?" he asked. "Actually"—and for a moment, I thought it was going to happen, but then, his tone changed—"everyone's doing great! Never better! How about you?"

"I'm fine." I was rubbing my temples now. "Would you ask Mom to call me when she gets back? I want to ask her something."

"Oh, um, she might be back kind of late. Maybe she should call you in the morning."

My insides were twisting in knots. I wanted to say something more, but at that point, there was nothing to say.

"Sure," I said. "Have her call me when she can."

I didn't hear from her the next day. When she finally called, the day after that, her words were so jumbled that I could barely understand her.

I wanted to be angry with her. I wanted to persevere and not care about her silent assassin and the brutal chemo treatments. Living in Orlando, it was easy to distract myself with entertainment every minute of the day. If I started to feel sad, there was always a parade somewhere that would cheer me up or a fireworks show or a musical revue. Who could be upset when there was so much *to do*?

But it was getting more and more difficult to keep myself distracted. Every time I thought of my family, I would remember why I came to Orlando in the first place, and the pixie dust would blow away. In the face of a dying parent, no Magical experience seemed so dreamlike anymore. They felt like an escape.

I needed to go deeper, to bury myself so completely in the Disney experience that even I wouldn't be able to see where my identity ended and my onstage Disney persona began. As far as I could tell, there was only one way to do it. *I had to become a character.*

Part of Your World

Being a character bore a heavy responsibility. As I mentioned before, characters were the reason people came to the park in the first place, and they were the reason they returned year after year. The average family would tolerate a forty-five-minute wait at most to get on a ride, but they'd stand in the rain for up to an hour and a half to meet Mickey Mouse. Parents would do anything for their kids. If the little darlings wanted a photo with Mulan, then by God, load the camera because they were going to be in that line for half a lifetime. That was exactly the point. Disney was created for children and children wanted characters.

As a character, I would be indestructible, a superhero as real to those kids as Saturday morning cartoons, more real than homework or bedtime. In wardrobe, I would get hit, kicked, head butted, and barfed on. I'd have my face licked, my hair pulled, and my fingers bitten. Child after child would squeeze my nose, punch my legs, pull my tail. And why wouldn't they? They'd seen characters take worse. Over and over, on the television screen, Goofy falls out of trees, jumps out of buildings, throws himself into impossibly grim situations, and still emerges without a scratch. How much damage could a five-year-old do?

As a character, I would be a celebrity, capable of doing anything.

I could bounce from one end of the Magic Kingdom to the other in no time at all. I could work all day in the diamond mines and navigate a magic carpet. I would be capable of feats that even a stuntman couldn't perform. On command, I would have to be a martial arts master, a contortionist, an artist—the ultimate Renaissance critter, no matter which skin I was in.

As a character, I would be a father confessor. Children told characters all kinds of secrets they wouldn't dare tell anyone else, secrets they knew would be safe with a five-foot-tall mouse. They'd check over their shoulders to make sure nobody was listening, then bring their popsicle-stained hands up to their mouths and whisper, "I have a new mommy now" or "I don't wet my bed anymore." Then, they'd giggle and hug me and wave at the video camera in Daddy's hands.

For adults, I would be therapy, more effective than a psychiatrist, more powerful than a prescription drug. I could always tell the ones who needed it the most because they resisted most vehemently. "Tigger's for kids," they'd say, "not mommies." They'd try to hide behind a camera or an autograph book held at arm's length. They pushed dark glasses up on stern noses and stood firm like Mr. Darling. Sometimes, a character only had to flirt a little. Sometimes, it took a little more convincing, but eventually, everybody gave in. That was part of the Magic. There was nothing like throwing tired arms around a life-sized cartoon character to revert a sensible grown-up into a cooing child. It was a flashback to a world of nap time and Nilla wafers.

Most parents played along with the game, but every once in a while, I'd see some dad who was just too clever to be fooled by kids in costumes. One day, I was shooting a little girl in Mickey and Minnie's kiosk. She was just standing there wide-eyed with a Cinderella bow in her hair and her heart in her open mouth, following Mickey's movements like a sunflower tracking the sun. Her dad gave Mickey a nudge and said, "Boy, I bet it gets hot in there." Then he smiled and gave his daughter a know-it-all wink as if he just told the Easter Bunny a dirty joke.

Right before I took the photo, I told the little girl, "You know what Mickey told me before you got here? He said he wants to see you stomp on your daddy's toes."

The girl tilted her head to one side. "Really?"

I nodded, solemn as a priest. "The harder, the better."

I kept that photo in my wallet for a week.

Anonymity was the luxury of doing fur. Face characters had to be present and witty from the moment they stepped onstage until the moment the break-room door closed, but inside a character head, the performers were totally anonymous. They became the soul of a cartoon, animation itself. Behind Geppetto's bewildered smile or Tigger's bounce, they could be sullen or hungover or horny or de-hydrated, but their true emotions were concealed within layers of fur and Velcro. Almost anything they did in costume was forgivable because it wasn't them doing it. If Aladdin flirted with somebody's wife, it was because that was part of his character. If Tigger stepped on a kid's foot, it was forgiven because Tiggers are bouncy. These characters were written to be unpredictable.*

To be approved in a character role, I would first have to go through a not entirely objective audition process. How well I would do depended as much on the panel of judges as my ability to portray accurate character animation. Two friends of mine, Katia and Cameron, were identical twins. They were genetically indistinguishable, from their long, thick eyelashes to their Scandinavian noses to the little dimple on the left side of their pouty mouths. In fact, they were both left-handed. However, while both girls had been approved for

---

*In 2004, a thirteen-year-old girl claimed that she had been molested by Tig-ger. Within days, character performer, Michael C. Chartrand, was charged with lewd and lascivious molestation of a child and taken into custody. During the course of the investigation, more complaints were filed against Chartrand, but none had sufficient evidence to press charges. Chartrand's lawyer (who was also a friend of fur) declined a plea bargain and took the case to trial, at which time he donned the tiger costume and demonstrated the difficulty of seeing and mov-ing inside the bulky fur. It took a jury less than an hour to deliver a "not guilty" verdict.

Ariel, only Katia could do Cinderella and only Cameron could do Belle. They were approved for different roles at different auditions by a different set of executives. Of course, they became equally proficient in all three roles so that they could switch to cover each other's shifts without the managers knowing. It was against the Rules, but the coordinators either didn't realize or didn't care. As long as there was a Cinderella on the float making eyes at Prince Charming and dancing with mice, everything was okay.

Once approved, I would have to go through a week of training before I could go onstage. In the training course, I would learn:

1. *Movement:* A performer had to move the way the illustrator originally intended for the character. Goofy loped from place to place. Tigger bounced. Any five-year-old girl knew that a proper princess stood with her shoulders back and her chin up and curtsied with her head tilted a little to the side. Baloo and Brer Bear and Liver Lips McGrowl, the Country Bear Jamboree bear, might all belong to the same species, but their movements made each one a unique persona.

2. *Speech:* Face characters had to speak with the accents and affectations of the original character. In the case of Belle and Princess Aurora, this meant being absurdly polite, and in Mulan's case, less so. Mary Poppins and Burt had English accents and Gaston was French. The Mad Hatter stuttered and babbled like a patient in a psych ward, whereas Tarzan spoke with a stunted jungle vocabulary.

3. *Writing:* Autographs, like orchids, were unique and highly collectible. Each character had a specific signature that needed to look the same every time that character put pen to paper. For instance, Aladdin signed his name with "best wishes" or "make a wish" and a little magic lamp under the double *D*. Eeyore put a little bow on the tail of the *Y*, made his two lowercase *E*'s backward, and drew a rain cloud over the name. Even the most obscure character had an autograph. Pain and

Panic (from Hercules) were jagged and bumpy like writing in the backseat of a car, whereas Belle's signature was flowery and feminine.

I would have to know the habits, poses, and animation of each particular character before I could go onstage in that costume, and even with all the proper training, there were complications. For example, Chip and Dale looked similar, so their mannerisms had to articulate the distinction. Both chipmunks scurried and circulated, using quick movements to animate their personae, but whereas Chip was composed and philosophical, Dale was mischievous bordering on chaotic. Dale could steal a guest's hat and wear it around the park for a while, but Chip was the one to give it back.

There were pros and cons to all the Disney characters, so I had to choose my audition wisely. Fat characters, like Pooh, carried extra bulk in the form of costume framing, which put asymmetrical pressure on the performer's spine and led to chronic lumbar problems. However, if a costume didn't have that extra framing, then the performer got very little ventilation, so thin characters, like Brer Fox and Tigger, had a tendency to overheat. In the summer months, Tiggers were always the first to go down with heatstroke and dehydration.

There were other characters whose costumes didn't allow them to hold a pen so that all they had to do was pose. Hades had long urethane fingers, which extended well past the ends of the performer's hands, and King Louie's arms hung down to the ground, an effect achieved using bars inside the sleeves of the costume that the performer manipulated like a puppeteer. Buzz and Woody negotiated tricky glove issues by using a stamp and inkpad for autographs.

One person could be approved in many different roles, so it was important to remember which character I would be animating. It didn't happen often, but occasionally I would see a character fall into a full-blown identity crisis, acting the wrong way, signing the wrong name during an autograph set. It wasn't such a big deal if they signed Tweedledee as Tweedledum, but there were times when a performer started the day with a couple of Rafiki sets, then Smee, followed by a quick stint as Drizella. And when it was time to get into the Flik costume, the performer didn't know if she or he should be signing "Ta-Ta for Now" or "Best Wishes" or "Merry Fucking Christmas."

Being a character presented philosophical issues as well. Child abuse, for instance. God knows, Disney had more than its fair share of crying children accompanied by irate parents, so this scenario was in my face every day. As a Cast Member, Disney had a policy regarding child discipline. If I ever saw an adult disciplining a child in a way that seemed too severe, I was instructed to report it to a manager, who would then make the call. But because of the speech and behavioral restrictions, characters were a little more isolated, and that sometimes meant turning off the voice of conscience.

Those restrictions, in fact, were a big drawback to any role in the character department. Because the actions of the characters had to be consistent with their animated personalities, performers were never allowed to break character, no matter what the circumstances. A friend of mine was doing the Mad Hatter one day when a desperate parent asked how to get to the nearest bathroom. The Mad Hatter, normally a confused, babbling caricature, broke character long enough to give the guest concise directions, and for that crime was issued a reprimand.

For fur characters, speech was strictly forbidden. Even if a Cast Member won her high school talent contest by mimicking the Mickey voice, under no circumstances was she allowed to use it on-stage. A fur performer couldn't cough or whistle or form any words whatsoever. The only acceptable sound was a kiss, usually applied to a child's cheek or the top of a guest's head.

While this might, at first, seem like an easy rule to follow, it presented more than a few awkward situations. One day, I was shooting in the Pooh kiosk, when I noticed a couple pushing a child in a wheelchair at the head of the exit line.* Pooh dropped to one knee and gave the child a big hug, and while he did, the greeter explained that this little girl was five years old and she had come all the way from Anchorage to meet her hero. She was in the late stages of leukemia, and at that point, it was irreversible. Between the lines was the understanding that we would never see her again and that her last, most heartfelt wish was to spend a minute with Winnie the Pooh before she passed away.

The little girl was crying as she got up out of her chair, and her parents were crying because they hadn't seen her this happy in months, and the greeter started crying because everybody else was. The little girl threw her arms around Pooh's neck and told him how much she loved him and how she wasn't scared anymore. And Pooh squeezed her tight and rocked her back and forth. He couldn't make a sound, so he made little kissing noises in the air around her head, but I could see that from the way his shoulders shook behind those brave, unblinking bear eyes, he was sobbing uncontrollably.

In silence.

As much as I appreciated the comforts of the big, furry animal characters, however, I knew that I could never be one of those anonymous, sweaty creatures. I had worked hard to establish myself at the top of the Cast Member hierarchy. I was the out-of-character photographer. I dated an Ariel. If I took a position as a fur character, I would be backsliding down the food chain. No, there was only one choice for me: I had to become a heroic Disney face character, someone who, like me, came from a humble station on the streets; who, like me, worked his way up the ranks to take his rightful place alongside the princes of the Kingdom; and who, like me, was prince height with Mediterranean features—*Aladdin.*

---

*Disney does a lot of charity work with the Make-A-Wish Foundation, honoring the final wishes of terminal children, so this is not an uncommon occurrence. More often than you might think, the wishes of these children have something to do with meeting a favorite Disney character.

It wasn't such a long shot. Ever since I showed up at Disney, people had been telling me I looked like Aladdin. "Uncanny," they'd say, or "Dead ringer." Stuff like that. So when I saw the notice on the Cast Member message board announcing face auditions, I decided to go for it.

From the moment I walked into the casting office, I could feel the tension in the air. A couple hundred people filled the waiting room, each one fiddling with a bag, smiling nervously, and trying to calibrate mentally the princess potential of every other applicant. I could tell by the way they did their makeup which girls were hoping to be cast as Belle or Cinderella. Darker-skinned girls did their eyes in exotic kohl-streaked Jasmine strokes. Fairer ones wore their hair away from their collarbones to show off their snowy white throats. Even the boys were affecting their proudest posture, puffing out their chests to imitate royalty. I filled out my casting sheet, lined up to be measured—I was, as I knew I would be, the perfect Aladdin height—and then sat down to wait.

Every fifteen minutes or so, a production assistant (PA) would read a list of names from the sign-in sheet, and the ten people whose names were called would file down a hallway and disappear for about ten minutes before returning one by one to the waiting room. Some carried slips of paper with character names and callback dates. These were the happy ones, the ones who had been invited to participate in the callbacks. The others emerged empty-handed and tried to exit as gracefully as possible.

I recognized one girl, a photographer, who came out of the back room with her hands in her pockets. Her face was a naked display of fear, insecurity, and disappointment. When she stopped near me to get her bag, I put my hand on her shoulder. "You okay?" I asked.

She didn't look at me for a moment while she fussed with her backpack. "They said my eyes are too close together, and"—her voice drifted off as she inhaled a staccato breath—"my nose is too crooked and my lips are too thin and my teeth are too small. My only chance of making Cinderella is cosmetic surgery."

As she scurried away, I tried to put her story in perspective. She was probably overreacting. Most likely, she had been turned down because she wasn't smiling enough or she forgot to bat her eyelashes, but her imagination had filled in all those horrible details. This was Disney after all, not *American Idol*.

Before long, the PA was clapping his hands together and calling a list of names that included mine. We walked into an empty rehearsal studio and stood in a row. Facing us, our casting sheets arranged in piles in front of them, four executives sat at a long table. They ignored our entrance, shuffling through their papers with bored nonchalance, like a team of supermarket checkout girls forming opinions of shoppers based on piles of groceries.

The PA instructed us to act natural. "Just converse with the person next to you," he said.

This was the first stage of the audition: natural movements in a pseudocasual environment. I became dramatic. I gestured grandly and put my hands on my hips. Disney loves big eyes, so I opened my eyes as wide as I could. When I spoke, I enunciated like Bambi learning to speak for the first time.

The woman who approached me was Mickey height, immaculately dressed with her hair in a dark bun. "After reading over your casting sheet," she said without looking at me, "we've decided that we would like to see you again as Clopin. Please arrive thirty minutes before your callback."

I was one of the lucky ones, emerging from the audition with a slip of paper. As I gathered my things, I couldn't help but glow under the envious looks of the other Cast Members. Of all the people who'd shown up, only I'd been chosen to play the part of Clopin. It wasn't until I got to the parking lot that it occurred to me I'd missed something. *Who the fuck was Clopin?*

According to my callback sheet, he was the narrator of *The Hunchback of Notre Dame*, a gypsy who was "mischievous and flamboyant," not evil, but not altogether good either. He spoke with a French accent and wore a court jester's costume, complete with a big, preposterous hat, curly-toed espadrilles, and tights.

What about Aladdin? I thought to myself. Aladdin didn't have to wear tights. He was crafty and fun loving, definitely a good guy. Everybody loved Aladdin. Who loved Clopin?

Maybe, I figured, that was how it worked in the character program. You had to get your foot in the door with a minor character before you could play a major one. Pay your dues. If I really got into the Clopin part and killed it at the callback, I figured, it would be easier to transfer to Aladdin. So I rented the *Hunchback* video and watched the stage show at the Studios. I tried to get a handle on my character, his nuances and motivations, and his raison d'être.

By the time I arrived for my callback, I despised Clopin. He was frenetic and pompous, a fool in a clown costume. If I had to spend even one minute onstage as Clopin, I knew I would never forgive myself the shame.

The casting office was a flurry of activity. A dozen Cast Members stood in various character poses, studying scripts and mumbling to themselves. They were perspiring, fidgety with jitters, and terrified that they might have come this far only to be turned away.

The well-dressed executive from the first audition approached me with a clipboard in her hands. "Clopin," she said, making a check mark on a piece of paper.

"Zat's me," I said in my ridiculous French accent. "Where do I sign?"

She studied me like a piece of gum on the bottom of her shoe. "Not so fast. You need to get into hair and makeup. Get your costume on and then come find me."

The hair and makeup room was easy to find because it was the central hub of the chaos. There were racks of colorful costumes and rows of wigs on Styrofoam heads. Everywhere I looked, Peter Pans primped and Alices curtsied. Two Mary Poppins were engaged in a desperate tug-of-war for the last umbrella. Within moments, a makeup woman corralled me into an empty chair and was doing her best to put out my eyes with sticks and brushes. Then she turned me over to a dandelion-haired lady wearing a lanyard of safety pins around her neck who looked me up and down.

"Aladdin, right?" She handed me a stack of comfortable-looking clothes. "I can always tell. Aladdin is my absolute fav'rite character. He's just so . . . naughty." She scrunched up her face in approval, like "naughty" was the finest quality a person could have. "Don't you think?"*

"He's a regular scoundrel," I agreed. "But I'm here for Clopin."

"Oh?" Her smile melted. "Him I don't like."

She took back the stack of comfortable clothing and assembled a different costume, one with sparkling spandex and jingly bells, then directed me to the changing room where I struggled to put everything together. When I was finished, I took one look at myself in the mirror—iridescent unitard, purple cloak, a masquerade mask—and resolved to make my push for Aladdin at the earliest opportunity.

The mousy executive found me in the hallway and shoved a script into my hands. "These are your lines," she said. "From the moment you get in that room, you *do not* break character under any circumstances. Do you understand?"

"While I have you," I said, pushing shiny brass jester bells out of my face, "I was hoping to ask you about my role."

"Ask me later," she snapped, already moving down the hall.

The audition was relatively easy. I'd taken theater in high school and booked one or two commercials in LA, so I knew what they were looking for. I spoke in my French accent and threw in some arm movements that the animated character used. The corporate judges wore blank expressions, but I knew I'd done well. In the hallway, I came face to face with the executive. This time, she was smiling as if we were now on the same team.

---

*In 1995, the *Wall Street Journal* published an article that highlighted a piece of whispered dialogue in Aladdin. The piece in question takes place when Aladdin meets Jasmine and her pet tiger, Rajah, on the balcony of Jasmine's palace bedroom. As the menacing tiger approaches our hero, he whispers, "All good teenagers take off your clothes." Disney's official interpretation of this line is, "Scat good tiger, take off and go." On closer inspection, however, the truth seems to lie somewhere in between.

"Congratulations!" she enthused. "We want to get you started as soon as possible."

"Yeah, about that." I pushed the jester hat back on my head. "I'm not really feeling the part of Clopin. Can I switch to another role?"

The smile froze on her face. "You're not . . . *feeling* the part?"

"Don't get me wrong," I offered. "He's a complex character. He has some really terrific nuances. It's just that I kind of had my heart set on another role. If I could just go back into wardrobe and re—"

"No, you cannot just *go back into wardrobe*. You tried out in Clopin. You have been *approved* in Clopin."

"I know, I know, but I don't really like Clopin, and I just thought maybe I could try out for Aladdin instead."

"Aladdin?" she spat. "*Aladdin*? No no no! I don't think so."

Something about her tone set my teeth on edge. "Why not?" I asked.

"Your proportions are all wrong." She stepped back to survey me over the bridge of her nose. "You're out of shape. You're too hairy. Plus, you are far too old to be Aladdin."

"I'm only twenty-five," I lied.

She threw her head back and laughed. "Nobody would believe that you're a teenage boy. Clopin is much older, much more your style."

"But I don't *like* Clopin," I repeated.

She put her hands on her hips. "Are you saying you don't want the part?"

Who did this woman think she was, standing there, giving me an ultimatum? I looked just like Aladdin. Everybody thought so, even the wardrobe lady. "That," I said, "is exactly what I'm saying!"

"Well then." Her smile was pure cotton candy. "Thanks for coming and don't forget, fur auditions are this Thursday."

That afternoon, as I sped home, I stared at my face in the mirror. I had laugh lines and crow's feet taking root at the corners of my eyes, and there were traces of gray at my temples. I'd just turned thirty and, while I didn't look much older than mid-twenties, I certainly wasn't getting carded anymore.

Maybe she was right. Maybe I was too old to be a storybook hero. The thing was, if I was going to be a character, I wanted to do it on my own terms. If I couldn't play Aladdin, I'd just have to find another way to integrate myself into Disney's world. It was a brutal hiccup in the fabric of my Magic carpet ride, and the beginning of what turned out to be a rapid free fall.

A Spoonful of Sugar

Every noble family has its embarrassing relatives, and the Disney clan is no exception. In addition to Mickey, Donald, Snow White, and Pinocchio, Disney also produced a few esoteric segments that won't show up on the home-theater system anytime soon. Notably, there was the 1946 animated film, *The Story of Menstruation*, which was produced for the International Celucotton Company (Kotex). Running approximately ten minutes, this most arcane of Disney films mentions neither sexuality nor reproduction, presenting a woman's period as an issue of morale. The original screenings were accompanied by a booklet titled *Very Personally Yours*, filled with promotional material for Kotex-brand feminine products. It is estimated that 93 million women in America have viewed this film, but copies are very rare. Also absent from the Zoo are the characters of Disney's 1973 animated STD awareness film, *VD Attack Plan*, which starred the formidable VD as a general, leading his troops, Gonorrhea and Syphilis, into battle against Mankind. A memorable film for sure, but Disney won't be licensing the rights to make plush toys any time soon.

The audition debacle was disheartening, but I didn't have time to wallow in self-pity. The days were at their summer longest, and working the dark pavement of DAK, my energy was drained by the time the sun was at its high noon highest. After one particularly exhausting day that included cleaning vomit off my shoes on two separate occasions—once from a sugary Canadian boy and once from a hungover Rafiki—I wanted nothing more than to spend a quiet night unwinding with Calico. Unfortunately, Wigger was having a going-away party, and I had promised to make an appearance. As it turned out, everyone else canceled, so I was the only person who showed up at Pleasure Island to say good-bye.

"Hey baby! How about a little good-bye kiss?"

He was already drunk by the time I got to the BET Soundstage Club, downing shots and trying to get action from any girl who wandered too close. Whenever he struck out, which was every thirty seconds, he punched me in the arm and shouted what a big mistake she'd just made. To make matters worse, we were at Pleasure Island on Sunday night—not Thursday—so there were no Cast Member benefits. I couldn't get my usual discount, I noticed that none of the regular bartenders were working, and I didn't recognize anybody in the crowd.

"You know what I'm gonna miss the most about this place? The fags!" Wigger laughed so hard, he slipped sideways off his barstool, spilling tequila down his shirt. "Oh damn! That was the premium shit too."

I handed him a stack of napkins. Even under the dim club lights, I could see the veins bulging in his forehead, thick as vines around Sleeping Beauty's castle. "Relax, I'll get you another one."

"Yeah?" He looked up from his soggy shirt, and for a moment, I thought he was going to start crying. "Thanks my man. That means something, you know? Come here." He shook my hand and pulled me in, throwing his other arm around me in a backslapping bro hug. I could feel the cold stain of tequila soaking into my own shirt.

"Don't worry about it," I said, pushing myself away. "It's a going-away present."

"That *means* something."

The night was at the tipping point when the after-dinner crowd was fading out and the party crowd was rolling in. The music shifted from old-school favorites to new pop hip-hop. Wigger pumped his fist. "Aw yeah!" he shouted. "This is my motherfucking jam!" His outburst caught the attention of a large bouncer, who edged closer to our table.

There was something dangerous in the air. Guests were rowdier than usual, security seemed surlier, and Wigger was on the edge of mania. A waitress wandered past our table, and Wigger pounced on her arm. "Hey sweet thing. You wanna put a tiger in your tank?"

With a little twist, she slipped out of his grip, and stood at a safe distance. "Can I get you two anything else?" she smiled.

"Two tequila shots!" Wigger commanded. "This Aladdin motherfucker is buying." As the waitress disappeared into the haze, he punched me in the arm and began to rap. "Yo, a Street Rat found a magic lamp in a cave. It was dirty and shit, but he decided to save it. So he rubbed the side and a genie popped out. He stretched his back and began to shout, 'I been stuck in that lamp for a thousand years. And I'm pissed as hell 'cuz you stuck me there.' Aladdin said, 'What the fuck.' Genie said, 'Shut up. Y'all repressed my people for far too long. And now I'm taking back the Middle East with this motherfuckin' song'!"

The bouncer, a weapon of mass destruction in a *Look* book haircut, tapped Wigger on the shoulder, and shook his head.

Wigger stopped rhyming and held up both hands. "It's cool, my man. I'm cool."

The waitress appeared with our drinks, keeping a strategic distance between herself and either one of us. "Eighteen dollars," she said.

I handed her a twenty and passed one of the shots to Wigger. "To Disney," I said. "Bon voyage." We clinked our shot glasses and downed the tequila, my first—and last—drink of the night. "Well, it's late, and I have to work in the morning."

"Yo, check this out!" Wigger tugged my sleeve. "That burly bouncer motherfucker that just interrupted my rhyme? I bet you the next round I can nail him with this lime wedge."

"Are you crazy?"

"The next round. Watch this!"

Before I had time to react, Wigger whipped his used lime at the back of the bouncer's head, then spun around in his seat, laughing like a maniac into his hands. "That was fucking awesome," he squealed between his fingers. "Don't look!" The bouncer was scanning the room, his neck bulging like a thigh. He walked past our table and disappeared into the crowd.

"Time's up," I said. "I'm out."

As I stood up, Wigger grabbed my arm. "Yo, I seriously want to thank you for coming out with me tonight." He had that extremely serious look on his face that drunks got when things were about to get really bad. "I mean it. I totally appreciate it."

His grip on my arm was painfully tight. "You'd do the same for me."

"Absolutely," he spat. "Absofuckinlutely. You know why? I'll tell you why. Because we're like brothers, you and I."

"Like brothers," I agreed. Wigger was getting loud again. People were starting to stare.

"That's why I'm so glad I met you this summer."

"Me too." The oversized bouncer was heading our way, the corners of his mouth jerking like a hungry dragon. I squirmed, but couldn't break his Kung Fu death grip. "Okay. Just let go."

"See my man," Wigger continued, not letting go, "you can appreciate a good piece of ass. Some fine titties. Not like those faggots at work."

"Excuse me?"

"That's why you and I can hang out so good, dog. We're different from them. The only two heteros in the whole fuckin' Kingdom!" He raised his fist, a maniac's smile twisted onto his face. "Come on, man! Give me some love!"

I let his hand hang in the air. I could feel every face in the bar turning toward us, the bouncer pushing his way through the crowd. Wigger's twisted smile faded to confusion, then betrayal, then anger, like a queen transforming herself into a wicked witch. He dropped his fist onto the bar. "What the fuck. Why you gotta bitch out like that?"

Finally, he loosened his grip on my arm, and I twisted away from his fingers. As I walked away, I brushed shoulders with the enormous bouncer, now focused on his target.

"Why you gotta be a bitch?" Wigger screamed at my back. "You a faggot too?"

I walked out the front door and down the midway where guests were lining up for The Adventurer's Club and break dancing under the video screen, psyching up for the nightly New Year's Eve celebration. I didn't look up when the bouncers pushed their simpering baggage out the exit gate and deposited him upside down on the parking lot pavement.

Wigger was not missed around the break room. In fact, I was surprised at the seamlessness of his departure. I wasn't expecting an emotional ceremony, but the guy had been a part of our lives for the past six months. It seemed appropriate that something would be said, and yet the subject never came up.

"Let's play story time!" Alan clapped his hands to get everyone's attention. "The rules are, it has to take place in modern times, you have to include the most obscure Disney character you can think of, and you have to tell the story in one breath—no inhaling—and it has to start with 'once upon a time' and end with 'happily ever after.' Okay. Sunny, you go first."

Sunny pushed her glasses up on her nose and took a deep breath. "Once upon a time, there was a clairvoyant pig who got kidnapped by terrorists and Taran had to save her, and they all lived happily ever after, the end." She took a deep breath, and beamed at her audience, applauding.

"A Black Cauldron reference." Alan rewarded her effort with a respectable golf clap. "Very impressive. Okay, Rusty, you go."

Apparently, the two were back together because Rusty was curled around Alan's legs. He stood up and took a deep breath. "Once upon a time, there was a little black centaur named Sunflower, who worked for the white centaurs; then one day she rose up and broke the shackles of her repression and she got her own Happy Meal toy and little girls everywhere finally had a black Disney role model and they all lived happily ever after."

The performers in the break room applauded, but it was clear they didn't understand the reference. "Thank you, thank you." Rusty blew kisses to his audience.

Nikki, who had been sprawled on the couch, raised herself up to her elbows. "Technically," she said, "Sunflower doesn't exist. Disney edited her out of the segment when they released *Fantasia* on home video."

Rusty hoisted an eyebrow. "Girl, you can't edit history. Sunflower is real and she is a symbol for African American centaurs everywhere!"

Alan stepped between them. "Okay, Nikki. Your turn."

"I'm not playing," she said, lying back down.

Alan turned to me. "Let's see what you can do."

"Once upon a time," I started in the traditional mannner, "VD, Gonorrhea, and Syphilis were battling against Mankind, but just as they were about to deal the final blow, a team of government scientists, working on powerful biological weapons to fight an unwinnable war in the Middle East, accidentally stumbled on a cure and decimated their troops forever and Mankind lived happily ever after."

The room was silent. "That's disgusting," Nikki said.

That evening, I got a call from Brady, inviting me on an adventure the following day. His words were vague, but the message was clear. I should dress comfortably, hydrate, and be ready for anything. I still hadn't figured the guy out. He worked at the Magic Kingdom, so we rarely crossed paths on property. The only parties he attended seemed to be his own, and he had been there long enough to know his way around the Rules. Then there was his philosophy of Guerrilla Philanthropy, which intrigued me with its thinly veiled self-indulgence. He fascinated me like an earthquake: unpredictable and potentially devastating. When I got home from work, I took a quick shower, powered down a shot of Johnny's Scotch, and sat down on the curb to wait.

"Where'd you find this car?" I asked as we pulled away from the Ghetto. I was sitting in the passenger seat of a convertible Alfa Romeo, with the top down, stereo blasting REO Speedwagon.

"It found me," he shouted over the music. "I woke up one morning and there it was."

"One day, you'll have to tell me how you come by all these toys."

He smiled, head bobbing like Goofy on Rohypnol. "No I don't."

"Seriously, Brady. What do you do exactly?"

He pretended to consider the question. "I gamble. I skywrite. On weekends, I host keggers and work on my tan." Taking off his aviator shades, he squinted at me more closely. "You look different. Happy. Are you on something? If I didn't know better, I'd say you'd been Disnified!"

"Give me a little credit."

"You met someone, didn't you? Tell me everything, and by 'everything,' I mean the dirty parts." I told him about Calico, leaving out the dirty parts. I was relieved that he didn't know who she was. "An Ariel," he said when I finished. "Not bad for a DAK photo jockey.

"She reports to your manager. She hates him as much as you do."

A cloud crossed his face. "Nobody hates him as much as I do."

Since it was the middle of the day—primetime for amusement park attendance—there was no traffic on I-4. Jetting north, I was surprised to discover a general discomfort growing inside me the farther we drove from Disney property as if I were moving away from a demilitarized zone and into a minefield. Faded strip malls surrounded by scraggly trees infected the swamp commercial zone around Kissimmee. Highways seemed too narrow, cars too reckless. I gripped the door handle and tried to concentrate on the BGM coming out of the Alfa's primeval stereo, but I couldn't shake the fear that there was a violent crime taking place in each home around Universal at that very moment. How long had it been since I'd been off Disney property? I couldn't remember the last time I'd dropped into a concrete bowl. It'd been months since I felt the buoyant caress of the ocean's tides.

As we passed through downtown, I spotted the alley where Nick and I had painted the walls, and I felt a tug of regret. We had the opportunity, back then, to create something beautiful, to do something constructive that might make people proud of where they lived, but we had opted to follow a villain's code instead. And for what? A magazine article? It was heartbreakingly insignificant.

Brady sped to an exit just north of downtown Orlando where he zigzagged through the streets until the billboards became Spanish, then turned into a large arena-shaped building with a sprinting greyhound painted on the side. The place looked deserted, but he led me to a side door, which opened at the touch of his hand.

Inside, the place smelled like Hooters: sweat and beer and testosterone. As my eyes adjusted to the darkness, I saw that I was standing at one end of a court that ran about fifty yards from end to end. The walls on three sides were green, the floor split from back to front into two parts: half black paint and half wood paneling. The fourth wall was nothing more than a thick nylon net, beyond which, there were fifty rows of stadium seating. Brady was smiling. "What do you think?"

"I've never seen anything like it."

"This is the Orlando Jai Alai Fronton. It's one of six in the state, the last six in the country."

As far as I could tell, we were the only ones there. "Are we allowed to be here?" I asked.

Brady tilted his head at me as if I had just passed my "sell by" date. Then he turned and limped down a hallway. I followed him to a locker room where he chose a locker seemingly at random and opened it to reveal a lineup of wicker scimitars and plastic helmets. "Try on one of these," he said, tossing me a helmet. It stank like disinfectant, but it fit. Brady was brandishing one of the wicker weapons.

"This is the *cesta*," he said. "Hold out your right hand."

He pushed my hand into a leather pocket at one end of the cesta, palm flat against the wicker, then strapped it to my arm using a long leather lace. It felt awkward, but sturdy, like an elongated baseball glove. After strapping himself in, we walked back onto the court.

Brady dropped a ball into the pocket of my wicker cesta. It was about the size of a baseball, but as hard as a golf ball. "We call this the *pelota*," he said. He placed me in the center of the floor about twenty-five yards from the front wall. "Now, what you *don't* want to do," he said, "is throw like a softball. Relax your arm and throw from the shoulder. The pelota will find its own course." I took my best shot, but the ball flew wide, into the net on the side of the court.

"Good start," he said with Disney sincerity.

He showed me how to lean over the cesta and follow through with the arc until, eventually, I was able to hit the front wall. Catching the ball was another story. I could never quite predict the placement of the little pelota. More than once, it bounced into my ankles, leaving quarter-sized bruises that turned blue almost immediately. Brady's throws were only a little better than mine, but he had more control over his catches. He was able to catch and hurl in one fluid motion that had me baffled.

After about fifteen minutes, a man appeared at the top of the stairs. He was whippet thin with dark hair and a dark mustache. When Brady saw him, he called out in Spanish, and the two embraced like brothers.

"This is Beltran from Mexico City," Brady said. "He's been teaching me the art of jai alai."

"Brady is a good man," Beltran said in a thick accent, rubbing the back of his head. "But I'm afraid his jai alai is a little unpredictable."

"I'll keep that in mind," I said.

Brady and Beltran sat in the front row of the stadium and spoke in hushed Spanish while I practiced throwing and catching. After a few moments, Brady called me over.

"How would you feel about going to a party in the Caribbean?"

"Are you kidding?"

"Not at all. Beltran's brother loves Disney, but he's too sick to come visit on his own, so he's offered to fly a couple of genuine Cast Members down to his beachside villa for a birthday party. Crystal blue water, exotic rum drinks, and we'll still be doing a good deed under the radar."

"You had me at 'Caribbean.' "

The three of us played jai alai together for a while and then Brady and I took off. I probably should have been more suspicious about this Caribbean birthday party, but it didn't really occur to me. Maybe it was Disneyfication, but it sounded just good enough to be true.

On the drive home, I felt less apprehensive, but I was still relieved when the untamed scrub brush gave way to gardens manicured by Disney gardeners. Brady dropped me off at the Ghetto, then sped off. No sooner had I pulled out my keys than my phone rang. I recognized Calico's number, but I could barely understand what she was saying through the tears. I was at her apartment in five minutes. I found her sitting on the couch under a potted palm with her legs pulled up against her chest. Her mascara was smudged and her eyes were red from crying. When she saw me, she jumped to her feet and ran into my arms. I made a few comforting sounds while I stroked the back of her head and waited for her to speak.

"There was this girl," she sniffed, her voice raspy. "This beautiful little girl. She couldn't have been more than ten years old. She had such enormous blue eyes."

Calico pressed her lips together, but fresh tears came anyway. She pulled her hands out of mine to wipe her eyes. "I had a special request from a Wish kid who wanted to meet Ariel. My coordinator asked if I'd do it and, of course, I said yes. I put on a fresh set of shells and got in the fin. When I was ready, my greeter brought her in.

I'm Wishing

She was wearing one of those straw sunbonnets with the Mickey swirl in front, pulled right down over her ears. I said something about how pretty she was and how she would certainly marry a prince someday. She put her hand on my fin and felt the sequins. She didn't say a word. When her mom put her down in my lap, she just kept touching me. My arms and my hands. So intently. Like she was mesmerized by the textures. She was so beautiful, I think I forgot to keep talking.

She asked if she could comb my hair, and I told her I didn't have my dinglehopper, but she could touch it if she wanted. That's when she started crying. She said she used to have long red hair too. Before the medicine. And she used to put flowers in it to hold it back behind her ear. She touched my face and my mouth. "You have everything, Ariel." She told me not to cry. I told her it was just the sea spray.

I couldn't talk any more without my voice breaking. I looked up at the little girl's mom and she was crying too, but I didn't want her to think she'd made me sad. I just held onto her while she stroked my hair.

She told me that she listens to me sing every day. "Mommy lets me put your movies on when I finish my homework. When I turn sixteen, I'm going to be a princess just like you, and I'm going to swim to the surface where a prince will find me." I told her that she'd make a beautiful princess and that I couldn't wait to hear about another royal couple in the Kingdom.

Before her mom came and took her off my lap, she gave me a hug and held my hand and said, "I've listened to your songs so many times. My dream was to meet you and know what you're really like, and now when I'm at home, watching your movie, I'll know. I'll keep you in here." And she showed me her fingertips that traced *my* face and *my* stomach and *my* arms.

Calico stopped talking and let the tears run down her face. She hiccupped and looked at me, startled, then laughed. I held onto her and let her wipe her face on my shirt. She was so vulnerable.

I thought about Orville's words: Disney would help me find Magic, but only if I dropped my journalistic defenses. More than anything at that moment, I wanted to be present for her; I wanted to show that I wasn't just an emotional voyeur, hiding behind a camera.

When Calico reached for a tissue, I took a deep breath and closed my eyes. "My mom has cancer," I said. "Lymphoma. She's back at home in LA right now going through chemotherapy and radiation treatments and macrobiotic diets and everything she can think of."

It was the first time I'd said the words out loud, and they felt horribly inadequate. I stood up and went to the window. Outside, I could hear the wind blowing through the leaves of the banana trees and a symphony of crickets. When I turned around, I saw that Calico was standing with the tissue in her hand, her eyes red, waiting for me to continue.

"At first, nobody told me. My dad said she had appendicitis, which was easy enough for me to believe because, I mean, what do I know about appendicitis? Or cancer? My brother was the one who finally broke the news months after her first treatment. But I should have known. There were days that she could barely stand up. It took her fifteen minutes to get from the couch to her bed. She stopped eating."

Calico walked over and put her arms around me. "It's okay," she said.

"And what did I do? I ran away to Never Land. I left her there. And my dad and my brother are dealing with everything."

"Ssshh."

"I'm an asshole."

She stroked the back of my head while she kissed my eyelashes. "It's not your fault," she said.

That night, we made love, and for the first time, I told her I loved her. There was a thunderstorm and the sky was exploding every few minutes with lightning. She was soft and gentle as if she were giving a part of herself to me. We started on the couch and finished on the balcony, where we could reach out and touch the curtain of rain that separated us from everything else in the world.

I could feel myself falling for her. She was so open, so honest with her emotions. In my weakened state, I was eminently grateful for her vulnerability and her willingness to trust me.

You Can Fly! You Can Fly! You Can Fly!

In September, love bugs descended like a plague on Orlando. They swarmed over the plastic picnic benches, swam through water fountains, and pranced around the parasols of baby strollers in a ubiquitous mating lambada. Other than the name, there was nothing cute about the love bug. It was black and spiny, no bigger than a Tic Tac, with a little red splatter right behind its head. It flew, but its flight was slow and drunk, like it was tripping over the wind, another species of languid Southern insect with nothing better to do on a sticky summer day.

They were called love bugs, but the "love" they experienced was entirely physical in nature. You rarely saw just one bug; usually they were a dual entity, attached at the butt. It was a mystery where they came from or where they went when September ended, but for one month, Florida was overrun with thousands of these creatures, fucking wherever they pleased.

It was kind of ironic actually, these bugs having sex all over Disney property. In August, Disney was the most pristine family entertainment park in the world, and less than a month later, it was a bordello. They were especially attracted to the color green, making it downright hazardous for any Peter Pan in September. I couldn't reach for a mustard packet or tie my shoelaces without uncovering an orgy of insects going at it. They dragged each other across my eyelashes, crunching under my feet like stale popcorn.

But as annoying as they were and as much as they ruined bowl after bowl of crisp, green salad, there was something sweet about their singular desire for companionship. Maybe it was just anthropomorphism, but people went out of their way to avoid killing these sex-starved insects. And if somebody happened to be in love when the bugs swarmed, well, everything took on a whole new level of symbolic meaning.

As summer came to an end, the crowds melted away like a snow cone. Park attendance dropped to a humble hundred thousand a day, and resort managers granted second-string masseurs extra days off. Little by little, the humidity evaporated, and each autumn day more closely resembled the lazy summer afternoons of Everywhere Else, USA. Guests were happier. Bouncing children laughed and waved at colorful characters from high atop the strong shoulders of kind-eyed fathers. Every couple took on the sappy posturings of a Honeymoon pair, holding each other close without the fear of sweat.

Backstage, life was more peaceful, too, without the constant rumble of air-conditioning machinery. Performers spent less time in the break rooms and more time chatting outside in the afternoon breeze. Powerade consumption declined. Tiggers didn't pass out as much. Parades were less torturous when Cast Members weren't tethered to a float like eggs frying sunny-side up in a pan.

Autumn at Disney wasn't like autumn anywhere else. The trees stayed green and the flowers continued to bloom. On property, landscapers replaced wilted plants with new growth, ripe with buds, bursting with color. You couldn't judge the seasons by the landscape, or you'd think it was always spring in Orlando. As for me, I had never been happier now that I was finally immersing myself in Disney culture, giving myself over to Walt's wonderful philosophy.

I spent all my free time with Calico, discovering the hidden gems of Disney World. One afternoon, we were light petting in a Pirates of the Caribbean boat when a solitary woman in the back row, right behind us, pulled out a mason jar. I probably wouldn't have noticed her since her black dress almost completely smothered her, but at the time, I was half turned around nibbling Calico's ear and noticed a gleam of light as the woman unscrewed the tin cap. Over the Jolly Roger BGM, I could hear the woman sobbing, her shoulders shaking out of sync with the drunken sailor tack of the boat's track.

Calico fumbled with my zipper as I watched the woman through a veil of dirty blond hair. Very carefully, she dislodged the contents of the jar into her hand. Under the dim light of the caverns, it looked like dirt, but I knew she wasn't mourning a few ounces of earth. Muttering a prayer to herself, she scattered a bit of the ash into the waters of the Captain's Room and again at the Wench Auction. When we got to the Burning Jail, she reluctantly opened her fingers and let the rest go.

When the boat brought us back to the Bayou, we disembarked and the woman disappeared into the crowd. I didn't say anything about it to Calico. Instead, I renewed my efforts to keep myself distracted. On the hottest days, I would take Calico to ride the waterslides at Typhoon Lagoon, then watch the sun set over martinis at the Yacht and Beach Club Resort bars. She showed me the hidden break rooms at Hollywood Studios, and I showed her the forgotten storerooms in the Magic Kingdom tunnels where we paid homage to the love bug lifestyle.

One bright September day, I clocked in five minutes early, whistling a tune from *Fantasia 2000*. I didn't notice Marco slithering in beside me until he spoke.

"Hola, chico."

His accented simper made my teeth hurt. "Hello, Marco."

"I hear you've been very busy." He smiled as he walked out the door. "It has been such a pleasure working with you. I will hate to see you go."

It was the first time we had spoken since Disneyana. After months of working side by side with Marco, I had become pretty good at avoiding him and ignoring his wisecracks, but these ominous words shook me.

Had someone seen Calico and me sneaking around beneath the Magic Kingdom? Had I been recognized and reported? Was Calico in trouble? Or was this another one of Marco's lame schemes? I stumbled through my morning schedule, distractedly taking photos of guests at Pooh's kiosk, constantly checking over my shoulder for my manager's arrival.

Sure enough, when I returned from lunch, Orville was there, and he asked me to join him in his office. While I pulled up a chair, he closed the door. I had never seen him so serious.

"What's up?" My attempt to sound lighthearted fell flat.

"I just spent the entire morning with the head manager of the character program." He cleared his throat, and I could see his chins struggling for recognition. "This is not a nice man. He oversees character coordination for all four parks: Animal Kingdom, Hollywood Studios, Epcot, and Magic Kingdom, and he's not someone I ever wanted to have to meet face to face."

To say that Sam was "not a nice man" was like calling deep space "kinda chilly." I immediately thought of Calico. I imagined her sitting down in a meeting just like this one across the table from him.

"This manager has been forced to take drastic measures, and he made it clear that my job was on the line if I didn't do the same. As you can imagine, he put me in quite a position. I had to promise him that I would do everything in my power to follow through on my end."

"Wait," I said. "What do you mean 'drastic measures'?"

"He has to take care of problems in his department, and I have to take care of problems in mine."

"Did he have to *fire* anyone?" In all my time there, I hadn't actually witnessed anyone being let go, but I was positive that my SOP trysts with Calico constituted fair grounds for both of us. My heart accelerated to techno BPM. I didn't care what happened to me, but I couldn't let Calico lose her job over something that would embarrass her for the rest of her life. Orville reached for a manila envelope.

"It was all my idea!" I blurted. "She had nothing to do with it."

"Relax." Orville put a hand on my arm and then pulled a photo out of the envelope. "You don't recognize this, do you?"

It was "Mickey Flashing Tit," one of my better pieces from an afternoon photo session. The girl wearing the Mickey head had a pierced nipple and a tattoo of a rose around her areola. I had focused on the tattoo and the nipple ring and let Mickey's face blur into the background. It was erotic and a little disturbing. Good color balance.

"Do you?" Orville was shaking his head, urging me to agree with him. "You have never seen this before in your life."

I nodded as everything fell into place. "I have no idea where that came from," I concurred.

Orville slid the photo back into the manila envelope. "I told the manager I'd ask around, but I probably wouldn't have any luck. I have a staff of professional photographers after all. Anybody could have adjusted the aperture, balanced the exposure setting, and added an off-camera flash. And since the negatives never turned up"—he gave me a meaningful look—"I have to assume that it didn't come from this lab."

"Um, Orville, about what I said . . ."

"I have no idea what you're talking about," he said as he stood up.

"And what about the girl?"

"Unfortunately, this little Mickey was recognized thanks to her—how should I put this—outstanding characteristics, and her contract has since been terminated. Oh,"—he turned to me, his face serious again—"should you happen to get any ideas about doing shots like this in the future,"—one two three—"don't."

The next morning, I went in early to take care of some "loose ends." That was Orville's way of telling me to destroy the out-of-character shots on the last few months of negatives. It was still dark when I pulled in to the Cast Member parking lot. The lab was locked, so I walked over the bridge in front of the Tree of Life to watch the sun rise. All around me, frisky animals were just beginning to stir: anteaters snuffling through palm fronds, macaws clicking and calling out like horny college coeds on spring break. I'd become so accustomed to the DAK soundtrack with the music and recorded animal sounds that I'd forgotten the nuanced beauty of authentic animal noises. It was so peaceful that morning, watching the hot air balloons float over the parks, and breathing the reclaimed irrigation water as it evaporated into the Florida humidity. As the sky over Cocoa turned Silvermist blue, a Space Shuttle launched from Cape Canaveral, and I watched it rise up and out of the atmosphere. I imagined its thin, white trail as a thread joining heaven and earth, as a long ladder that allowed free passage between people of both worlds.

Backstage, somebody pushed play on the BGM, and once again, Disney asserted its dominance over the animal kingdom, as the real animal noises became indistinguishable from the recording. Shredding the negatives didn't take long, but it affected me on a profound level, like I was extracting pieces of my soul. I could feel myself transforming into a corporate automaton, erasing history for the conceit of the Company. Had I slipped so far that I wouldn't be able to return? I needed to ground myself again with somebody who knew the difference between right and wrong—even if he didn't always choose the obvious answer.

I went through the day with a bad taste in my mouth, then clocked out and called Brady. He picked up on the first ring. "Moshi moshi."

"Where are you? Can you talk?"

"Honto desu." He sounded like a bad voice-over on a martial arts video game. "I'm at home. What's on your mind, gaijin?"

"Why are you butchering Japanese?"

"I went fishing today, and caught my dinner. Sashimi-wa oishii desu. If you want to come by, you're welcome. There's plenty."

Fresh sushi sounded pretty good, so I accepted. After a quick shower, I walked over to Brady's apartment. It was one of the identical units in the Ghetto, not far from my own. He answered the door dressed in a kimono, holding a Samurai sword. He had painted his face white and accented his eyes and forehead with thick red lines like a kabuki actor. On his head, he wore a Shang wig, slick black hair tied back into a fist-sized bun.

"Irashaimasen!" he exclaimed, throwing the door wide. "Welcome, tomodachi!"

His living room was decorated to look like an eighteenth-century European parlor. Overstuffed sofas and chairs made from rich, dark woods and decorative fabrics were meticulously placed around the room in a way that ensured ease of conversation. Strategically positioned halogen spots highlighted textured oil paintings of fruit bowls and European landscapes done in the Renaissance style. Side tables displayed antique treasures: silver candelabras, a snuffbox inlaid with mother-of-pearl detail, and a blown-glass candy dish filled with inedible butterscotch candies that only ever seemed to exist in the sitting rooms of very old ladies. The BGM was *Madame Butterfly*.

"My, Grandma," I said, "what a fantastic interior decorator you have."

"Hate all you want," Brady said. "When the Queen comes to Orlando, we'll see where she wants to dine."

I looked him over in his long silk kimono and painted face. "From what I can tell, the Queen has already arrived."

He flashed the Samurai sword in mock menace, then stepped aside. "Please sit." He gestured to the dining table, a massive baroque hunk of wood, surrounded by eight formal antique chairs, patterned with pink silk. The space above the table was dominated by a crystal chandelier that refracted the light magnificently around the room like a Gothic disco ball. Two places were set with simple black plates and chopsticks. Brady arranged a single orchid in the center of the table, then disappeared into the kitchen.

Instead of sitting, I wandered over to a bookcase whose shelves were bowed beneath the weight of an enormous stack of books. There were books on every subject from financial theory to fairy tales, Agatha Christie mysteries, self-help manuals, poetry, pop-up books and books on globalization. And in the center of the case, a hardcover edition of Ayn Rand's *Atlas Shrugged*, the novel that had set me on my path of self-reliance as a professional skater.

"Have you read all of these?" I asked.

Brady looked up from the serving plate where he was arranging cut rolls and sashimi, using the edge of the Samurai blade. "Those are the ones I liked enough to read more than once," he said.

"How many times have you read *Atlas Shrugged*?"

"Actually, I never really stop reading it. I use it as a reference manual every time I start to lose focus."

Like all philosophy, Randian objectivism meant different things to different people, but the fundamental principle was universal: A person must take responsibility for his actions.

"I could use a little focus right now," I said. I told him about the pictures and how it had made me feel sick to destroy what I had created. Brady placed the sword on the counter, and walked past me, into the living room where he picked up a framed picture off the coffee table, and handed it to me. It was my picture, "Mickey Flashing Tit." I had only given copies to one other person: the subject of the photo. "How did you get this?"

"She happens to be a very special friend of mine," he said, taking the picture back. "And now she's applying for a job at Starbucks."

"Maybe she can go to Universal," I said.

"Maybe *Sam* can go to Universal," Brady spat. "So she took a couple of pictures. So what? She didn't hurt anybody. They didn't end up on the Internet or go home with a guest. Everybody takes out-of-character pictures. Here." He handed me a stack of photos, each one depicting a different character in the Disney roster, behaving inappropriately: Aladdin on a cell phone, Cinderella on the toilet, Prince Eric kissing the Snow Prince. "Everybody does it. Nobody gives a fuck. Except Sam. So he made an example out of my friend."

"Couldn't you talk to him?" I suggested. "You used to be friends."

"Friendship is a tandem bike," he said. "You have to work together or you're never gonna make it to the ice cream shop. For ten years now, I've been pedaling and Sam's been putting on the brakes. No, the time for talking is long gone. I promise you this: before the end of the year, one of us will be gone from Disney." Brady looked at the framed photo affectionately. "Good color balance, by the way."

Brady went back into the kitchen and reappeared with a tray of sushi and a large bottle of cold sake. No sooner did we begin eating than I heard a scratching at the bedroom door. Brady pretended not to hear it. "I suppose I could just spend some time researching Sam—dig up a little dirt—stuff that Disney would salivate over. It wouldn't be hard to find . . ."

The scratching behind the door became more insistent. It stopped for a moment, then started again with a muffled whimper. "Either your hostage is trying to escape," I said, "or it's dinnertime for man's best friend."

Brady wiped his mouth with the back of his hand, smearing white face paint across his lips and knuckles. "Just ignore it," he said, filling my sake cup. "But if I got Sam fired, I suppose they'd approach me again for a management position, and I'd politely decline again. And some other douche bag would slip in to make my life miserable."

"You wouldn't want to be a manager?"

Brady popped a plump piece of octopus in his mouth and chewed without mercy. "Do I look like the management type?" He spat a piece of rice as he said this. "Seriously, twenty years in Disney characters does not make me the best candidate. It makes me crazy. Wanna know something? I never dreamed of being president or leading an army. When I was a kid, I wanted to be Batman. I wanted to be the sniper who got behind enemy lines and got the job done while the system languished under its own bureaucratic bulk."

"A lone wolf," I said. Behind the door, the whimpering got louder, the scratching more frenzied. "So what's a sniper doing working at Disney World?"

He shook his head and swallowed the octopus. "You're not asking the right question," he said. "First, you need to understand my goals. What am I trying to snipe? Batman fought evil. Robin Hood robbed from the rich. John Galt stole the most creative, productive minds in the world. You need to understand the motivation before you can figure out the mission."

"Okay, then, what's your motivation?"

Suddenly, the dog behind the door started barking, mean, throaty, growling yelps that physically disturbed the air and made the crystals in the chandelier shimmer. Brady put down his chopsticks and went to the bedroom door. He opened it as if he were going to slide through, but the door flew open and a dirt-colored pit bull bolted through and headed straight for me. I fell backward off my chair, covering my face with my arms, and rolled myself into a fetal ball until I realized I wasn't being attacked. The dog was standing on my chair, wolfing down my sushi.

Brady helped me to my feet, where I watched from a distance as he pushed the pit bull away from the table and led her back to the bedroom. She was healthier and fatter, and her fur was no longer patchy, but she was familiar. "Is that the same dog—," I started.

"We rescued," Brady finished, closing the door again. "Yeah."

"I thought you gave her to an animal trainer."

Behind the heavy face paint, Brady looked embarrassed. "Turns out she kinda liked me."

I thought back to the night we had kidnapped the dog. There had been something nostalgic about his posture and the ridiculous ease with which he had found the unmarked mobile home in the dark swamp, far from anything that would show up on GPS.

"That night," I said, "how did you know that place?"

Brady nodded as if he had been waiting for me to ask. "I spent a couple years there in high school, before I moved out on my own. It was my dad's place—still is, technically. I never should have left Jake behind."

"You named her Jake?"

"Don't judge me. Ever since I was a little boy, I wanted a dog named Jake. My dad called her Zelda, after my mom." For the first time since I'd known him, Brady looked shaken, his lips taut, the lines around his eyes deeper. In the refracted light of the chandelier, behind the makeup, he seemed his age. I felt sorry for him. He'd obviously had a rough childhood. But then, who hadn't? A sense of betrayal took shape and floated to the surface of my emotional soup.

"Why didn't you just tell me we were taking back your dog? You made up that whole story about a DAK trainer and rehabilitation. And being a philanthropist."

"Guerilla Philanthropist," he corrected. "And I didn't make it up. I truly believe people are capable of doing something more if they just stop living within their comfort zone. Look, I shouldn't have lied to you. I'm sorry. I just didn't know how you'd take it if I told you the full story."

I looked down at my plate where Jake had turned my sushi into a disastrous mix of rice, seaweed, and slobber. "I'm no Puritan. I can take it," I said. "But I don't want to be kept in the dark. If you want me to be a part of your Guerilla Philanthropy missions, I want full disclosure."

"Full disclosure." Brady smiled. "Deal." We toasted saki cups, happy to be past that brief challenge.

Still, something wasn't sitting right. "You call yourself a Guerilla Philanthropist and yet you study Ayn Rand. How do you reconcile objectivism with altruism?"

"Let me be very clear here," he said through a mouthful of tuna. "Altruism in the ideal sense only exists in theory. When you give a coin to a blind man or when you donate anonymously in church— even if nobody ever finds out—there's still a benefit, some sense of well-being or pride or divine grace, something that turns the act into a zero-sum exchange rather than an unequivocal gift. There's always a payback."

"You didn't answer my question."

"Rand wrote that the purpose of a man's life is the pursuit of rational self-interest. Before I die, I want to hike Machu Picchu. I want to see the aurora borealis. I want to sleep with an Icelandic girl. And I want to prove that altruism can exist by committing one purely unselfish act. I want to do one thing for somebody else that gives me no benefit whatsoever."

"Wouldn't work," I said. "The Karma dividends would nullify the altruism. The Catholic Church would canonize you. Some reality TV producer would want to follow you around, broadcasting your good deeds for big advertising dollars, and you'd be back where you started—selfish, ego driven, hungry eating sushi off designer plates."

Brady pointed his chopsticks at me. "You remember Beltran from the jai alai fronton?"

"You said his brother wanted to fly us to the Caribbean." I hadn't given it much thought since then. I assumed it was just banter.

"That's the one." Brady smoothed the front of his kimono. "His brother lives in Havana where he's sort of an independent relief worker. He receives medicine from other countries and distributes it to hospitals around Cuba."

"Aren't there government agencies that do that? The Red Cross or something?"

"In theory, yes." Brady refilled our sake cups. "However, pharmaceutical companies are charging astronomical prices for medicines to try to recoup the billions of dollars they've invested in research. Nobody in the undeveloped world can afford their medicine, and they're the ones that need it the most. Diseases like AIDS are ripping through the population, virtually unchecked, and the Western world is unable to do anything above the line because of our cold war trade embargo."

"You lost me."

"Since Castro took over Cuba in the early '60s, the U.S. has imposed a *global* restriction on trade with the government; that means, anybody who trades with Cuba gets cut off from trade with America. It's created a unique society of complete independence, and provided the world with a shining Communist success story,

but it's also built a healthy underground railroad for Western pharmaceuticals. Cuba's not the only country being ransacked by HIV,
and Beltran's brother isn't the only person doing something about
it. Resistance movements are popping up in Brazil, India, and all
over Africa."

"Guerilla Philanthropists."

"For real." He smiled and shot his sake. "So what do you say? You
want to be a part of the revolution?"

"What!" I nearly spat my sake through my nose. "Smuggle drugs
into Cuba?"

"Bring lifesaving medicine to people who need it. Actually, it's
not nearly as exotic as it sounds. It's a very small quantity, and I'd
be the one carrying the stuff. I just need a spotter in case anything
happens to me. All expenses paid. There's no actual risk for you."

Cuba's an entire country off-limits to Americans, just ninety
miles off the coast of Florida. I had always been intrigued by those
mid-century images of Havana at night, glamorous and swanky,
textured with cigar smoke and rum-drunk gangsters. Deep inside
me, something was stirring. It was a feeling I hadn't allowed since
I'd internalized the Disney lifestyle: the thrill of stepping outside the
box, of following my shadow down a mysterious alley at breakneck
speed, and of dealing with the consequences much, much later.

"We're balancing the odds for people who have no way to help
themselves," Brady was saying. "The point is we're doing something
altruistic here. We're the good guys."

"What if something went wrong? Who goes after the 'good
guys'?"

"Good question." He frowned. "The American government. The
CIA. The pharmaceutical companies. And probably the WTO, but
it'd take them *decades* to work out what we did."

"How illegal is it?"

"It's more illegal than stealing a dog from a trailer park," he said,
"but not nearly as illegal as premeditated genocide." He noticed a
mauled piece of octopus on my plate. "You gonna eat that?"

I pushed the plate toward him. "Tell me, Nemo, how did you catch this octopus?"

Brady paused, the sushi halfway to his open mouth, ready to launch into a story, then his face cracked. "Fine. As it turns out, I caught a trout, and I'm told they don't make very good sashimi. So I stopped at the Publix fish counter on my way home, and there you have it."

For the rest of the evening, we talked about politics and philosophy, subjects that had turned mushy in my head. It felt good to stretch my mind beyond desert island fantasies and Disney trivia and to debate topics that used to matter to me like foreign policy, social issues, and art. Before I left, I agreed to go with Brady to Cuba, to assist in his quest to perform one truly altruistic act. I went home that night with a Zen-like sense of calm, a feeling that reinforced my belief that I had made the right decision, that dropping everything else in pursuit of the Disney Dream was an inevitable stepping-stone on my path to Enlightenment.

Just Around the River Bend

Disney World is a municipality with its own governing body, post office, and fire department. They write their own building codes, patrol their own properties, and enforce their own rules. If they wanted to, they could build a nuclear power plant or a golf course made of cheese. They don't need anybody's permission because, in Disneytown,* Disney is the alpha and the omega. One upside of this sovereignty is that it assures them a direct role in Florida's legislation, even when it comes to laws that affect the other theme-park residents in and around Orlando. Another bonus feature is that they have the ability to contain and defuse any embarrassing situations before the mainstream media can get hold of them and blow them out of proportion. The downside? Well, come to think of it, there isn't one.

Throughout the month of October, the Disney parks had become crowded with families in a rush. They needed autographs, pictures, and souvenirs, and they weren't letting anything stand in their way. These were the late vacationers, the ones who had to cram in two weeks before the end of the year, but still wanted to avoid the

---

*Actually, it's the Reedy Creek subdivision of Lake Buena Vista.

airlines' exorbitant holiday fares. They were in Orlando to have fun, and they were merciless about it.

On one especially hot October day, we were short a couple of photographers, so Orville had me running all over Animal Kingdom, covering a character breakfast in Dinoland, Tree of Life shots on the bridge, and all the character kiosks in Camp Minnie-Mickey. It was almost noon before I was finally able to take my break, and I was so dehydrated, my legs were shaking. As I left the kiosk, Mickey gave me a thumbs-up and a sympathetic pat on the back. I rode one of the blue Schwinn bikes to the lab where I deposited my last few rolls of film and collapsed in a chair.

"Hola, chico."

I pressed my thumbs to my temples and began vigorously rubbing. "Hello, Marco."

"Boy, it sure is crowded today," he said. "I wouldn't want to be outside shooting with these crowds."

"It's not so bad," I said. I stood up too fast and my head spun. I had to hold on to the processing machine for balance.

"At first," Marco continued, "I was upset that Orville put me in the lab, developing photos, but when I saw how many people were here, I realized he was doing me a favor."

"Good," I said. "I'm going to lunch. If Orville is looking for me, I'll be back in an hour."

"Oh, one thing. Some of your photos came out really dark."

I stopped, my hand on the doorknob. "Which photos?"

Marco flipped through a stack of character shots. "This roll," he said, "and this one. Actually, pretty much all of them."

"Let me see," I said, reaching out for the folders. "I could've sworn—" Sure enough, they were all underexposed, and not just a little bit.

"I know. I was really surprised." Behind Marco's concern, I could hear something that sounded like satisfaction.

When a photographer picks up a camera, he goes through a basic checklist before ever taking a picture, starting with adjustments to the exposure settings. There was no way I could have been shooting the wrong exposure all day. There was another possibility, however. Sure enough, from where I was standing, I could see that the digital numbers were all screwy on the processing machine.

Marco moved to stand next to me. "Oh no!" he said, his hand over his mouth. "You mean the machine has been broken all day?"

"It's not broken," I said. "But we have to reset this thing before it ruins any more film." As I punched in the proper processing information, I realized that something wasn't right with the numbers. While the machine had underexposed my film, making my photos come out dark, the numbers I was changing were for *over*exposure. Sure enough, the stack of photos in the tray was way too bright as if somebody was shooting wide open on high-speed film.

Marco dropped into Orville's chair and stretched his arms behind his head. "So"—he arched his eyebrows—"is the machine all fixed?"

His smug smile was a half-eaten worm in the poison apple of his face. "What is this? A tantrum? Revenge? Are you having a bad hair day?"

He shrugged. "Just doing my job."

"Nobody will buy these," I said. "What do you think Orville's going to say?"

"Orville is never going to find out."

"Yes, he will," I said. But I knew he wouldn't. Marco probably planned to set the numbers right before anyone knew any better. Nobody else in that lab would know what Marco was doing, and I certainly wasn't going to tell. Never rat on a rat. At Disney as it was in the skate park.

He pouted. "*Pobrecito*, now you're beginning to understand. All these Rules. They only enforce the obvious. I'm not eating onstage or pointing with one finger. I smile—" His wicked grin turned into a dazzling happy face. "And if that isn't enough, I have insurance." From his chest pocket, he produced one of my out-of-character photos, "Suicide King," in which King Louie was holding a prop pirate gun in his mouth. "You see, chico, Disney World is exactly like the rest of the world where you're innocent until proven guilty. But with one little exception: once you're proven guilty at Disney, you're finished. You get kicked out of paradise and you're never allowed back in." He saw me eyeing the picture, and slid it across the counter to me. "You can have this one," he said. "I have plenty more."

The conversation with Marco upset me on levels I barely understood. It wasn't so much his bitchy attitude (which I had come to expect) or the thinly veiled blackmail attempt (which could indict pretty much the entire DAK character department if it came to light) but the looming threat that lay just beneath the words. When I had first arrived at the Magic Kingdom, I came in as a casualty of the outside world, my wounds still fresh, seeking a sort of sanctuary within the hallowed walls of Disney. As cynical and solipsistic as I had been, Disney World had accepted and comforted me while I healed. I was living proof that Disney Magic could mend a broken heart. I was a convert.

But Marco was insinuating that this Magic was an illusion, that the world beyond Disney's border was no different from the world within. His disenchantment was what offended me the most. His attitude was blasphemy, worse than my brother's stoic practicality, worse than my own early cynicism had been because Marco was a Cast Member. He was a disciple of Disney, and his false witness was a shit stain on the shiny surface of my born-again devotion.

I left the photo lab intending to go to the cafeteria, but I wasn't hungry, so I spent my lunch break riding the blue Schwinn bike around backstage, stopping at the monkey habitat and the canoes behind the Tarzan stage, every place that had ever given me good memories. Leaning the bike against a wall behind Asia, I went back onstage through a Cast Members Only door, and headed for the lab. In Dinoland, I came face to face with Nick Elliot, now sporting long hair and a brow ring.

"Duuuude!" He was with three other guys, a wakeboarder, a pro

BMXer, and some other guy I didn't recognize who had a tattooed nose. "You're still at Disney? What the fuck!"

I glanced around to make sure nobody had heard his swearing. "I'm still here," I said. "Living the dream."

"The dream?" Nick shouted. "The dream is being in Daytona for Rick *motherfucking* Thorne's bachelor party, bro! We just finished a demo in Tampa, where we all made *cash* so we're road-tripping! I wanted to do a pit stop at Disney so I could show these guys the Rat Factory before we hit the bars." His friends laughed, fist bumps all around. "What do you say? You in?"

I could feel the Magic unraveling around me. People were noticing Nick and his friends, their tattoos and saggy jeans, the "Chronic Masturbator" T-shirt, the stench of kneepads. Parents pulled their children a little closer, rushing them down the path. "I dunno." I tried to look casual. I leaned against the Dino-Rama railing, then remembered I was onstage, in wardrobe, and stood upright. My shadow had fled. "I have to get up pretty early tomorrow," I said.

"That's bullshit!" Nick shouted. "Dude, you gotta come. We're gonna ride the concrete bowls, and then Thorne says he's buying everybody a hooker!" There were more fist bumps and some inappropriate hand gestures.

I tried to memorize the guests' scowling faces as they hurried past us, so I could track them down later and provide some semblance of recovery: free pictures maybe, a Tree of Life photo frame, a stuffed Piglet. "I'll call you later," I said, backing toward a Cast Members Only door. I could hear a dozen kids crying, and I was certain it was my fault.

"I know you, bro!" Nick's voice rose above the din of Dinoland. "You can't hide here forever!"

I was off my game for the rest of the day, and then, to make matters worse, I couldn't get the air conditioner in my Jeep to work. By the time I got back to the Ghetto, I was dripping sweat. I couldn't remember the last time I'd seen my roommate. The demands of his regular job and his secret project had kept him away from the house so much I'd begun to imagine that I lived alone, so I was surprised to see his Firebird parked in front of the apartment.

"Hey stranger," he said when I walked through the door. "You look like you got thrown in the pool." The Scotch bottle was within reach, but as far as I could tell, he wasn't drunk yet.

"My AC died today," I said.

Johnny picked up a sweaty highball glass from the counter. "Let me take a look," he said. "Ah might be able to work some magic."

He followed me to the parking lot where I popped my hood. He rested his glass on my bumper, then leaned over the engine and began twisting caps. The sun had begun its descent over the Disney golf course, with a gentle breeze blowing from the direction of the Clermont Muscat vineyards.

"You're home early," I said.

Johnny opened up his car, and rummaged through a box in the back. "Ah took the day off," he said. "Ah'm writing up a press release for Project Jericho and ah wanted to get it right."

"Project Jericho?"

"It's just a working title." He opened a plastic bottle and poured a bright blue fluid into my engine. "We have so much work to do, ah may have to take tomorrow off too."

"Two days of hooky." In all the time I'd known him, he'd never even been fifteen minutes late. "Can you tell me about it yet?"

"Not yet—nondisclosure and all that mumbo jumbo—but ah promise you'll be the first to know as soon as we go public. Oh, that reminds me, we want to have the launch party here this weekend. You don't mind, do you? It won't be anything crazy. Just a few close friends." He lowered my hood and adjusted his Jeff Gordon cap. "Now fire it up and switch on the AC."

I started the Jeep, and right away, the cold air began to blow. "Perfect!" I shouted over the engine.

Johnny smiled. "Ah'm a one-man pit crew."

I showered and put on a decent shirt. I had promised to take Calico out to dinner, and I was looking forward to getting beyond this stressful day. Her apartment was only about fifteen minutes away, but the traffic on I-4 held me up for almost an hour. As usual, Calico's door was unlocked. I found her in the bathroom, putting on makeup.

"Humph. I was *just* about to give up on yew." I wasn't sure, but it sounded like she was talking in an English accent. She looked over my shoulder, into the parking lot of her apartment complex. "Which cah did you bring this evening?"

"My Bentley's in the shop," I teased, "so I brought the Jeep." I moved to hug her, but she turned her back and fiddled with a selection of lip gloss. "Sorry I'm late," I said. "You wouldn't believe the traffic. Everywhere you look, overheated Geo Metros on the side of the road. It's like tourist stew out there."

"Is that sew?" she called out from the bathroom. Then, she mumbled something I couldn't quite hear.

"Beg your pardon."

She stuck her head around the corner. "I said, I'll be right out. Make yourself at home."

I went to the kitchen and poured myself a glass of water, then flipped through a fashion magazine that was holding down a pile of bills on her kitchen table. Calico's kitchen was the most lived-in room in her apartment. It served as an office, a waiting room, a library, and a den. Her kitchen table was stacked with mail, magazines, phone messages, and any other odds and ends that didn't fall into the category of cosmetics or clothing. About the only thing she didn't use her kitchen for was cooking.

The way she decorated her apartment had always intrigued me. She had an eclectic collection of souvenirs, haphazardly displayed beside mundane objects. In the cupboard where she kept her Diet Coke was a bottle of Andoran wine in her birth year. Under a stack of old *Vogue* magazines, an autographed poster and front-row ticket stubs from Cirque du Soleil. And scattered like Easter eggs on every flat surface, hundreds of photos of herself in provocative poses around Orlando. "Here I am partying at PI—I was so drunk! Oh!

And this is me cuddling a tiger cub. Isn't he gorgeous?" Finding objects d'art among the piles of junk was like making an archaeological discovery.

"I had the most annoying confrontation with Marco today," I said, stretching out on her couch. "And then, out of nowhere, an old skater friend of mine showed up at the park, and he was acting completely inappropriate. I spent the rest of the afternoon chasing kids around, giving out stickers and coupons."

"A scandal?" Calico appeared in the doorway, wearing bright red lipstick and long, fake eyelashes. "How delicious!"

"Well, 'scandal' might be a little dramatic, but, you know." My words derailed. "Are you going onstage?"

She smiled, and I could see a smear of bloodred lipstick across her teeth. "Of course not, dahling. Why do you ask?"

"I've never seen you in this much makeup outside the Grotto,"

"I felt like dressing up tonight," she said, her voice taut with impatience. "Yew *are* taking me out to dinner, aren't yew? I'm famished."

She went to get her purse. As I waited on the stair landing, I noticed Venus twinkling through the tree branches, and it reminded me of when we went skating in Celebration, the magical night when we first kissed. "Star light, star bright, first star I see tonight." I smiled at her, but she gave no indication that she had even heard me. She shut her door and walked toward the stairs, swinging her hips like a catwalk model. I offered my arm, but she brushed past me, knocking me to the side. "Hey!" I cried out, clutching at the handrail. "What's with you tonight? And what's with the accent?"

For the briefest moment, her eyes lit up with anger, then her expression melted. "I'm sorry," she said. "I forgot to tell you. I got approved in Cruella de Vil."

"Oh." I pulled a splinter out of my hand. "That's terrific. Congratulations! I didn't even know you were auditioning."

"I didn't want to say anything until I knew for sure I had the part." She had dropped the accent and was normal again.

"Okay. I get it. You're Method acting."

"That's right," she said. "This is my technique."

"That's so Meryl Streep." Finally, she let me kiss her. "This calls for a celebration. I'm taking you anywhere you want for dinner. Sky's the limit."

"Anywhere, huh?" Calico chewed her lip. "Actually, there's a new place on I-Drive I'd love to try. It's called Morton's."

"The steakhouse?"

"It's supposed to be good."

"But you're vegetarian."

"Yeah, but—I just think it might help me to get into the role." She raised an eyebrow. "Is that a problem?"

"Not at all. I love steak."

"Good," she sniffed in her Cruella voice. "Then let's go."

At that point, almost ten months into my Orlando experience, I was so far gone down the rabbit hole, so *loyal* to the Disney Dream with its pixie dust and its wishing wells, I was no longer able to distinguish between Wonderland and terra firma. The truth was, I had become everything I despised: a generic clone in a team jersey, censoring the lyrics of my life's anthem so as not to offend the convention geeks or the honeymooners or anyone else who crossed the border into Never Land. At that time, if Calico had asked me to renounce my citizenship and defect to Disney World, I wouldn't have given it a second thought. I was no longer a mere believer; I had pledged allegiance, signed the declaration, and tattooed my soul with Disney's colorful flag.

For the rest of the night, Calico practiced her English accent, and I tried to keep a straight face. Over the next few days, she honed the dialect to a perfect North London inflection, and even learned a few words of Cockney rhyme. And from that day forward, she ate red meat with every meal.

A Whole New World

The call came late at night, after Calico had fallen asleep. I picked it up without checking the caller ID. "Hey rock star." Brady's voice was strained as if he were trying to talk without being overheard. "Can you be packed and ready to go by Friday?"

A week's notice was plenty of time to set up my schedule. "Cuba?"

"Don't forget your board shorts and your Disney smile."

"What happens in Havana stays in Havana."

"I'll pick you up at 8 A.M."

I didn't hear from Brady for the rest of the week, but on Friday at 8 A.M. sharp, he pulled up in a VW minibus ("It just showed up on my doorstep."), and we drove to the airport. I had packed a small duffel bag for the occasion, but it was mostly filled with sun block and aspirin for my forthcoming hangover. Brady had a backpack and an enormous stuffed Mickey, which he tossed gracelessly into the overhead compartment.

For the short flight to Jamaica, we sat on opposite sides of the plane. In Montego Bay, we breezed through customs and into the terminal where Brady pulled me into a souvenir kiosk and bought a few schlocky Jamaican souvenirs.

"In case anyone asks," he said, stuffing a *Hey Mon* shot glass into my duffel, "you went barhopping, got sloppy, and passed out on Cornwall Beach. You can fill in the details."

The next flight was even less eventful. Nobody cared that we were Americans going to an off-limits destination. We were simply a group of pilgrims on an Epicurean quest, looking for revelry and relaxation in a tropical paradise, disconnected from the rest of the world. As the plane banked around the coastline of Cuba, I felt a familiar tingle on the bottoms of my feet, the playful stretch of an old friend, my shadow, who handed me a rum drink with a silent wink.

Once again, I was off on a bona fide international escapade with real adrenaline and real consequences. I was fulfilling a lifelong dream, but I found that after months of soldering a Disney mien onto my own persona, shaping my entire being into a demeanor of placid *Look* book certitude, I was unable to define my expectations outside of a Disney framework. I imagined Havana as a real live Magic Kingdom where the characters wore white linen shirts and danced to salsa BGM on crystal blue beaches or an uncharted pavilion in Epcot where the entertainment was cigar rolling and the Drinking-Around-the-World selection was a bottomless mojito.

Our flight landed without a problem at Jose Marti International Airport in Havana, and we navigated through the terminal until we were standing curbside beneath the clear Cuban sky. Within moments, a bright blue 1957 Chevy sedan pulled up. Sure enough, the driver was smoking a cigar, tapping his fingers to the salsa music blaring out of the speakers.

"It's showtime," Brady said, smiling broadly. "Papi!"

Papi was a small, tan man with a shaved head and a bright smile. Every inch of him flashed gold: necklaces, bracelets, earrings, and sunglasses. He had a gold brow ring, a stud in his nose, and his teeth were lined with gold bridges and caps. On each finger, he wore at least three gold rings set with enormous stones. He had a gold-plated pinky nail, pierced with a gold chain that attached to a gold bondage ring. He was dressed all in white from his linen shirt to his drawstring trousers to his pristine white espadrilles. I had to squint to look directly at him.

Papi and Brady hugged and then Papi clicked his tongue. "Welcome to Havana, boys." His voice was a soft falsetto, like the Blue Fairy gone to Buenos Aires. "You're just in time for my birthday party. Cuban specialties: salsa and sexiness!" He noticed the stuffed Mickey. "Is that what I think it is?"

"Sure is," Brady said. He handed Papi the Mickey, then pulled a bright yellow, plush Winnie the Pooh from his backpack. Papi squealed with glee, and danced around the car with Mickey and Pooh in his arms.

The Chevy was in terrible condition. It looked as if it had been sanded down and spray painted blue. The chrome was dull, the upholstery held together with duct tape. The interior smelled like gasoline, and the whole contraption rattled as Papi pulled away from the curb.

"Ain't she a beauty?" Brady asked from the passenger seat. He stroked the cracked dashboard. "She's one of the best-kept cars in Havana. Of course, she's got one of the most loving mommies!" He reached over and pinched Papi's cheek, a square of brown in a sea of gold. As we turned out of the airport onto the main street, my door swung open, and I grabbed the front seats to keep from flying out of the car.

The two friends talked in Spanish while I stared at Cuba just outside the window and watched my Disney framework dissolve away like a hand-painted fairy tale dipped in turpentine. The buildings were tall and narrow, crowded together like books on a shelf, their dust jackets faded and torn from years of use. The windows had no glass, and through the broken shutters and open doorways, I could see paint peeling away from the vaulted ceilings or, sometimes, no ceiling at all, just cracked wood and concrete where the roof had collapsed inward onto faded mattresses. Barefoot children played baseball from one side of the street to the other, using sleeping dogs as bases in the middle of the road.

The Cubans sat in their doorways, leaned out their windows, and crouched in the streets to watch us drive by. Papi drove slowly to avoid the obstacles, but still the car grumbled every time he sank into one of the monstrous potholes. The whole country smelled of smoke and decay.

Papi pulled up to the sidewalk and cut the engine. "*Venga*," he cooed in his Latin singsong. "I will introduce to you my friends."

His house was cluttered with artifacts from around the world: porcelain Buddhas, Peruvian mosaic flowerpots, Russian nesting dolls. Here, too, there was no glass in the windows, only brilliant blue shutters, which had been thrown open to let the sunlight into the living room. Every room featured framed photos of Papi with smiling people.

"He's a very generous man," Brady said, handing me a glass filled with something dark. "If he likes you, he'll let you stay in his house forever. In exchange, people bring him gifts from all around the world."

"What is this?" I held up my glass.

"Rum." He flashed a wicked grin. "If you want, you can dilute it with cola, but don't ask for Coke. They haven't seen it here for forty years. Salud!"

People continued to pour into Papi's house. Everyone was greeted with smiles, warm hugs, and rum. Eventually, I found myself on the rooftop where a group of people were toasting Cuba's future. When he saw me, Papi waved me over.

"I wanted to thank you," he said.

"You're welcome. Thank you for inviting us to your party."

"That is nothing," he said. "After your generous charity, it was the least I could do."

"Charity?" I was so engrossed in the scene, I had forgotten that we were on a mission of Guerilla Philanthropy. "Oh, right. You're welcome."

He leaned close, his soft voice an excited whisper. "What did you bring?"

I had no idea how Brady had even transported the drugs, much less what they were. "It's a surprise," I said.

Papi's gold rings sang as he rubbed his hands together. "I can't wait!" He crossed himself. "Come with me." He led me to his room where the stuffed Mickey and Pooh were sitting on his bed. Before I knew what he was doing, he had produced a knife and plunged it into Mickey's stomach. Then he did the same to Pooh. Where the knife ripped the fabric, white pills poured out onto the bedspread. "If I'm not mistaken, it looks like Crixivan! And Epivir! Oh, this is wonderful."

I recognized the names as pharmaceuticals used in AIDS cocktails. "I hear they're hard to get."

"You have no idea!" Papi pulled a handful of plastic bags out of a drawer and began to fill them with pills. "Cuba's cut off from American business so that means they're cut off from American medicine as well. Cuban scientists are trying to make their own versions of the brand-name drugs, but it's not easy and it's very expensive. You and Brady are helping to bridge the gap." In the dim light, Papi's face was the epicenter of a golden borealis. "Thank you."

I left Papi to organize his shipment, and wandered back into the party. It was a good feeling, this Guerrilla Philanthropy. It was something I could get used to. I climbed the stairs to the rooftop, where the party was in full swing, and took a spot by the railing. From my rooftop perch, high above the streets of Havana, it was impossible to fit Cuba into my Disney paradigm. Here were worn building facades that hadn't known rehabilitation since Disneyland's Autopia was remodeled, wandering dogs that snuffled over bird carcasses in the alley, and bootleg cigar salesmen and sex peddlers who patrolled the sidewalks below.

I looked up to the sky and tried to imagine that I was in a sound booth in a pavilion at Epcot, waiting for the fireworks to begin, but the *reality* of Cuba was simply too grand. Sure, there were white linen wardrobes, live salsa BGM, and rum-laced beverages to keep me drinking around the world, but this was no theme park. I was on an adventure in Realityland. It was magnificent and dangerous, and like being in the ocean, I had to keep reminding myself not to turn my back to the experience. I felt awed and humbled to be a part of it.

As the night progressed, the music got louder and people started dancing. I sipped from rum bottles whenever they came my way, then passed them along. Every so often, Cuban girls would grab my arm and dance up against me. Brady flashed through the room, grinning like a Lost Boy, clinging to one girl or another. And so the night went, with rum, salsa, and laughter, and eventually, I curled up on a sofa and closed my eyes.

Brady was making breakfast when I woke up, whistling "Buena Vista Social Club." "How you feeling?" he asked.

I sat up, expecting the worst. "Not too bad, actually."

"Havana Club rum," he said. "Best stuff in the world. Too bad we can't get it back home."

The sun was just peeking over the rooftops. Through the glassless windows, I could hear a muted salsa rhythm. "Why are you up so early?"

"I never went to sleep," Brady said. He transferred a pile of scrambled eggs to two plates and laid them out on a tile-topped coffee table. "I've been up all night, talking with Papi and thinking."

"Uh-oh."

"Yeah, no shit, right?" The eggs tasted different but good. He had used herbs from Papi's garden and powdered milk. He cleaned his plate and put down his fork, all serious and sincere. "I've made a decision. I'm moving here."

"To Havana?"

"To Cuba." Brady wiped his mouth on the back of his hand. "I feel good here, like, really good, like I'm supposed to be here, doing good things. Remember I told you about my dream? To do one altruistic thing that gives me no benefit whatsoever. Well, I think this is the place. Cuba! It's not a capitalist society, so I wouldn't be doing it for the money. I have no family here, so I wouldn't be doing it for the tribe. In fact, I have no real ties to the community, so nothing I do would come back to me. It's perfect!"

"What about your life back home?"

"Home will always be there. I've gone as far as I can go with Disney." He leaned back with his hands behind his head and stretched out his arms like a king on a throne. "This is what comes next."

I cleared our plates, poured myself a cup of coffee, and got in the shower. It made sense in Brady's eccentric way. I would miss our benevolent mayhem, but the guy was chasing down a dream. I could relate.

"Papi left early this morning on his distribution run," Brady said, as I put my duffel bag together. "So we have to find our own way to the airport. I hope you don't mind if we stop to pick up a couple of cigars."

"Can we bring Cuban cigars back?"

"No," Brady smiled. "But I know a place where they wrap them in Dominican labels. Come on."

I followed him through streets with no real concept of direction, right-angle turns that led from one potholed, dog-paved road to another. Clusters of children wearing school uniforms scampered down sidewalks, hopping over divots in the pavement and crossing the streets whenever they found a break in the traffic. Quick Belgian taxis and Czech motorbikes dodged huge, lumbering Detroit autos: Oldsmobile, Chevy, Ford, Pontiac, cars with proud hood ornaments from postwar America.

Dogs draped like Dali clocks from windowsills and doorways. Old women peered through slats in the window shutters, watching the streets with curiosity. From every house, the strains of low-fidelity salsa filled the living rooms and spilled onto the sidewalks. Everything seemed to be under construction, but there was no sign of a crew. We hopped over bags of cement, stacked on wood palettes, covered in dust that could have been months old.

The city was really warming up now, beams of sunlight slanting through windowless windows, reflecting off silver hood ornaments the size of Barbie dolls. People crowded one another along the sidewalks, lined up in front of dark warehouses where sober counter attendants doled out bags of powdered milk and white rice. Urban chickens scratched in the dirt, fighting over space in sidewalk cracks and compost piles. The smell of freshly baked bread lingered everywhere.

"Wait here." Brady ducked into a nondescript building, then reappeared a few minutes later with two boxes of "Dominican" cigars. He handed one to me. "From me to you," he said. "Thank you for trusting me."

"The pleasure was all mine," I said.

He winked. "Still is." Suddenly Brady broke into a run, and I narrowly avoided a parade of rusty cars following him across the street. He jumped up on the running board of a weathered flatbed truck and addressed the driver, "El aeropuerto?" he asked.

"Si," the man behind the wheel said. "Diez minutos."

Brady smiled at me. "Climb in."

We were barely in the back when the truck pulled away from the curb. There were ten other Cubans standing there already, riding the flatbed like a giant surfboard, leaning from side to side when the road bent. The experience was wonderfully surreal; hundreds of miles away from Disney, and yet the air around me was electrified with Magic. I glanced over at Brady, eyes closed, smiling against a golden morning sunbeam. He had made this possible. If my life was a Disney story, Brady was my Genie, my Blue Fairy, my Magic broker.

After about twenty minutes, the driver pulled up to the airport terminal and honked his horn. Brady and I boarded our flight without a problem and switched planes once again in Montego Bay. When we landed in Orlando, I had a thought.

"Brady," I asked as we moved toward the customs desk. "Why did you invite me on this trip? You carried the stuffed animals. You didn't really need a spotter."

He smiled. "I wondered when you were gonna put it together. The delivery to Papi was just the first half of the project."

Our line was really moving. We were just a few steps away from the customs desk. "What's the second half?"

"Last night, after you passed out, I arranged another shipment—this time, meningitis vaccine—really top grade stuff."

"Medicine?"

"That's right. The Cubans have done wonderful things with meningitis inoculations, but of course, the USA won't allow it into the country. You remember my friend Beltran from the jai alai arena? Well, his daughter has developed spinal meningitis—a pretty advanced case. There's not much we can do for her, but there are thousands of others who can benefit from Cuban science, so I volunteered us to bring some stuff back over the border."

I hissed. "Now? You're carrying the stuff right now?"

"Technically, we both are," he said. "Keep smiling. They're looking right at us."

"But how—" And then I remembered the cigars.

Brady was beaming a Zen-like calm. "He's one of the best cigar rollers in the city. He worked on these boxes all night, making them look just right. Don't screw it up now."

We were next in line to greet the customs officer. I could feel beads of sweat beginning to roll down my back. When the officer called us up, I put on a Disney smile.

"Papers?"

"Here you go."

"Jamaica, huh?"

"Yep."

"Did you visit any other places?"

"Just Montego Bay."

"Did you see Ocho Rios?"

"I was only there for a night."

"Any souvenirs?"

"Just a couple of shot glasses. I collect 'em so—"

"You're sure you didn't visit any other countries?"

"Positive."

"I'll be right back."

The customs officer stood up and disappeared behind a wall of two-way glass. I looked at Brady, but he was flipping through a Jamaican magazine, his face cherubic. I tried to hum a Disney tune, but I couldn't remember any. After what seemed like an eternity, the officer returned.

"Okay. Have a good day."

When we got outside, I pulled the cigar box out of my bag and threw it at Brady. "You son of a bitch!"

"What." Brady was laughing. "You did great!"

"What happened to full disclosure?"

"I know, I know. I'm sorry." He rubbed his face, sheepish. "It all happened so fast."

"That is not okay." I put my hand in the air, and a taxi pulled forward.

"Listen, that was the last time. I swear. From here on out, I tell you everything."

It was like being in LA again, having friends lie to my face. Had I come all this way, spent all this time developing what I thought were real relationships, just to be on the butt end of betrayal again? It was the same at Disney as it was in the skate park. I threw my bag in the back of the cab and shut the door before Brady could get in.

"Hey, come on." He was being melodramatic, standing on the curb, looking forlorn. As the car pulled away, I could faintly hear his voice. "It's for a good cause!"

I didn't stay mad for long. I spent the next day feeling sorry for myself, but by the day after that, I couldn't remember what had made me so upset in the first place. He hadn't slept with my girlfriend or wrecked my car. He was just doing what came naturally. But by the time I called, his phone had been shut off and his apartment was empty.

Brady was gone.

Beauty and the Beast

"Is that you?"

"Yeah. It's been awhile, so I just—"

"It's been two months!" Michael shouted into the phone. "Didn't you get my messages?"

"I know I know. I'm sorry." I was already trying to think of a graceful way to get off the phone. "How are you?"

"How am *I*? *I* am fine. *I* have never been healthier."

I closed my eyes. "How's Mom?"

He sputtered a little, and I thought he was really going to lay into me, then he took a deep breath, and I could tell by his silence that he was rubbing his temples. "Not good," he said finally. "She's nauseous most of the time. Her hair is gone. Her fingernails are all cracked. And she has persistent neuropathic pain in her hands and arms." He spoke about her condition with professional objectivity, but his words painted a detailed illustration in my mind of our mother's wasted body lying alone in a room that was never warm enough to keep her from shivering, never bright enough to make her smile.

"I thought the treatments were supposed to help," I said.

His professional tone turned hollow. "Chemotherapy is a last resort." The bottom line was, the cancer may have been life threatening, but the chemo was sure to kill her.

Michael took a deep breath, and when he spoke again, it was with a level of vulnerability that I rarely heard in him. "Come back to LA," he said. "Florida will always be there, and Mom and Dad could really use your support right now."

I was touched by the honesty of his plea. He must have been exhausted, bearing what surely would have been an endless barrage of questions and concerns, during this crisis. At least if I was home, I could take some of the pressure off my brother. Once again, he was the lifeguard, trying to drag me out of the waves before it was too late. "Never turn your back on the ocean," he had taught me. But wasn't I turning my back at that moment, doing my stubborn utmost to disregard the real issues in my life?

I wanted to say yes. I wanted to rush back to LA, to be there for my family, but I was stuck in place, nailed to the cross of my own self-interest. Frantically, I tried to come up with reasons that sounded sincere. If I left Orlando, I'd be leaving Calico. I'd be walking away from Disney and the wonderful life that I had worked so hard to create, and returning to a place where I had nothing. I dredged up my martyr's justification that I had been excluded, that within our convoluted family structure, the cancer still did not exist. Sure, Michael knew the real story, but as far as I was concerned, Mom was out "running errands"; she was "taking a nap." If I went back to help her, I rationalized, I'd be challenging their complex cover stories, which had somehow become the foundation of our interaction for the last year.

"I can't go back yet," I told my brother. "I have a job here. And a girlfriend. And it's just not the right time."

"Fine," he said. "It's your decision. I just don't want to see you do something you'll regret for the rest of your life."

Hanging up felt like I was cutting away a piece of my heart. I needed a shower and a home-cooked meal. Calico wasn't picking up, so I stopped at the supermarket and bought a six-pack of beer and a bottle of Scotch. At least, there was good ol' Johnny. I could always count on a little generic sympathy from my roommate.

The sun was setting as I crossed the parking lot of the Disney Ghetto with my Publix bags and my duffel, the sky streaked with cloudy wisps of Pluto orange and Minnie pink.

On the stairs, two boys nearly knocked me over in their rush to get past. They ran directly into my apartment, leaving the door wide open. I couldn't believe what I was seeing. My living room was filled with people, Cast Members draped over the furniture in the living room, giggling and kissing and getting high. I recognized a Mickey, three Poohs and a Pluto, but there were at least a dozen other people whom I had never met before. One partygoer, a shirtless boy with nipple rings and spiky hair, took the beers out of my hand and began passing them around. Within seconds, Johnny's face appeared at my side.

"Isn't this great!" His cheeks were flushed deep red, his eyes glassy with Scotch. "Ah haven't been this excited since the prerelease party for *No Strings Attached*."

"What's going on?" I asked as calmly as I could.

"Ah mentioned it the other day," he said. "It's our debutante ball—sort of a *coming out* party. Ah didn't want to tell you too soon because ah didn't want to jinx it, but . . . ah am the producer of what is going to be the first ever gay boy band!" The shirtless boy—who I guessed to be about fifteen—lay back on the kitchen table while Jazz Jericho poured beer into his mouth. "And ah have you to thank."

"Me?"

"You said if ah don't follow my dreams, somebody else will come along and screw it up."

"I never said that," I said. "That was Jazz."

"Well, this is my dream." He grinned. "And ah'm doin' it!"

When I first moved in with Johnny, I admired his shallow simplicity. A glass of Scotch, a Jeff Gordon ball cap, and everything was rosy. But now, he was complicating his life with aspirations and mixed up with people like Jazz Jericho, who was a sure recipe for disaster.

"Ah've been doing a lot of research," Johnny swirled the ice around his glass. "Ah mean, it's unbelievable, but nobody has done this angle yet. Everybody is so focused *on ethnic* diversity or *personality* profiles—you know, the Nice One and the Brooding One and the Tough Guy—We are going to be the first ones ever to do sexual orientation! We even have a token Bi. Jazz knows some guy who has his own recording studio so we'll be able to get a demo together no problem. And ah have access to the airwaves so . . ." He shrugged. "You want a beer?"

Jazz sat down behind the bar and began fumbling with a New Kids on the Block CD. Drop. Conceal. "So what did he say?" he asked no one in particular. "Will he do it?"

Johnny cleared his throat. "Ah have a favor to ask." His tone was slurred, yet businesslike, Dean Martin pitching a used car. "Would you do us the honor of shooting our first album cover?"

I looked from Johnny to his Scotch to the spiky-haired kid who was now making out with one of the other young boys on Johnny's sofa. Jazz had poured a pile of cocaine onto the New Kids CD and was dividing it into lines with a business card.

"Tell him the concept," Jazz said.

Johnny shifted into a director's pose, his hands held up like the frame of a lens. "Picture this," he said. "Five beautiful boys. They look frightened. Not terrified. Not teeth chattering, but just . . . vulnerable. They're wearing society's wardrobe: the starched collar, the power tie, the blue blazer with shiny naval academy buttons. Their hair is neatly combed, everything in place. Spic and span."

Jazz looked up from his coke, beaming. Flick. Reveal. "And here's the kicker . . . they're in *a closet*. There are clothes on hangers and shoes at their feet. Hats in turn-of-the-century hatboxes, and maybe some naughty blue magazines just out of reach."

Johnny motioned Jazz to go on, so he did. "But then, the cover unfolds to reveal—The beautiful boys have come leaping from the closet, no longer wearing expressions of *fear* and *uncertainty* but of *pride* and *confidence*! Their hair is *styled* now. Not just combed. And some of the boys have piercings. And of course, they're dressed differently. They're no longer clad in society's garments. Now they're wearing the clothes that were just hanging around them in the closet: lightweight, surplus, ripstop pants. Shirts of silk fabric in bright colors, unbuttoned to the waist to reveal their hard, sculpted bodies. Society's clothing is left on the hangers and strewn around the closet behind them. And, above everything . . . a rainbow. Shimmering over them."

"So." They were both a little breathless, staring at me, waiting for my reaction. "What do you think?"

I was careful to keep my expression neutral. "A gay boy band?"

"Ah know!" Johnny gushed. "It's so simple. But then all the best ideas are." He held up his Scotch glass to toast Jazz and the spiky-haired kid who was scratching his nose, staring at the CD. Johnny and Jazz and the rest of the gay boy band and their friends were staring at me, waiting for some reaction, some pledge of allegiance to their cause. Over Johnny's shoulder, I could see my Publix bags, now filled with empty beer bottles.

"You don't have to decide right now," Jazz broke the silence. "Just think about it for a while and figure out if you're ready to make a strong political statement."

I helped myself to a Corona and settled on the balcony where I could ignore the revelry and watch the stars come out. What the hell was going on here? Johnny wasn't the kind of guy who took chances. He did the same safe thing day after day. Nevertheless, here he was, tipping back Scotch, demonstrating Pearlman-sized delusions of grandeur.

He had generously attributed his burst of ambition to my influence, but there was another puppeteer pulling his strings. Eventually, the balcony door opened, and a girl joined me. I'd seen her around. She was a Cinderella at the Magic Kingdom. She had a soft, round face and dazzling blue eyes.

"Interesting day?" she asked.

"You have no idea."

"I wasn't always a princess, you know. I used to be a paramedic.

I took EMT courses and everything. So, if you choke on that lime in your beer, I can resuscitate you."

"That's a relief."

"Actually, I don't have a choice. When I got my EMT license, I took an oath to help people whenever and wherever possible. So, even if you were a jerk"—when she stirred her cocktail, she did it with her fingers fanned out, glossy French tips hovering over the rim of the glass—"I'd be duty bound to try to save you."

After Johnny and Jazz's ambush, I was feeling the opposite of flirtatious, but the girl showed no sign of leaving, so I threw some words together. "Have you ever saved anyone's life?"

She sipped her drink, careful not to smear her lipstick on the glass. "The other day, this man in my line just keeled over. My greeter thought it was dehydration, but I could tell it was a heart attack." When she smiled, she wrinkled her nose a little. "So I had this one side of me that knew what was going on because of all the EMT classes and whatever. Then there was the other side of me— the princess side."

I shook my head. "Which side is that?"

She clucked her tongue as if I had forgotten the very essence of Disney. "You're a Cast Member. You should know this."

"I'm not a princess."

She set her drink down so she could talk with both hands. "When I'm onstage, I must stay in character at all times. Cinderella has a working knowledge of sewing and scrubbing—maybe a little singing—but not CPR. Under no circumstance is it acceptable for a princess to perform mouth-to-mouth!"

It was an ethical predicament. Should she break character in order to save the man's life or preserve the Magical Experience for all the children who came to see Cinderella?

I was interested now. "So what did you do?"

"What do you think?" She picked up her drink and took a sip.

"I think you dropped to your knees and pounded his chest until he started breathing again."

"Are you kidding?" She practically spat her drink through her nose. "Do you know how long it took me to get approved for that role?"

The girl's phone rang, and she drifted to the other side of the balcony to take the call. Just then, the door opened again, and Johnny's face appeared, grinning like a Cheshire Cat. "So," he said, shutting the door behind Cinderella, "have you given it any thought?"

I couldn't hold my tongue any longer. *"A gay boy band?"*

"You don't like it?"

"Ever since the Beatles, boy bands have relied on a fan base of screaming females."

"Exactly!" Johnny stabbed the air with his finger. "There is nothing out there for the *screaming male* fans. That's why it'll be such a huge success!"

"I hope it is," I said. "But I just don't feel comfortable shooting your cover."

He nodded and sipped his Scotch. "Ah understand."

"Johnny," I said. "Have you heard about anyone who died at Disney World recently?"

"Died?" He made a face. "No, why?"

I glanced up at Cinderella, still gushing into her phone. "It was just a rumor I heard about a guy having a heart attack."

"Ah haven't heard anything," he said, his cheeks flushed Queen of Hearts red. "But then Disney's got one hell of a medical team. And an even better PR crew. As Walt was fond of saying, 'You can dream, create and build the most beautiful place in the world, but it takes people to make that dream a reality'!"

The next day, the temperature skyrocketed to well over a hundred degrees. Even the Florida natives were uncomfortable, laid out in armchairs or draped over the vented slats of benches, fanning themselves with soggy maps. It was so hot that by noon Magic Kingdom had already lost a Meeko, a Gideon, and two Captain Hooks to heatstroke and the Mad Hatter's nose kept melting off his face. Hydration reminders were posted on the tunnel walls, at every stage door, and on corkboards hung over the urinals. Still, Cast Members were dropping like popcorn, dizzy and gasping for air, drowning in the humidity.

When I finished at DAK, I went to the Magic Kingdom to meet up with Calico. I hadn't been able to reach her the night before, so we rode the Monorail while I brought her up to speed on all the events of the past couple of days. I told her about Havana and Brady and then Johnny and his boy band party. She was shocked.

"You have to be careful who you make friends with around here," she warned. "Not everyone's as sweet as me."

"I tried calling you last night," I said.

"I know," she said. "I am *so* sorry. I got your messages, but my mom was really sick last night, so I went over to her house to take care of her and fell asleep watching a movie."

"Is she alright?"

"She'll be fine." Calico waved it off. "It's mostly in her head. She can be *such* a hypochondriac."

Through the window of the Monorail, I could see a small crowd gathered around a wedding party. The bride and groom were standing in front of the Disney Chapel, waiting to get into Cinderella's horse-drawn carriage. Mickey and Minnie flanked the happy couple. The BGM was "A Dream Is a Wish Your Heart Makes."

I nodded toward the scene. "What would you do differently?" I asked.

She shrugged. "Put the groom in black leather, the bride in barbed wire."

"Artsy."

"Or dress them in meringue and hose them down during the vows." Calico gave a dark chuckle. "What's the point? They're doomed anyway."

Everything went suddenly dark as the Monorail went around a corner and into the Contemporary Hotel. My head ached from the crush of the pressure change. "You're not going to be a very popular wedding planner."

Calico's smile was without joy. "Wedding planners don't have jets."

That weekend, I made reservations for us to stay one night at Universal's Portofino hotel, a five-star resort with spa treatments and gondola service to their theme parks. I told her to take Saturday and Sunday off, but I didn't tell her why. I wanted it to be a surprise.

It was noon when I rang her doorbell. Check-in time. I smiled to myself, imagining her delight at a mud treatment and body exfoliation. Would she be in a frisky mood or would she be sweet and gentle? Lately, it was kind of a coin toss. I rang the doorbell again and checked my watch. It was 12:05 and clouds were just beginning to darken the sky, so I retreated to my Jeep and left a message on her voice mail. An hour later, I still hadn't heard from her.

As I thought about it, it occurred to me that she might be with her mom. Calico had been there a lot recently, helping her plant new rose bushes in the garden. Her phone didn't get service at her mom's house, so I couldn't call, but I remembered the address. Calico's mother was wearing gardening gloves and sunglasses, talking on her portable phone when I pulled up.

"So good to see you!" she said when she finished her call.

"Hi, Sandra. How are the roses?"

"Wonderful!" she said. "I just clipped a dozen perfect Dutch Centifolias. Would you like some iced tea?"

"No thanks. I was just looking for Calico."

"Oh," Sandra pulled a strand of hair away from her face. "Let's see, if I remember correctly, she is working today."

"Really?" I said, chewing on a fingernail. "Because I could've sworn she had today off."

"Well," she laughed gaily. "I've been wrong before. My memory isn't what it used to be, and we see her so rarely these days."

"Is that right."

"I've hardly seen her since she got the part as that dog lady." She pocketed her gardening shears and smiled. "Are you sure you wouldn't like to come in and have some iced tea? I'd love to hear what you two have been up to."

As I sped away from her parents' house, I could hardly breathe. Nothing made sense. Calico told me she had been over there at least three times in the past week. Either Sandra was in the middle of a full-blown delusion or Calico was lying to me.

What did I really know about my girlfriend? In the few months we had been together, I had learned that she was a Method actress and a box of Godiva could pretty much get me out of anything, but beyond that, it was hard to describe her personality.

Most of the time, Calico was the perfect princess, sensitive and genuinely sweet. She said "please" and "thank you" and blushed when she heard an off-color joke. She called everybody by a pet name, nothing creative, usually "baby" or "honey" worked for people she had just met. For me, she reserved "sweetie" or "sweetheart," a term of endearment that comforted me because nobody else got that one.

She was vivacious and hungry for experience. If you knew how to say "I'll have the chicken, please" in Catalan, she wouldn't let you go until you taught her the exact pronunciation. She commanded attention whenever she spoke and took no more than half an hour to become acquainted with an entire room full of strangers. She was pretty—not cover-girl beautiful, but possessing a very confident aura of sexual awareness. She knew her strengths and didn't waste time covering her naturally attractive features with makeup—unless she was rehearsing a new part.

There was something else there too. When she talked to you, she made you believe that you were the only guy who understood her and that for the first time in her life, she was baring her soul to a kindred spirit. You got so caught up with the hidden tumultuousness of her life and the secret camaraderie of her confessions that you began to think of yourself as her personal savior, as the *only person in the world* who could offer sanctuary from her tragedies.

The catch was, she had this effect on everybody: the busboy who poured water at her dinner table, the shoe salesman at the outlet mall, the gas station attendant. No encounter was too distant or too brief for her to weave a total stranger into the tapestry of her charms.

I didn't hear from Calico that night or the next day. At sunset, I drove back over to her apartment and waited. I felt like a stalker, but I didn't care. I had to know what was going on. I downloaded some phone apps. I switched my ringtone from "Ev'rybody Wants to Be a Cat" to "Be Prepared." Eventually, her car pulled in to the parking lot. I was standing there when she stepped out.

"Did you get my messages?"

"Oh! Sweetie, you startled me." She put her hand to her chest and took a couple of breaths.

"I waited for you all day yesterday."

"I am so sorry. I tried to call you from my mother's house, but I couldn't get any signal and—you're not gonna believe this, but her power line went down, so I couldn't even call you from her phone."

"Really?" I fought to keep my voice even. "That's funny because when I went over there yesterday, the phone was working fine."

Her lips tightened around her smile. "You saw my mother?"

"She was gardening and making iced tea. She wanted me to tell her about all the things we've been doing lately, since she never sees you anymore. What's going on, Calico?"

Calico's chin began to tremble, and she put her hand up to her face. Before I could react, she collapsed into her car seat.

"Oh God," she moaned, her eyes moist with tears. "I can't do this. It's just too much."

"What's wrong?" I was confused, caught between loving consolation and righteous indignation.

She sniffled and blew her nose. "I don't know," she wailed. "I don't know if I can talk about it yet."

I had already imagined the worst. She had met someone. She wanted to break up but didn't know how to tell me. I had had two days of solitude to work it all out in my head and it wasn't pretty, but not knowing was far worse.

"Try," I urged.

She took a deep breath and looked up at me through the tears. "Are you sure you want to hear this?"

"Yes."

"I have cancer."

The ten months that I had been hiding out in Orlando did nothing to soften the blow of those words. Ten months of fireworks shows, of following the Rules and providing immediate recovery. I had traveled across the country. I had chased the Disney Dream and caught it by the tail, only to find myself confronted with the very thing I had struggled so hard to escape.

Now, however, I didn't feel like running.

"Oh Calico."

"I'm not even thirty." Her words were barely audible through the sobbing.

"Shhh." I put my arms around her and told her as many comforting things as I could. I assured her that modern medicine was practically unbeatable. I reminded her about my mom, how she was bravely fighting lymphoma, how if she could confront cancer in her seventies, a healthy twenty-something woman would have no problem. "What kind of cancer is it?" I asked.

"I don't know," she said between sniffles. "That's where I was this weekend. I had to spend the night at a hospital in Tampa while they did a biopsy. I should know the results in a couple of weeks."

I held her close and stroked her hair. "Why didn't you tell me?"

She wiped her face on my shirt and looked me in the eyes. "As of now, you're the only other person who knows."

A silent agreement passed between us. I carried her bags up to her apartment and left her alone to get some rest. She said she would call me if she needed to talk.

The next week, everything was back to normal. We visited each other at work with little gifts and rented romantic comedies. She didn't mention her illness, so I didn't push her on the subject, but I wouldn't let her do her own dishes. And when she pulled out the vacuum cleaner one day, I made her sit down while I vacuumed the carpets. We were redefining our relationship, and I had never been happier.

Painting the Roses Red

"How is everything in the Sunshine State?" My father's voice sounded unfamiliar over the phone.

"Supercalifragilistic, Dad," I said. "But this hammock's facing the wrong way and I can't quite see the sunset."

"Oh," he said. "Right." His tone suggested that he was struggling to align his worldview with a place where hammocks and sunsets weren't fantastic, imaginary creatures. "Well, I hadn't heard from you in a while. I just wanted to make sure everything was going well."

"Yep," I said. "Things are great." I felt a chill like a cloud passing in front of the sun. There was a long silence.

"Okay. Well. I guess that's about it. Feel free to call whenever you like."

"Okay."

"Okay."

"Dad!" I blurted out before I could stop myself.

"Yes?"

"How's Mom doing?"

He took a deep breath, and for the first time, it occurred to me that he was crying. "It's been a hard week, I'm afraid, not much sleep—not really sleeping at all. But she's eating a little more now, so that's good. The thing is though, that, well, she . . . she decided to stop the treatments. She said she can't do another one . . . and I don't blame her. Not really. They're awful . . . they're just . . . But Michael says she should continue, just for one or two more. Just one more. But I don't blame her. And she says if it comes back, she'll just let it take her." He sniffed. "Every day, I ask myself what's the right thing to do."

Hot tears were streaming down my cheeks. I tried to think of something decent to say, but my whole body was shaking and I was afraid to open my mouth.

He took a deep breath. "We just have to keep our fingers crossed."

He had opened up to me. Finally, after a year of secrecy, he had broken the silence. "Dad, I'm sorry," I said through the crying. "I am so, so sorry." For his pain. For leaving. For not being there at that very moment. We talked for a while longer, and promised to talk again soon.

I hardly slept that night, and the next day, when I clocked in, Orville was quick to pull me aside.

"Take this to the bathroom," he said, pressing a bottle of Visine into my hand, "And for God's sake, tuck your shirt in. Today is Thanksgiving, not casual day."

I stumbled through my photo sets in a daze, mechanically loading and unloading film while my father's words echoed through my head. He had opened up. After a year of silence, he had dropped the pretension of the game and spoken honestly about my mother's condition as if I were somebody who could handle the truth. And all I had done was ask the question.

I wasn't trying to fool myself. I understood that his honesty was less a reflection of my actions and more an indication of his own condition. He had simply reached a critical crossroad in his life, a place where he needed to talk about what he was going through despite decorum or consequences. Still, it was a step. I was worried and terrified and utterly disoriented.

Mom couldn't quit her treatments, not after coming so far. Michael was in touch with her oncologist—she needed to heed his advice, even if the chemo was rough. Did Mom know something that we didn't know? Maybe cancer was the kind of illness where you could feel yourself getting better, like a hangover or a sprained ankle. Or maybe she was just giving up.

Many times throughout the day, I made up my mind to move back to LA. But then I would remember Calico, who was scheduled to start chemo treatments later that month. How would I break the news to her? Was it possible to go back to my mother in LA without abandoning my girlfriend in Orlando?

All through the afternoon, as I stood in the character kiosk, snapping pictures of giddy Newlyweds, giggling Japanese girls, and Wish kids, I tried to imagine what my mom looked like, what she was going through, how she felt. Every time an older woman put her arms around Mickey and Minnie, I imagined *her* smile, her courageous eyes. I performed my job with Rule Book aplomb. I put on a Disney face like a big cartoon head, and I smiled and I waved. And when I went to the bathroom or got a drink or left the kiosk between character sets, I walked down a forgotten path behind the hibiscus shrubs, and I wept like a frightened child.

Near the end of the day, Orville showed up at Camp Minnie-Mickey where I was shooting the mice. He was smiling his big onstage smile, but I could see concern crinkling the corners of his eyes as he watched me stumble through my duties. The mouse greeter that day was the elderly gentleman who had been there the day Sunny was kidnapped by the Brazilians. He was as forgetful as ever, picking his nose and admiring hibiscus flowers in the back of the kiosk, but on this day, I didn't have the energy to cover his job duties. When it was time to switch the mice, Orville announced a cheese break, then pulled me into the back of the kiosk.

"Why don't you clock out, go home, and get some rest," he said under his breath. "I'll finish up the rest of the day here."

"I'm fine," I assured him through a forced smile. "I only have an hour left anyway, but thank you. Seriously."

"Here come Mickey and Minnie!" announced the old greeter, suddenly alert. As he ushered two fresh mice into the kiosk, a pair of Newlyweds rushed forward to receive the holy blessing.

I stepped forward to get their photos, but Orville grabbed my arm. "Keep an eye on those two," he nodded at the Newlyweds. "They're Collectors."

They couldn't have been more in love, standing there, grinning in their mouse-eared top hat and veil. "Those aren't Collectors," I said. "Look at the wedding bands."

Orville didn't take his eyes off them as he moved out of the background of my shot. "Everybody smile," I announced with as much brio as I could muster. "Say Mickey."

The Newlyweds had their left hands on Mickey's shoulder, showing off their wedding bands, which I thought looked nice, so I made them pose for a couple of extra photos. Everybody smiled and hugged, and the Newlyweds disappeared out the gate as I reloaded my camera for the next set of guests.

"Oh no, Mickey," the old greeter said under his breath. "What happened to your wardrobe?"

Sure enough, the sleeve of Mickey's safari shirt was tattered, a gaping hole where his Camp Minnie-Mickey scout badge used to be. Before I knew what was happening, the elderly greeter shot through the exit gate and was sprinting after the couple.

I handed my camera to Orville and ran after him, dodging greasy children and sweaty parents, vaulting a bench as I narrowly avoided a battalion of wheelchairs, but it was no use. The couple had disappeared into the crowd. I saw the old greeter by the restrooms, leaning against a wall. He was wheezing, a froth of spittle on his chin, his face Jafar red.

"Are you alright?" I asked. "You want to sit down?"

He nodded and sank down on a nearby bench, in the shade of a blooming jacaranda tree. The BGM was "Zip-a-Dee-Do-Dah." "You should get back to the kiosk," he rasped. "I'll be fine."

"I'll be right back," I said. I grabbed a Styrofoam cup from a coffee cart and filled it at a water fountain, then ran back to the bench. "Drink this," I offered.

He took the cup, then froze. He made a few gasps for breath, then looked over at me, and as he did, the color drained out of his cheeks and he smiled. His eyes glazed over and his head rolled back. And then he stopped breathing.

I shouted for help, and slapped his face. I couldn't believe how cold he was all of a sudden. I had no CPR experience whatsoever, but I had to do something. I knew I had to try to force air into his lungs, so I pounded on his chest. I held his nose and put my mouth over his, trying to push air through his throat. It wasn't working; I couldn't find a pulse.

Crowds were beginning to form now, but nobody stepped forward or offered to help, so I kept going. I pushed his body into a lying down position on the bench. As I raised my hands above me to pound his chest again, I was pulled away. Three medics in blue jumpsuits moved in. They quickly set up a stretcher and transferred his limp body onto it, then pushed through the crowd to a Cast Members Only door.

Orville had disappeared from the kiosk, and my camera was nowhere to be found, so I stood in as greeter until a pimply kid came to relieve me. I walked back to the photo lab with my hands in my pockets. The old greeter couldn't die—not at Disney World. There were statistics. Nobody had ever died here. No way could he be the first.

Marco was the only one in the lab when I arrived. He sneered when he saw me. "Your shirt is untucked," he said. "That's at least one reprimand."

"Fuck you," I said.

His sneer faded into mortified shock. "Excuse me?"

The little trailer rumbled. The door opened and Orville walked in. "Marco, will you excuse us." It wasn't a question.

Marco hissed. "Do you have any idea what he just said to me?"

"Marco!" Orville snapped, then his voice changed. "Honey.

Please." A signal more intimate than workplace camaraderie traveled between them, and Marco left without another word.

I dropped into a chair, and Orville pulled up a seat next to me. The walls of the little lab suddenly felt very close. I was choking on the smell of development chemicals. "You and Marco . . .?"

"Please. I need to talk to you about what just happened." Orville removed his spectacles and ran a wide hand down his face. "As I'm sure you know, the character department has a new manager. What you may not know is that she was in Camp Minnie-Mickey today giving her boss a tour when that whole scenario went down. As I'm sure you can imagine, they weren't pleased that one of my photographers was assaulting an old man in the middle of the character kiosks."

"Assaulting him? I was trying to save him."

"That's not what it looked like," he scowled. "To the children in the park, it looked like you were beating and kissing him, and that is very difficult to explain to a child."

"No, it's not, Orville." I was fighting an impossibly strong current, and I had no hope of winning, but I had to put up a struggle. "Tell them I was doing my best—"

"A Cast Member may never *ever* perform a medical operation onstage." His voice swelled. "Do you remember Guest Guideline 6? Preserve the Magical Experience! And let me tell you about that experience. Sleeping Beauty pricked her finger on a spindle and fell *asleep*; Snow White ate a poisoned apple and fell *asleep*. As far as they know, that man fell asleep too, until you started in."

"This is bullshit."

"Plus, the medics were right behind you!" he shouted. "Now, I'm going to have to provide a lot of immediate recovery. A LOT!" He leaned back in his chair and put his spectacles back on. "I'm sorry. There are just some things that are out of my control. . . . You understand what I'm saying, right?" The collar of his khaki shirt was dark with sweat and one of his shoelaces was untied, but still he was a Disney Cast Member with management responsibilities.

When a wave crashes over you, and you're being tumbled under hundreds of gallons of water, your immediate instinct is to struggle against the forces holding you down, to fight your way to the surface where there is air to breathe and a board to keep you afloat, and to prepare, most likely, for another wave coming. But your instinct is wrong. In this situation, you don't know which way is up, and all the struggling in the world will only wear you out. You have to relax and let the wave take its course. Eventually, the water will settle and you will rise to the top.

"How did you know they were Collectors?"

Normally, he would have delighted in the clever chain of deduction that led him to his discovery, but on this day, there was no mirth in his eyes. "The wedding rings," he said. "They're replicas from the Haunted Mansion. . . . One from here, one from Paris."

I unclipped my nametag, and set it on the counter next to the cameras. "What happened to the old greeter?"

Orville shook his head and lowered his eyes. One two three. But he didn't say anything.

There was nothing more to do. For the last time, I clocked out and crossed the Cast Member parking lot. My Jeep was unbearably hot, but I sat inside, sweating, trying to process everything that had just happened. I was no longer a Disney Cast Member, no longer a part of the Magical Machine. And what about the old greeter? The unthinkable had happened; I had watched a man die at Disney World. I vowed to watch the news for details of this momentous story.

By the time I pulled in to the Disney Ghetto, it was dark, and the moon was just peeking over the treetops. I was exhausted, emotionally drained, and dirty. I wanted a shower and a good night's sleep. Unfortunately, it wasn't meant to be.

The apartment was blazing hot, pounding with the overproduced rhythms of some boy band phenomenon. Every light in the place was on, including the floor light from my bedroom, which had been angled over the bar and draped with red silk. And there, standing on a chair, wearing nothing but a pair of boxers and a backward Jeff Gordon racing cap, was my roommate, Johnny. He was pointing a disposable instamatic camera at a pile of young men who were writhing around on the kitchen floor, completely naked save a headband, a plate of French toast, five stuffed tigers, and a pirate flag, in no particular order.

"Hey!" came a startled shout from the linoleum. "Shut the fuckin' door!"

Johnny stepped down from the chair. "Hi, roomie. You're just in time. Ah want you to meet Boy Banned." He ran through a roll call of names and then presented me. Sure enough, Jazz was right in the middle of the stack, the pirate flag draped casually over his thighs.

"Johnny," Jazz pouted. "Can we keep this moving please? We still have to do individual head shots, and I have a thing."

"Ah'm out of film in this one." Johnny shook the little instamatic as if it were an empty light bulb. "So, like, take five, kids,"

As Boy Banned stood up and stretched, I kept firm eye contact with my roommate, who appeared to be in charge here and who, not incidentally, was the only guy in the room besides myself wearing at least a couple items of clothing.

"What the hell are you doing?"

Johnny's eyes were rheumy with Scotch. "Guess what. We recorded our first single today. "Love Is a Four-Letter Word." It's a bit rough, but—you wanna hear it?"

Jimmy, the spiky-haired kid, wandered by, scratching his crotch and eating an apple. I shifted my gaze to the ceiling. "No. I've had a hell of a day, and I want to know why the apartment is filled with naked people."

Johnny was swaying like a pirate on a choppy ocean. "Well, you remember you told me you didn't want to shoot the cover—and that's not a problem—but ah needed to do something because people are going to want press photos and stuff, right? So ah decided to take matters into mah own hands."

"You're shooting nude press photos?"

His smile was Cheshire. "It's original."

"Hey Johnny, check this out!" Jazz was beckoning from the kitchen floor, where he had arranged four of the guys in a tight group, so that each one was covering another's genitalia. It looked like amateur gay porn. "What do you think?"

Johnny beamed, "Perfect!" He moved to pick up a new disposable camera.

I grabbed his shoulders. "Johnny, that is not perfect. It's pornographic. And it's bad. This whole idea of yours, from start to finish, is bad. And now you've turned the apartment—my apartment—into a clubhouse for the young gay community of Orlando! Can you see how this might be a little stressful for me?"

He thought about this for a moment, but the strain of thinking was too much for him. "Hey, did ah tell you, we recorded our first single today."

I lost it. I don't remember what I said, but by the time I was finished with my tirade, I had managed to pack everything I could into my duffel bag and backpack and was loading it into my Jeep.

"Call me soon, okay?" Johnny was tilted against the sliding glass door, blinking in the glare of my taillights. Behind him, in the kitchen, Jazz was rolling the band members into the pirate flag like pigs in a blanket.

As I sped down the highway, I wrestled to put order to everything that had just happened. My mom was quitting her chemo treatments, my photographic career at Disney was finished, and my roommate was such a useless alcoholic, he couldn't even hold a thought in his head. I was homeless, friendless, and jobless, but at least I still had Calico. I turned down her street and pulled into her driveway. I didn't think she'd be off work yet, so I was surprised that her car was in the lot. As usual, her door was unlocked.

"Hello?" I didn't want to call out too loud because I didn't want to alarm her. I made my way to her cluttered kitchen and poured myself a glass of water. Clearing a space on her table, I noticed a bunch of photos that I hadn't seen before: Calico lying on the deck of a boat, water skiing, posing on the sand. Occasionally, I saw a photo of some guy that I almost recognized, but couldn't quite re-member. His face was never clear enough. I pushed the photos to the side and set my water glass on an unopened credit card bill.

Something about those pictures was bothering me—not Calico or that vaguely familiar guy, but something else. And then it hit me: the time code. According to the date stamp on the bottom of the prints, the photos had been taken the weekend I'd made reserva-tions at the Portofino, the day Calico had been in Tampa getting her biopsy.

A sudden crash from Calico's bedroom startled me, and I dropped the snapshots. On the soft carpeted floors, my footsteps fell dead silent. I could hear music coming from her room and the sound of somebody sobbing.

Her bedroom door was open wide enough for me to see her na-ked body bucking and contorted on the bed. What I had thought was sobbing was actually gasping through a sheet that was bunched in her teeth. Crouched naked, with his face in her crotch, was the same guy from the photos, but this time, I recognized him. It was her greeter.

"Bad dog," Calico was growling in her fake English accent. "You're a miserable, naughty little puppy."

I stood there, frozen in the door, unable to take my eyes off them, but unwilling to tear myself away. I felt sick to my stomach. When her greeter mounted her, I decided to get out of there. I backed out the doorway and into the living room where I could only vaguely hear the sounds of their fucking, and sat down in a chair.

Should I wait for them to finish and come out of the bedroom? Should I write a good-bye note? Should I trash the living room? A thousand thoughts raced through my head, but I decided that it would be best just to leave. I made sure the door was closed behind me.

I Will Fly No More

"Zip-a-dee-do-dah, honey." My mother's voice sounded faded and distant over my mobile phone. "What time is it?"

"It's about 10 A.M. my time." I winced. I hadn't realized I was calling so early. "So about seven for you. How are you?"

"Me? Oh, I'm fine. Everything's wonderful here." She cleared her throat. "Are you at work?"

Through the slats of my window shade, I could see a few thin lines of daylight. At Animal Kingdom right now, somebody in maintenance would be cranking up the AC on Pride Rock to lure the lions out near the tour buses. "Not exactly," I said. "I left the photography job."

"But you loved that animal place."

I wanted to tell her everything, but I didn't have the energy. "It was time to move on," I said.

"Does that mean," her voice turned hopeful, "you'll be coming home for Christmas?"

Christmas. Three weeks away. Now that I wasn't a Disney Cast Member anymore, I could do anything I wanted for the holidays and the weekends and every day in between. "I don't know," I said. "Go back to sleep. I'm sorry I woke you up."

"Call anytime," she said. "And let me know about Christmas. I'm really looking forward to seeing the whole family together one more time." The way she said it sounded like "one *last* time."

"I'll call you soon." I rushed words in to fill the silence. "I promise."

I held the phone to my ear until long after my screen had gone dark. I felt weak, winded from the effort of holding back words that needed to be said. In months past, I would have simply gone to one of the parks and extinguished my misery with garish celebration. But this time, there was nothing to distract me—not a parade, or a hot air balloon, or even so much as a sparkler to take my mind off the disastrous events that had left me alone and out of work in a dark motel room that smelled like Swisher Sweets and Glade. I closed my eyes and sobbed into the pillow, my Disney Dream shredded around me like a bed of decaying kelp.

I struggled to remember why I had come to Orlando in the first place. What had I been trying to find? Magic? Immortality? I had a vague memory of my own blind faith and the promise of a better life. When I first arrived in Orlando, I had clung to that promise, and everything it implied. I was hopelessly optimistic and positive that I would be able to refurbish my job, my relationship, my friends—I had been looking to upgrade my LA life to some Disney version of it where people were always happy and trust was unquestionable, and I had failed.

Twelve months in the Magic Kingdom, and I had nothing to show for it. At least I finally understood the wisdom of Marco's words: life at Disney was just like life in Everywhere Else, USA; no matter where I went, I would always have to contend with good *and* bad. From now on, I resolved, I would make better choices. I did not know what I was going to do exactly, but I was prepared to take the next step with my eyes wide open.

In the bathroom mirror, my reflection looked older. I had a four-day-old five o'clock shadow and my eyes were bloodshot. I shaved and styled my hair into something respectful, then pulled on a nice pair of slacks and a dress shirt. I tasted blood when I pushed my labret back in, but I didn't care. I'd earned that pain; for abandoning my identity, I deserved it.

Throwing open the front door, I surveyed the grand expanse of parking lot in front of the World Famous Budget Lodge. It was the same place I'd stayed when I first drove into Orlando, and the closest place with a VACANCY sign above the door. The night attendant wanted $56 a night, but I talked him down to $50, since I had my own towel.

As I drove away from the garish mini-malls of Kissimmee, the landscape turned wild. Crabgrass spread, ivy grew unchecked along the cracked streets. Here and there, plants were dying, giving way to new growth. Thinking back, I couldn't remember the last time I had truly interacted with nature outside of Disney's cultivated communities. In LA, outdoor adventures had been an integral part of my life: surfing, backcountry skiing, rock climbing. I had surrounded myself with natural beauty right up until the time I moved to Orlando. How had I slipped so far from something that made me so happy?

The service for the elderly greeter was being held at a cemetery near the orange groves of Clermont. It was quiet here, away from the highways and the BGM; I could hear wind—not recorded climate conditions, but actual blustery weather—and real birdsong, so voluminous and full of natural timbre, that it felt as if I could ride the wave of sound. For the first time in almost a week, I was feeling something other than self-pity.

His name, it turned out, was Walter. He had died in transit on the way to the hospital and pronounced DOA. There were only a few people gathered around his urn, including Orville and Marco. Halfway through the somber service, it started drizzling, and we stood beneath umbrellas. From the sparse words his family offered, I got the impression that Walter had been that eccentric relative people liked to forget about until Christmas cards were due. Neither Orville, Marco, nor I spoke.

At some point, it dawned on me that I had been to this cemetery before. In fact, all I had to do was look over my shoulder to see the tombstone where Nick had done his infamous wall ride. At the time, it had seemed like a harmless prank, an interesting backdrop for a sepia-toned action shot, but from this perspective, I was struck by the irreverence of what we had done. Had it really seemed significant back then? Progressive? A year and three thousand miles later, I was right back where I started: without a home, without a job, without a sureness of whom I could trust. Disney World had turned out to be no more Magical than any other place in the world. My life had become a grim fairy tale, an unfinished story without moral or meaning.

When the service ended, I stood with Orville and Marco until everybody was gone. When it was just the three of us, they held hands, leaned against each other, and cried. Eventually, Orville walked back to the car, leaving Marco and I side by side under our umbrellas.

There was a metallic taste in my mouth, something like blood. I swallowed against it. "I didn't know about you and Orville."

"Nobody knew." He looked down at his shoes, shiny wet and flecked with little pieces of grass. "Orville is the reason I stayed in Orlando."

I considered all the petty things Marco had done to annoy me over the past year. None of it seemed so insidious now. "You hungry?"

He shrugged. "A little."

We agreed to meet in half an hour, and I watched him and Orville drive away. There was one more thing I had to do before I left Orlando. I crossed the slick lawn and put my hand on the tombstone where I imagined I could still see wheel marks from Nick's wall ride. I ran my fingers from the rough surface to the polished part where the letters were etched into the stone. "I'm sorry," I said to the cold granite. "Rest in peace."

Universal CityWalk was close. I parked in the Spiderman lot and shuffled along the people mover until I reached the crowded square with all the shops and "streetmosphere" entertainment. Over sandwiches, we talked about our lives, and Orville and Marco told me how they had ended up in Orlando. Orville had grown up in the panhandle of Florida and dreamed of one day owning a comic book store. Always shy, he had picked up photography as a way to meet people, then discovered he was pretty good at it. Marco had studied photography in Puerto Rico and saved up all his money to come to Florida. His dream was to be a fashion photographer in Miami, but he had learned quickly that New York photographers shot most of the Miami jobs, and he didn't have enough resources to get to New York. At first, Disney had just been a way for him to get money together, but he had quickly fallen in love with the place.

"It was the colors and the cultures," he explained. "I loved how Disney could bring people together, no matter where they were from or what they believed in. Disney was a common ground for everybody. And for the first time in my life, I was the best photographer around." He flashed a sheepish smile. "At least until you came to Animal Kingdom."

"You're way more technical than me," I protested. "I don't know half the techniques you do."

"It's true," Orville agreed.

Marco put down his sandwich. "When I started dating Orville, I felt like I had everything in one place. I thought 'I don't need New York or Miami.'"

"It's so easy here," Orville said. "You settle down at Disney and you meet all these people who are more deviant than you could ever be—weird and wonderful—and it's like, for the first time, you're not the black sheep of the family. You're just a part of somebody's Magical Experience."

Marco rested his chin on his hands and closed his eyes. I felt a touch of regret that I would never again be able to experience that backstage Disney world of blue Schwinn bike rides and Julie Andrews discussion groups.

"You know what's really crazy about this whole situation?" I stirred the ice around my glass. "I came to Disney because I wanted to get away from drama and tragedy. I wanted to go backstage where the fun never stopped and everybody lived happy ever after in Never Land. I found this amazing, magical place where nobody ever dies, like the Bermuda Triangle, only in a good way, and I actually started to believe that I could settle down here. I honestly thought I had it in me to be a lifer."

Marco looked at me, puzzled. "What are you talking about? People die at Disney World all the time."

I shook my head. "There's never been a death at Disney. Even Walter. The paper reported he died in the ambulance on the way to the hospital."

Marco and Orville exchanged a look. Orville took a deep breath before he spoke. "Nobody's ever been *pronounced dead* on Disney property because that's Disney's policy. If somebody passes away at one of the parks, the body gets loaded into the alpha unit and pronounced dead *in transit*. Remember the guy who had a heart attack waiting in line to see Cinderella last month? His heart stopped beating before he hit the ground. It was probably the same with Walter, but Disney doesn't want anyone to know that because death ruins the Magic." He reached across the table. "Hey, don't look so sad. I didn't mean to upset you."

In reality, I wasn't at all that surprised. Somewhere in the back of my mind, I think I knew that was the case the whole time. What really threw me was my apparently innate talent to deceive myself into believing the most absurd fantasies: that I could escape reality in an amusement park, that I could continue to live a life unexamined. After all, hadn't I deserved to be fired from my old job? Hadn't I pushed my ex-girlfriend away? I ran from my mom when she needed my support the most. I was a shallow, self-centered bastard.

Marco leaned his chair back and squinted up at the sun. "You know what I've been thinking about the last few days?"

"What?"

"When I first came to this country," he said, "I was amazed by how big everything was. The cars, the houses." He held up his sandwich. "The chickens! I thought, wow! This must be the best place in the world. Everybody has such wonderful big things! But then I found out the other side to the story. The big cars guzzle gas and ruin the air. The big houses have the same problems as little houses, only bigger. The big chickens are only big because they are pumped up with chemicals! But by that time, I had become too involved, and I couldn't escape. I kept thinking about my uncle—the words he said to me after he dragged me out of the waves one day when I was first learning to surf in Sitches. He said, '*Jamas le des tu espalda al mar.*' Never turn your back on the ocean."

The moment he said it, the second it was out, everything came to an abrupt halt. Music stopped playing and jugglers quit juggling. Lovers paused their kisses to listen. And in the eyes of every child on the CityWalk, a smile, as they waited for Marco's words to sink in.

It was like an awakening—what Disniacs call a "pixie dust moment"—when your vision clears and you suddenly see your life in perspective. Orlando wasn't my destiny. It was a detour, a wonderland of fantastic stories and people who covered my retreat into false magic. Disney had been a convenient location for my escape, considering the hours of happiness and fantasy I'd found at the feet of my Disney heroes, but running away to live at Disney hadn't made my life any better. It hadn't healed my heart or made me happier. It had only taught me how to *appear* happy until I was finally able to confront my issues.

Of course, I had tried to believe the fantasy. I wanted to think that I was moving toward enlightenment every time I guided somebody up a wheelchair-accessible ramp or photographed a fellow Cast Member doing whip-it hits in a Donald costume as if happiness was a goal that could be achieved by making people around me smile.

I wanted to believe that I could successfully plug myself into the theme park world, that all I needed was a support group of entertainers and a book of rules outlining wardrobe, hairstyle, and attitude—a neat, prepackaged lifestyle that would work for me the way it worked for hundreds of other happy Disney Cast Members. I had listened to the legends of sex and drugs in the Magic Kingdom and come to believe that they were a kind of inspirational legerdemain, a mythology that might guide me to acceptance and, ultimately, happiness. But I had miscalculated.

The truth was I didn't have it in me to be a lifer. It had taken me no more than a month to shatter the veneer of Disney's chaste brand of Magic and only a few weeks more until I, myself, was distorting the Experience with out-of-character photos and SOP trysts. No wonder I had burned out on Disney so quickly.

I didn't need Walt's wonderful world to make me happy. I didn't have to be a part of anybody else's Magical Experience. I only needed to be there for the people who mattered most in my life: my mother, my family, my friends. For them, I needed to Provide Immediate Recovery. As Tarzan once told me, everybody can be a hero.

At that moment, with my former boss and nemesis sitting across the table, it occurred to me that even with all the stories and the parades and the music and the character sets and the fireworks shows, it was time to leave Orlando.

"So," Orville smiled as the music revved back to life and, all around us, guests and waiters and street atmosphere performers went back to doing what they were doing. "What are you going to do now?"

"Now," I said, imagining my mom and dad opening presents under an impossibly tall Christmas tree. "I'm going home."

Circle of Life

I took me four days to drive back across the country, ample time to chastise myself for dropping my safe, journalistic objectivity and getting carried away with the Disney Dream. In New Orleans, I changed my ringtone from Jiminy Cricket's "Give a Little Whistle" to Nine Inch Nails' "Closer." In Dallas, I uploaded a hazmat icon as my avatar. By the time I crossed the Arizona state line, however, my self-immolation had run its course, and I was glad for every single experience at the Magic Kingdom.

Nikki left a message to say that she and her partner had been selected to adopt a Colombian child. Johnny left me a couple of messages describing the awesome ascendance of Boy Banned, but by the time I got to New Mexico, he had given up calling. Calico, on the other hand, called me every day, crying, commanding, begging, cajoling. She ran the full gamut of emotions from martyred to manipulative, but I let all her calls go to voice mail. I couldn't decide if she was schizophrenic or if she really thought she had me fooled.

I hated the fact that I had fallen for her. Orville had warned me not to get involved. He had told me stories about people like Wigger who shoplifted their personalities from the lovable Disney characters. The day Calico and I went skating, she had said something that sounded like a line from *The Little Mermaid*. And it probably was.

In retrospect, it was clear as Cuban rum: there was no Calico. In her place was only a dull, ordinary girl who took on the personalities of Disney characters the way Silly Putty copied a comic strip from a newspaper. Only she did it in serial succession, one character at a time. As Ariel, she was soft and dreamy, a wedding planner who sought beauty and love. She wished on stars and cried for terminal children. When she was approved in Cruella, she became downright wicked. She wore makeup. She ate meat. Only a woman who killed puppies could lie about having cancer.

So what kind of woman could lie to *cover up* cancer? There was no easy Disney archetype for my mother. Walt's world was a place without maternal influence, an oligarchy of eternally youthful heroes and aging villains. I didn't for a second think that she was lying to spite me; more likely, she was doing what she'd always done: protecting me from the truth, letting me have my Fantasyland.

LA smelled like sweaty kneepads and smog, like home. Since it was my first night back in LA, mom insisted on cooking dinner for my brother and me, and she wouldn't take no for an answer. Michael lived about an hour east of our parents, so I stopped there and let him drive us the rest of the way. As expected, he forced me to sit through fifteen minutes of well-rehearsed lecturing before he warmed up.

"I'm glad you came back," he said.

"Me too." I watched the cars move past us on the freeway, shiny imports with polished chrome parts. Of course, the weather was perfect, arid, with just enough sea spray that I could taste the salt. I closed my eyes and felt the sunshine on my face. The sounds of traffic, the radio stations that I had known since I was a kid.

My brother looked over at me. "Are you still upset that Mom and Dad kept you in the dark?"

I stretched my fingers through the sunroof. "No," I said. "Well, yes. I mean, I guess I understand that they didn't want to scare me."

"That's part of it," Michael said. "But there's a part of Mom that doesn't want to admit she has cancer. She thinks if she doesn't talk about it, it might just go away." He shook his head. "I know it sounds preposterous, but it's true."

Actually, it sounded quite reasonable. Hadn't I been doing the same thing for the past twelve months? "But she talked to you."

"Barely!"

"Really?"

"If I hadn't stayed in touch with her oncologist, I probably wouldn't have had half the information I got. It was really frustrating. She's like you." He paused here, and for the first time, I recognized something like envy in his silence. "Living in her own little Fantasyland."

Nothing he said could have cheered me up more. "So how is she?" I asked.

"She's good." Michael nodded. "Recovering."

"Is she . . .?"

He looked at me. "What?"

"You know."

"What? Cured?" He turned down the radio and cleared his throat. "You have to understand something. Cancer doesn't just go away. The best you can hope for is that it goes into remission." He took a deep breath. "Right now, it appears that Mom's cancer is in remission, but we have to wait a few weeks for more accurate test results, and we'll never know anything with one hundred percent certainty. Not ever."

I fidgeted with a loose string on my jeans. "Does she *feel* better?"

Michael smiled. "She feels great."

I was struggling across the driveway with my bag when she opened the front door. Her hands left little streaks of stuffing across my cheeks when she hugged me.

"Look at you," she exclaimed. "Such a nice haircut."

"Disney makes everybody wear this haircut, Mom," I said. "It's in the Rule Book."

"Well, it's very handsome." Her hug was surprisingly strong.

Sure enough, she looked great. Her hair was coming back in, grayer than before, but thick and stylish. She had lost a lot of weight and the wrinkles on her face were a little deeper, but she had a natural flush to her cheeks and she smiled constantly. I couldn't take my eyes off her as she ran around the kitchen fixing dishes, checking the roast, setting the table. She didn't want anyone helping her, but Dad and I did little chores behind her back, using involvement as an excuse to steal snacks from the table.

At one point, she caught me watching her. "What?" She stopped mixing a brown sauce and sat down next to me. "What are you looking at?"

I shook my head. "Why didn't you tell me you had cancer?"

She wiped her hands on her apron and frowned thoughtfully. "Didn't I?"

"No, you didn't. You told me you were feeling tired or fluish or had allergies or something, but you never told me the truth. And you never told me about the treatments."

She smiled and patted my hands. "Well, luckily, that's all behind us now."

"Really? Because Michael said—"

"Oh, pishposh," she waved her hands in the air between us as if my concern were an annoying fly, and she could make it go away by swatting at it. "Look at my hands."

Her nails looked strong and healthy again. "Nice manicure," I said.

"No, look. Here. No veins. The chemo treatments disintegrated my veins. Don't my hands look young?"

I laughed. "There's a benefit I bet the doctors never thought of."

"The wonders of science," she said, tousling my hair. "I can't believe how well-groomed you look. You say Disney makes everybody do that?"

I wanted to know more about her experiences, but I could tell she wasn't going to subject herself to my questioning. Maybe it was me. Maybe it was the intense nature of the illness and the treatment. Or maybe, like Michael said, she just wanted to have her own little Fantasyland where there was no such thing as lymphoma or sadness. Either way, we had come full circle, not talking about things. I was home and I was happy to be with her.

"Disney makes their employees do a lot of things," I said.

She affected a thoughtful pose. "I seem to remember you telling me something about a girlfriend," she said. "A lovely mermaid?"

"A *little* mermaid," I said. "It didn't work out." It was too onerous to relive the whole escapade, so I left it at that. "I love you, Mom."

"I love you too." She gave me another firm hug and stood up. "But if I catch you or your father ruining your appetite before dinner, so help me!"

That night, as we ate, I told stories about my Disney adventures, the good stories about Magic and Pixie Dust Moments, not the ones about deviant characters or manipulative Cast Members. Everyone laughed at the funny parts and smiled when it was poignant and begged for more stories even when I couldn't think of any more to tell.

When dinner was over, somebody put on *Peter Pan*, and I sprawled out on the couch to watch. I made it as far as Never Land before I fell asleep, smiling.